I, ROBOT

HOW TO BE A FOOTBALLER 2

PETER
CROUCH

WITH TOM FORDYCE

Also by Peter Crouch with Tom Fordyce

How to be a Footballer

CONTENTS

PROLOGUE

A footballer's book is supposed to be a simple affair. 'I was born here. My mum and dad look like this. I was good at football and I got better at football. Here are some matches you already know about and some you forgot. This guy was nicknamed Trigger and that guy we called Smudge.'

But I never was your typical footballer and so see no reason why my book should follow conventional suit. Rather than the same old same old, a tour through the familiar and the banal, I'd rather show you how it really is: the secret tricks and the inside stories, the madness and the mistakes, the truth behind the puff and the magic behind the curtain. When you've played at the top for two decades, you see things that you can't forget: the players who are so scared by the idea of cooking for themselves that they get the canteen staff to clingfilm up the same lunch they have just eaten so they can have it again for tea; the one who sustained a tiny cut on his leg yet went to the club doctor every day to ask to him apply a Band-Aid on his behalf; the player who shut himself away in his hotel room every night to have his dinner opposite his smartphone, a smartphone showing his wife on FaceTime eating exactly the same dinner at exactly the same time.

You might think you know what football chairmen are like. You don't. Not until you've heard about the one who propositioned me from an open-topped sports car, or the one who spent so much on their house that they could have bought the entire local town. You don't really understand what agents are until you've heard about the one who rides a motorised trike lit by UV lights around Marble Arch, wearing a fur coat and smoking a cigar. Over the following pages, you'll also discover which position on the pitch produces the most selfish human beings in existence, what the stretches substitutes do on the touchline really mean and why grown men who play football are unable to choose their own pants.

I've done a few things myself as well. It's time I got the story about the worst 100-metre race of all time off my chest, and explain why my early career was nearly derailed by me and my friends inventing the thrilling new sport of bush-jumping. I also did something on holiday once involving a pleasure craft, a sudden nautical storm and a bottle-opener that I cannot carry with me any longer.

Not for us the straightforward analysis you've become accustomed to on television. Instead, I'm going to reveal why the outswinging corner is always better than the inswinger, what really happens when you pull out of a tackle and why Rafa Benítez's pet Alsatians are the best-behaved dogs in Europe. Find out what secret gift the Real Madrid president gives out when he makes a big signing. Come with me onto Roman Abramovich's yacht and discover what happens when you spill a drink on his deep-pile carpet. Step inside the Golden Rhombus of Football and understand how a man can lose himself within it.

You may be familiar with Mickey Rourke. You won't be familiar with what happened with Mickey and me in Miami one summer: I've had to corroborate several subplots with friends to remind myself that all of it actually took place. It will shock you when you find out which board game obsesses Premier League dressing-rooms and which international player intimidates all the others with his dominance of it.

We will talk about the silly little games we play. There is one so childish yet so addictive that the truth about it has never leaked out before. Until now. We will dig into the curious and often disturbing world of referees: the strange clothes they wear; the mysterious so-called training they undertake; and why they are reminiscent of the worst defensive midfielders of all time. We will discover the identity of the greatest tackler I have ever faced and try to fathom his obsession with stonewashed jeans.

I've been lucky in football. I have gone to places and experienced things that I could never have dreamed of. I know the best trophies to drink champagne from and why the bubbly you get for man-of-the-match performances cannot always be trusted. I've seen a lumpy clogger of a player transformed into an inadvertent elegant genius, simply by being in the wrong place at a very bad time. I have witnessed one of Fabio Capello's assistants parting the arse hair of England legends with a highly unusual hairdryer technique.

It hasn't all worked out. There was the time with Madonna when the Robot only got me so far. There was the incident when a member of the British royal family made a disparaging remark about my ability to attract women. And don't get me started on what happened the time my dad and I found ourselves teeing off in front of one of the legends of modern golf.

Still. There are secret rules that need to be brought out into the open. Why managers can never drive players' cars. The secret platform at the London train station that is football's equivalent of Harry Potter's Platform 9¾. The cut that an agent can expect to make off your big transfer move. There is strangeness everywhere you look: midnight curries with Tony Pulis and Cameron Jerome, eaten in an empty stadium; the fitness gadget that works wonders for your hamstrings but looks like a sex toy; the kickabouts with kebab-shop owners that were as intense as a Champions League showdown.

It's been the most enormous fun to be part of. Of course it has. I am Peter Crouch. This is *I, Robot: How to be a Footballer 2* – The Big Stuff. Shall we?

FANS

You're lucky, as a Premier League footballer. Lucky for what you do, for what you earn, for how much fun you can have. And lucky, too, for the adoration you can get for just doing what you always wanted to do.

You can find football fans in the least expected places. After the World Cup in 2006 I went on holiday to Miami with my mates from home. The plan was for some nights out, some sunshine, some time away from all that pressure and madness we had with England in Germany. On our third or fourth evening on the town we walked into a bar and past a bloke who looked exactly like an older, more rubbery version of Mickey Rourke.

'That bloke looks exactly like Mickey Rourke,' said one of the lads. The bloke who looked like Mickey Rourke looked at me and did a double-take.

'Hey, it's Robot Boy!' shouted the bloke who looked like Mickey Rourke, who we could all see now actually was Mickey Rourke, and started doing a bad version of what was now clearly my trademark.

You can't fight these things. 'Yeah, I'm Robot Boy,' I told him. And so began the sort of surreal forty-eight hours that you don't see coming when you're a kid in the Spurs youth team.

First, we had our photo taken together, both of us Roboting, me considerably better than Mickey. Then Mickey took us into the VIP section and began to back up his reputation as something of a hell-raising maverick. Drinks kept coming over. Girls kept coming over, more for Mickey and the drinks rather than any wider appreciation of his new friends. The night became purely about one long adventure with Mickey Rourke, at least until it became the next day and then pretty close to sunrise.

Mickey didn't appear to own a phone. As we left he was insistent that we meet again the following evening, and wrote down the name of a bar on a piece of paper. We went to bed, woke up marvelling at what had just gone up and agreed that we might as well go to the bar he had mentioned, not because he would be there – Mickey was just being polite, going through the motions – but because if Mickey had recommended it, it would probably be quite a spicy venue.

But he was waiting for us when we walked in. 'Robot Boy! Robot Boy's boys!'

If anything this was a bigger night. There was no awkward first hour this time. We were straight back into it. Mickey, drink after drink, all manner of dancing and new friends.

We got in at four in the morning. One of the last things I remembered doing before going to sleep was to hang the 'Do not disturb' sign on the door, which made the constant banging that woke up me and my mates at 11am intensely irritating.

'Fuck off!' we all shouted from under our duvets. 'Fuck off, we're asleep!'

The banging increased in volume. 'What is wrong with these people?' I muttered as I stumbled to the door. 'Can't they read?'

I stuck a bleary eye to the peephole in the door.

Mickey.

I turned back. 'Lads, it's fucking Mickey Rourke.'

The chorus was instant. 'Ah, pie him off.' 'He can do one!' 'Give it a rest, Mickey, won't you?'

There was no thought about his film-star status, the kudos of his company, or the good times that we had shared. We just wanted to be asleep. I got back into bed and we ignored one of the great Hollywood character actors of the past forty years until he went away.

When we awoke a couple of hours later, we noticed that a letter had been shoved under the door. It was written in the most insane script, as if it was the first time the author had ever held a pen, or if he was experimenting with the Daniel Day-Lewis method. It took a while to decipher the words.

'Hey you guys! Such a fantastic couple of nights. Let's do dinner right? Meet you 8pm at this place. Mickey.'

We were in a heavy state. A two-day bender and hangovers to match. The last we wanted was another huge one. I was ready for room service, a film in bed and lights out about ten. The conversation was a simple one. 'Shall we swerve it?' 'Yeah, let's pie him off.' 'Agreed?' 'God, yeah.'

We never saw Mickey again. I didn't even think about keeping his letter. These sorts of things just happened at that point, when you played for England at World Cups. It wasn't that you took them for granted. You simply had no time to reflect on them before the next random encounter took place.

I don't want to give the impression that it was all glamour. I enjoyed my three-month loan spell at Norwich in 2003; lovely club, great supporters, huge fun helping out with a successful promotion push. But it did get shitty at times. When you park in the players' car-park at Carrow Road you have a short walk through the crowds to get to the home dressing-room. That's fine. It gives you the chance to have a chat with a few of the fans. I was on my way in when I spotted a teenage girl running towards me. Autograph, I thought. I have been playing well. Not a problem.

My dad, who had got there slightly earlier, was just behind her. He was waving and looking panicked. What was he trying to tell me? It looked like he was shouting, 'No!' but what could be the problem? She just wanted a photo. Why was he staring at me like I was bobbing about in the ocean with a shark's fin approaching at pace?

I was concentrating so much on my dad that I wasn't really looking at the girl. She was clearly excited, but I was the big-name striker powering her club into the Premier League. Could you blame her, I thought, signing her shirt, squeezing up close to her for the photo. Dad had stopped going bananas and was now hunched over with his head in his hands, a figure of dismay. I gave the girl a smile and turned back to my dad.

'What is wrong with you?'

He shook his head. 'I tried to tell you. I tried …'

He pointed at the girl as she walked away. Poo, all down her leg, smeared all over her back. There were bits dropping onto the ground as she went. I'm not saying it happened because she saw me. Maybe she was oblivious to it all. We've all been caught out at times. I've never had a laxative effect on any other autograph-hunters, at least not that I'm aware of. But I tell the story only to underline that not all interactions with admirers end up with free drinks with superstars in the best clubs of one of North America's great cities.

You can never let it go to your head because the memories of when you were on the other side are too strong. At the age of ten

I spotted QPR defender Justin Channing bowling about in Ealing. I couldn't believe he was actually human. I couldn't believe he was wearing jeans. I had assumed, without ever really thinking about it, that footballers spent all their time wearing team kit, possibly with a warm-up tracksuit over the top. A full kit, walking to the shops. I shouted at my mum in disbelief. 'Mum! Justin Channing's got *jeans* on!'

My aim was always to get in The Shed at Chelsea when I went with my dad. I wanted to be in with the proper fans, with the singing and the shouting, right in the guts of it all. Dad kept refusing and taking me to the seats in the big East Stand. When he finally relented and we made it in I couldn't see a thing, but I didn't care. I finally felt like a real supporter.

I used to buy *Match* and *Shoot!* magazines every week. A regular feature that had a deep effect on me was when a player was pictured sitting surrounded by the most enormous pile of readers' letters, tipped out of several brown mail-sacks. One day, I thought, I'll have bags of fan-mail like that and will be sitting on the floor in a heavily branded Reebok tracksuit.

Eventually, after a long crossover period when I went from being occasionally shouted at in west London (QPR) to moving to Aston Villa and suddenly being recognised on Alcatraz (day visitor rather than incarcerated; even David O'Leary wasn't that bad), it came to pass. At Southampton the letters started coming, and I would try to reply to every one. The dream scenario was a request for a signed photo (big stack, pre-prepared) with a stamped addressed envelope included. It saddens me that there is a whole generation of fans growing up who will never know the acronym SAE.

Come the move to Liverpool and a regular place in the England squad and it all went ballistic. I didn't want to let anyone down but there were too many for the old system to cope with, so I took the stack of pre-signed photos to my mum and let her at it. As at many other times in my life she came to the rescue magnificently.

Social media changed all this. You barely get anything through the post these days but you will get an instant deluge on Twitter. I see it mainly as a good thing: it brings fans closer to players, as if they have a direct hotline, and if some of those use the opportunity to make predictable jokes about the relative attractiveness of my wife and me, then so be it. The rise of the smartphone can also sometimes break down too many barriers. People are so used to intimate contact that they try to shake your hand when they spot you in a pub toilet. You've just been touching your old chap, you think, as they mangle your palm. It's either that or the surreptitious photo, taken as if staring intently at a message, given away by the audible shutter sound and a blinding burst of flash.

You never complain because you never forget what football can do. When I first signed for Villa, the East European bloke who was doing some decorating for my mum asked if I could get a pair of tickets for him and his autistic son. I'd got them a couple at Portsmouth and apparently the lad had loved it. It was the easiest thing in the world for me to sort, so when reports came back that the trip to Birmingham had also been a success, the request kept coming and the tickets followed. Milan and his boy ended up coming to every home match, and his son started to change. He had been struggling at school, not talking to anyone, unable to cope with much in his day-to-day world. As he came to more and more games, he began to come out of himself – talking to other kids in his class about football, showing them his programmes, actually having mates go over to his house for tea for the first time. I was so chuffed. It wasn't even a big deal for me. You always get four tickets for every home match as player. My dad wanted one. Milan and his son could have two others. If more of my family wanted to come I could easily borrow a couple of spares from team-mates. To hear that football had helped bring about such a transformation was wonderful. It was exactly what I thought football should do.

During that time I moved into a new flat in the little Warwickshire village of Knowle. It needed painting, and not knowing anyone else I asked Milan. He came up with his mates on the weekend of our next away match, stayed over and decorated the whole thing. He then refused any payment. I tried to reason with him – you've worked flat out here, at least let me pay your lads. Not a chance. And so I remember, every time a kid stops me, or when we do a trip to the children's ward of the local hospital: it's not a big thing to you to have a chat for a few seconds, but it can be powerful for them. Justin Channing and a Polish painter. Not a bad pair of nudges.

What comes back to you can be just as wonderful. You score a goal in a big game and you see thousands of people leaping around and screaming and looking like the best possible thing in the world has just happened. You run to them with your expression mirroring theirs, all of it feeds back in a glorious happy loop, and you think: *I* did that!

When I scored England's opener against Trinidad at the 2006 World Cup, twelve million people were watching in Britain. Even taking into account the proportion of those in the Celtic nations hoping we got turned over, that's an awfully large number of people to make happy at the same time. A musician might have the same size audience cumulatively over a period of time, but only a footballer is privileged enough to have it as the accidental instantaneous reaction to his day job. It's a good feeling to go back to as you reach the end of your career. After you've been beaten at home by Shrewsbury you do let the mind drift back a little. You hold those memories close, feel the warmth, go to your happy place.

The strangest fans I ever came across were those awaiting us in Japan when Liverpool played in the World Club Championship in 2005. The whole trip had a weird haze about it: we had one day to adjust to the eight hours of jet lag before our first match, so we didn't adjust. I remember playing *Mario Kart* with Steve Finnan at 3am, wide awake, with a game against the Puerto Rican champions a few hours later. I scored twice. Who knows how many I might have banged in had both my eyes been open.

We knew something was up when we came through the arrivals lounge in Tokyo and there were banners for individual players with big hearts drawn around them. Hundreds were waiting outside our hotel. We tried to sneak out of a side-door to go for a stroll, but word got out that we'd escaped. First there was one person following us, then two, then fifteen. By the time we got to the nearest mall we had three hundred fans in a tightly-packed group, ten yards behind us, saying absolutely nothing and never attempting to get any closer. We would walk into a shop and they would all stop outside. We'd walk out and they would wait until we were ten yards on and then resume the world's politest stalk. We made it all the way back to the hotel before, freaked out by it all, I turned around and waved. 'You alright?'

Suddenly it was all photographs and autographs, girls screaming and other girls crying. They loved Steven Gerrard. They were in love with everyone. 'Where is Bišćan?'

I cannot speak Japanese. I probably pronounce Hidetoshi Nakata in a way that no Japanese person would recognise. So I had sympathy with the difficulty the locals had with my name, even as it gave some of the team-mates a new nickname for me. Months later, training on an autumn day at Melwood, I would hear reminders of that trip floating through the Liverpool air. 'Feeter!' would come a plaintive shout. 'Feeter ...'

The politeness was remarkable. When they took a selfie they announced it by shouting, 'Selfie!' Before the shutter was pressed they would count you in: 'One. Two. Three!' You were constantly being given presents – little trinkets, or chocolates, or beautiful bits of nothing that they'd made themselves. In Burnley I had a spicy sausage named after me. Different vibes.

For pure noise, it's hard to beat the experience of playing in Istanbul. When Liverpool played Beşiktaş, the İnönü Stadium – the old one, with the open ends and the Kapali stand at the north side where all the beautiful lunatics went – was like nothing I had witnessed before. Everyone in that stand appeared to be male, exclusively between the ages of twenty and fifty. There were no women, no kids, no older men. It was pure aggression, all of them bouncing in unison for hours, flares going off, fireworks, wild banners. I had absolutely no idea what any of the big signs read but it made you shiver with excitement. 'Robot Boy! Mickey says hello!'

You couldn't not be up for a game in an atmosphere like that. Fans waiting at the airport to give you grief rather than chocolates, shower you with ear-splitting whistles as you came out onto the pitch. We don't whistle like that in Britain. We can't do it loud enough. We'd try it like that and end up sounding like a load of postmen. It would actually be quite relaxing. In Istanbul it's like a different technique entirely. It sounds like the buzzing of thousands of angry crickets. Perhaps the Turkish method also involves rubbing arms and legs together.

We talk about the architecture of great stadiums but it's the supporters who fill them that make or break them. I loved the look of the San Siro as a kid, the way its towers made it look like a football castle. I loved watching *Football Italia* and Arrigo Sacchi's Milan team of Van Basten, Rijkaard and Gullit. But it was the noise when I played there in the Champions League that made it my favourite away ground of all time, just as it is the noise that Manchester United's away fans make that underlines what sort of club they are. I played for Liverpool. My mum's family are all Manchester City fans. Old Trafford can be ghostly quiet sometimes. But I'd rate United's away fans as the noisiest there are. They don't shut up. It's the same with Newcastle. They travel well. There's been little fun to be had as a Newcastle fan in recent years; everything except Rafa Benítez has been rather depressing. Yet they still go every week.

As a kid growing up in west London I used to go to Wembley for England games whenever I could. It was an awful stadium by that point. You couldn't see very well and people would be pissing up every available wall because the toilets were so poor. The new stadium is a million times better. But the atmosphere has not survived. I spent a decent amount of time sitting on the bench during Fabio Capello's regime, and the posh Club Wembley seats around us would either be empty for long stretches after kick-off and around half-time or be full of punters who had bought debentures as much for the concerts they'd hope to see as England World Cup qualifiers. I can understand the corporate vibe. I've done it at the Emirates to watch Spurs in the Carabao Cup and I've done it at Wembley itself when Spurs were rebuilding White Hart Lane. The food was amazing and the seats deep and comfy. You were closer to a relaxing snooze than a jump up and down while singing. But you lose so much when the balance goes too far that way. Football is not snooker. It's not Test match cricket. It feeds off the noise and it has to get you to your feet.

You get the same types of fans at all grounds. The joker, always trying to get a laugh at one of the subs when it's quiet. It's seldom funny and it's never original. 'Give us the Robot, Crouch!' You grit your teeth and try to duck out of sight by pretending to tie your bootlaces. The lonely one, who tries to start the wrong chant at the wrong point and ends up doing a self-conscious solo that soon tails off. The angry man, the one who apparently supports the home team but spends two hours abusing it at the top of his voice: a life of frustration, and suddenly he's in a space where it's both legal and acceptable to call a complete stranger a fucking useless bastard while he's trying to do his job.

Crowds turn more quickly now. You look at the abuse heaped on Manuel Pellegrini and Unai Emery after the first two games of the Premier League season in 2018–19. They had barely begun at West Ham and Arsenal and some fans were trying to get rid of them. You can't always be leading. You can't always win. It never helps a player and it seldom helps the club. I remember defender Jean-Alain Boumsong being singled out at Newcastle in a team that also included the not universally appreciated Titus Bramble. When I played there for Liverpool in March 2006 he had a stinker – losing me for our first goal, then early in the second half completely miskicking the ball before rugby-tackling me as I galloped into the box. Penalty, red card, game gone. He stood there for ages afterwards, boos ringing out, staring at the sky, and then trudged round three sides of the pitch to the tunnel, rather than the quick and easy route, getting absolute pelters from the crowd as he did so. I mean, he was bad. He did have a nightmare. They had paid £8 million for him, and he looked like a man playing centre-half for the first time. While he did move on to Juventus, it was only after they'd been relegated to Serie B. But I did feel sympathy for him.

You see things like that happening to fundamentally nice people and you always appreciate a good reception when one comes your way. In the middle of your career it's easy to think that adoration is normal, but it's gone fast, and nothing else you ever do in life will ever see you treated the same way. There was a time at England when I seemed to score every game. Even on the bench I'd come on and score. I thought nothing of it. I associated England with goals. Before a match the same thing would always happen: a player flicking through the programme would come over looking surprised and say, seen your goal-record? Yeah. Why are you on the bench, then? I'm not sure. But you've scored in every game! Yeah. I thought it was normal. I thought it was great, but I couldn't imagine it ending. Then it gets a bit harder, then you start being left out of squads, and then you look back and think, oh, that was fun ...

Your idea of what is normal changes when you get that sort of attention and love. You pie off Rourke. You chat to Daniel Craig and Jude Law in a bar at the Sir Thomas Hotel, there to meet the Liverpool team. Prince Harry comes over during a tour of the England dressing-room, looks at you and says, 'How did *you* bag Abbey?'

Now no one wants to talk to me about my goals. They want to talk to me about my podcast. I was in a central London hotel recently and the actor James McAvoy waved at me. He was with Samuel L. Jackson. 'Just want to say that I love the podcast!' he told me, although Samuel couldn't have looked less bothered. Perhaps Mickey had had a word.

I missed it when it was all gone. The bedsheet banner, the giant flag. I always wanted to be under one of those. The songs! When you hear thousands of people singing something just for you, it's hard not to feel a bit special. I remember my first one, at QPR, inspired by the fact they thought I looked like Rodney from *Only Fools and Horses*. *'No income tax, no VAT, a sixty grand transfer fee/ Black or white, rich or poor/ Peter Crouch is gonna score ... / God bless, Peter Crouch! Long live, Peter Crouch! C'est magnifique, Peter Crouch ...'*

I was nineteen years old when I first heard that. Amazing – and so much better to be the subject of a unique one, rather than a generic one that every club has. I was lucky again at Liverpool: *'He's big, he's red, his feet stick out the bed, Peter Crouch, Peter Crouch ...'* At Stoke too: *'Everywhere we go, everywhere we go. Six foot seven tall he's bound to score, everywhere we go ...'*

If you do get a good one, you can feel like you're the fans' favourite. I think of one of the first I heard at Anfield was to the tune of 'You Are My Sunshine': *'Luis García/ He drinks sangria/ He came from Barça to Liverpool/ He's five foot seven, he's football heaven/ So please don't take our Luis away.'* Sometimes you get a good song, but find you've been lumped in with others. Liverpool's Spanish stars had one to the tune of 'La Bamba'. *'Ra Ra Rafa Benítez/ Ra Ra Rafa Benítez, Xabi Alonso, García and Núñez ...'* Alonso won the World Cup and two European Championships with Spain and the Champions League with two different clubs. García won the Champions League and played for Barcelona and Spain. Antonio Núñez ... Antonio Núñez spent the majority of his career in the Spanish second division.

Football can give you so much. It can open doors and it can put you in the same chant as a player three times your equal. But sometimes even football is not enough. On the same trip to Miami that saw the Mickeyfest, me and the lads were in a restaurant when one of them recognised the tiny woman in dark glasses and baseball cap sitting behind us. 'Hang on, isn't that Madonna?'

It looked like she was having a conversation with one other person. Only when you'd been staring for a while did you realise there were four massive security guards parked at a nearby table, keeping a careful eye on anyone that went near. At one stage I got up to use the toilet. One of the big men followed me out.

'Crouchie?'

Turned out all four of them were English. All Southampton fans. I chatted to them for ages. They asked for signatures. I obliged. They asked for videos for their kids. Go on then.

After about half an hour, keen to be reunited with my mates, I asked them a question. 'Alright if I get a picture with Madonna?'

Suddenly it was all serious. 'No.' 'What?' 'She doesn't like to be disturbed. Please sit down.'

What? I thought. Neither do I, and I've just sorted you boys out ...

I'd been outranked. The Robot gets you Mickey, but it doesn't get you close to the Material Girl.

MANAGERS

You never forget your first manager. I was eleven years old when I met mine. It was a time of youthful fun and innocence, a time of pure excitement at playing in an actual team for the first time, a time of your dad being absolutely furious that you were being subbed off so that the kid with glasses who hadn't got on could have a crack playing the dashing goal-scorer role up front instead of you.

The manager was Mr Waring, one of the school teachers. He was a Derby fan, a football purist, a man who understood that his role was to instil a love of football into us and give everyone in the year a chance to shine. That contrasted with my dad, a Chelsea fan, who believes football is purely about winning. If I'd scored three goals and be looking to press on for a double hat-trick, Mr Waring would reason – quite fairly – that perhaps someone else should have a go. My dad would start raging on the touchline. 'You what? He's on fire! They can't handle him!' The other side would stage a rousing fight-back. The kid with glasses would do his best. We would lose. My dad would annihilate Mr Waring on the walk back home as if we had just witnessed England being humiliated by Iceland at Euro 2016.

As you rose through the football pyramid you began to understand that Mr Waring's philosophy was not the dominant one. When I was still at school, the coaches at Spurs would get me in to train with the youth team, who were often two or three years older. I was always rather nervous. The lads were confident, full of chat and the expanding vistas of young men who were playing football for a living. They had an easy camaraderie. I had a constant sense of intimidation.

Des Bulpin was a Glaswegian-born coach who defined the old-school approach. He loved me as a player. The other lads would get on a bus to an away game and he would tell me to jump in the car with him, so I could arrive more rested. The others used to terrorise me for that. Being the golden boy when all around you are becoming men is not as much fun as you might think.

There were other downsides. Because Des rated me he would be harder on me than the others. There was the sense that I might be going places, and that to do so I would have to toughen up. One afternoon during the holidays he took me aside.

'Peter,' he said. 'You can have a day off tomorrow like usual, or if you like you can come in and train with the lads again. What do you reckon?'

I wasn't quite sure whether it was an honour or a curse or a test or nothing at all. So I was honest. 'Er, I might play football with my mates in the park, cheers.'

When I came back in for the next scheduled session a few days later he was straight into me. 'Here he is, the part-time man!'

All the other lads were watching, all of them creased up.

'Had a good time at home, did you?' Des continued. 'Watching *Back to the Future* with a Big Mac in one hand and something else in your other hand, playing with yourself?'

I was devastated. I was humiliated. All the way round the pitches on the warm-up the lads were ridiculing me. But I can understand why he did it. He was testing me. Did I really want to be a professional footballer? Was I just a nice kid from a nice part of Ealing, or could I handle a little of what I would get much more of if I ever made it into the professional ranks? I never turned him down for training ever again, and he never stopped rating me and telling others that I was good enough – even when I didn't look like a footballer to some eyes, more of a lumbering siege engine rather than someone who could actually control a ball.

Sometimes you need that tough love from your manager. With the Spurs youth team we would train on the pitches at Chigwell in the morning and then go down to White Hart Lane in the afternoons to work in the old ball-court there. Occasionally, there would be a little time to kill. One time, we decided to detour via a snooker hall on Edmonton High Street. The fruit machines were fun. The lure of the giant rectangle of green baize was intense. The six of us were soon deep in an endless game: Ledley King and I were the tallest and thus the best equipped to actually cue somewhere near the white ball.

Then someone noticed that training had already started. Snooker can do that to you. It's why they stick it on telly in the afternoon. One minute you're having your lunch and you're bored, the next you're five frames in and it's gone dark outside and the back of your legs have stuck to the sofa. Our manager Bob Arber did not see it that way. We ran all the way there, but he was waiting for us as we sprinted in, look of incredulous fury on his face.

'Snooker? Flipping snooker? Gonna be professional flipping snooker players, are you? Using the spider as your flipping cue, were you? Standing on each other's shoulders to reach the blue?'

It was exactly what we needed. It kept us young dreamers grounded and switched us on to the standards required. Making a joke to a teenager about Big Macs and small personal assets these days would get you sacked, but in the same way that PE teachers at school are often the strictest, so these early managers knew that we needed boundaries. One of my jobs was to clean David Ginola's boots. If I didn't do it properly I would have to stay late to do them again. By the end I was polishing them so intensely that I actually got told off for obscuring the large white Nike swoosh with black polish. In my keenness to impress I was jeopardising David's lucrative sportswear contract.

Without discipline we were awful. To make up for our otherwise lack of interest in a more formal type of education, Spurs brought in a teacher to get us through an NVQ in Leisure and Tourism. We may have experienced the lure of a snooker hall in north-east London but we had absolutely no interest in how they were run. Because the teacher wasn't used to footballers and the fact they needed constant corralling, he gave us an inch and we took the whole of the classroom. It was horrendous. You had kids who were naturally the loudest and most disruptive in a normal class, and then combined into one uber-rabble. A recipe for disaster, and one that left a grown man in tears. I still feel bad about it to this day. Although I did get my NVQ, so at least one of us was paying attention.

For all that has changed in football, you still tend to address your manager as you did all those years ago: Gaffer. It used to be a fifty-fifty between 'Gaffer' and 'Boss', but sadly Boss is dying out. The last true Boss was probably Fabio Capello, who was so strict that Gaffer felt too familiar, as if you were asking him out for after-work drinks. The foreign lads tend to prefer 'Mister', which dates back to when Britain exported association football to the world through ex-pat coaches in the early part of the twentieth century, and the formal was all-important. They'll have a pop at pronouncing

Gaffer like a local yet lose track of the correct intonation and make it sound instead like a walled city on the Mediterranean.

All managers have nicknames with their players. None of them can be used in front of them. There was no player in England brave enough to address Capello by his, let alone Harry Redknapp by the one Jonathan Woodgate came up with. The best ones are always the convoluted ones: the manager who was known as The Judge because his hair resembled the white, curly wig of a legal man; the kit-man further down his chain of command who had a similar style and was thus The Magistrate.

Capello had other issues. At his first press conference he promised to learn English. He made this promise through an interpreter and obviously enjoyed the experience because he continued to use an interpreter for the rest of his time in charge. He didn't even learn an English swear-word, like a student on a school exchange programme. When he was angry it thus felt as if he was furious with the man on his right with multiple degrees in major European languages rather than the ones with NVQs in Leisure and Tourism sitting slumped in front of him.

He would stare at the poor bloke, spraying rage and disbelief, waving his arms about, red with anger and indignation. The interpreter would then have to try to be furious with us, even though he was a very pleasant, calm individual, and have to get the essential message across in more palatable fashion: 'The boss says you are a something of a disappointment and that he is banning mobile phones from the dinner table. Also the next person he catches wearing flip-flops to breakfast can, ah, go quickly back to where he first came from and procreate at their leisure.'

I had loved Capello at Milan. I was so looking forward to working with him, but his lack of effort in learning even the most basic phrases – easy ball, man on, Grey Goose Wanker – came across as a lack of real interest in doing the job properly. He and most of his staff still lived in Rome, and usually only came over for training camps. He had a seventy-something assistant called Italo Galbiati who had worked with him everywhere from Milan and Roma to Juventus and Real Madrid, but no one was really sure what that job was. He mainly used to run around the training pitches with a ball under each arm, screaming in Italian about topics we could only guess at. His enthusiasm was magnificent, like an Italian Sammy Lee, and he was clearly a pure football man. But none of us ever exchanged a cogent word with him.

Galbiati used to take over the communal areas of the hotel, the ones where we had enjoyed relaxing, and kick back with his fellow Capello underlings: Franco Baldini, who coached vigorously in Italian; Massimo Neri, who did fitness work vigorously in Italian; and Franco Tancredi, who worked with the goalkeepers on things that they did not understand. They would sit there drinking espressos, talking with great intensity and passion, and we would wave at them half-heartedly and trudge back to our rooms. You felt like you'd walked into the wrong hotel. You felt like you'd walked into the wrong country.

The permanent interpreter is never a good look. Eventually it will start to fail. The manager will talk at pace for five minutes, waving his hands around to signify complex tactical moves, varying his tone and emphasis, thumping his fist on his heart. He will then nod at the interpreter. The interpreter will nod back. 'He says knock it long.' Those overseas managers who make the effort to learn English – maybe before their arrival, as Pep Guardiola did, or quickly in their first year, like Mauricio Pochettino – always give themselves a better chance. If you struggle to communicate in post-match interviews, how have you managed to get complicated tactical plans across to your players? How can you persuade a potential new signing to commit to your club for three years when you're acting like someone on a week's holiday?

All managers have their biases. When you're stressed, you fall back on old certainties, and you see that with how overseas managers tend to recruit from their domestic leagues. A Portuguese manager brings players he knows from his homeland rather than taking a punt on a young British kid from the Championship. A German brings in Germans. It used to be the smaller clubs in the Premier League who would take a chance on young British talent. That's now changed: Fulham and Huddersfield, during their brief time in the Premier League, looked to various overseas leagues. Watford are all about foreign signings. Harry Redknapp is meant to take me, Jermain Defoe and Niko Kranjčar wherever he goes, although Harry actually sold me more times than he bought me.

The manager makes a real difference when you're thinking about signing for a club. Word gets around with players. This guy's good, he'll push you but he's fair. This one's a nightmare, he'll take the praise when the team does well and throw you under the bus when you lose. You hear about their tactics and you hear about whether training is fun or a classroom on grass.

I loved Rafa Benítez as a manager. He signed me for Liverpool at a point when many doubted, and he was obsessive about football and the myriad ways it can be played. But I never felt I got to know him as a person. He was emotionally closed to you as a player unless you wanted to discuss last night's game in the last sixteen of the Europa League between a team from Slovenia and the Maltese runners-up, in which case he would light up and hold court for hours.

Rafa's entire life is football. He has a wife and children but I still find it impossible to picture him taking his kids to school. He has two Alsatians which he has drilled like he drills his defences. I can't imagine him in the supermarket, or if I can it's wandering around with a confused look on his face, trying to work out why the oranges are arranged in that pyramid formation in the fruit and veg aisle, making a mess of the self-service check-out because he wants detailed video analysis of how it coped with the last customer. 'UNEXPECTED ITEM IN BAGGING AREA. PLEASE WAIT FOR ASSISTANCE.'

You take what you can from all of them. Gerry Francis at QPR was old-school in some ways but secretly quite forward-thinking for the time. He had good attacking formations, some of the flair still there from the days when he played alongside Stan Bowles and Rodney Marsh. He gave me my league debut when I was nineteen and returned to my life fifteen years later when he went upstairs at Stoke under Tony Pulis. He still had exactly the same haircut.

Sven-Göran Eriksson was in some ways the antithesis of both Rafa and Gerry. His mullet days were long gone and he could talk about anything but football: Japanese poetry, the architecture of John Nash, the music of Grieg (Edvard not Tony). I absolutely loved him. He was the calmest man I have ever met, in or out of football. His record with England was very good: qualifying for every tournament, reaching the quarter-finals in each one, which was how good we were. We shouldn't have beaten Brazil at the World Cup in 2002, yet it took a lucky goal to defeat us. Portugal were better than us in 2004 and 2006. Sven also exuded power and charisma. That may be at odds with your mental image of him, and indeed the geeky nickname us players had given him. But he had it. You could see where his successes away from the pitch came from. I'll say it: Sven was sexy.

Tony Pulis is not sexy. But Tony Pulis knows he isn't sexy, and that the clubs he's at aren't sexy, and that the combination of him and the club and the players he has at his disposal means he can't pretend to be either. Instead he works on all the other attributes, and it works for him. He would have loved Stoke to have passed teams off the pitch. We couldn't so we had to do other things: unsettle the opposition, get the tackles in, develop our long throws, work on our set pieces and hold off on them until the big lads had come up from the back ... to join the big lads from midfield and the big lads up front who were already there. We had to keep the ball alive in the opposition box and make their defenders head it and head it and head it, until they were so sick of it they were almost begging for the chance to play a nice sexy pass out from the back instead. Teams used to give away corners to us rather than face another long throw. I once saw Spurs' goalkeeper Heurelho Gomes have to take a knee like a boxer who had just been floored, so tenderised was he by Rory Delap's relentless aerial bombardment.

Pulis understood that you could try to play beautiful football and be relegated, or be horrible to play against and stay up. Stoke stayed up for ten years. It's like if I played basketball against LeBron James. I'd have to be up in his face, stand on his toes, use the sharp bit of my elbows in the soft part of his back. It's why the Premier League is so different to La Liga; their smaller teams try to play the same style as Barcelona and Read Madrid without the players to do so, and they get taken apart. Use what you have rather than what you wished you had.

Even fine managers can struggle to adapt as the football around them changes. Most have a period of success with their methodology and tactics and then find themselves superseded by the younger and funkier. George Graham had it cracked from 1988 to 1994 and then became gradually outmoded. Arséne Wenger was the king of all that was new and glamorous but by the end was too close to a cliché for a man of his abilities and achievements.

It happens because you get stuck in one philosophy. The best have the ability to adapt to the players and budgets they're stuck with. I've always felt that Harry Redknapp could have had success at the top of the Premier League and the bottom of League Two just the same. His teams could play different styles; he could find players if given £50 million or £500,000. Harry had a big enough character not to be intimidated at a top-four club but also the man-management to motivate Dagenham & Redbridge. Rafa got Newcastle back out of the Championship but, partly as a result of his obsession with tactics, could sometimes overcomplicate things. At Liverpool we played a poor Wolves at home and Rafa went for two holding midfielders. Keeping it simple can he harder than you think. Harry was fantastic at the obvious. Put players on the right side for their dominant foot. Keep a good defensive shape. Give each man no more than two straightforward instructions.

The greatest British manager of all time could do all that. Sir Alex Ferguson might look like a man who never changed, but he did, as football transformed across his twenty-seven years at Old Trafford. The way you could treat players changed completely but his values were solid even as his tactics adapted. He went from Bryan Robson to Cristiano Ronaldo, a revolution in players' characters, nationalities, lifestyles and needs, and he won all the same. A first league title in 1993, his last twenty years on, but done totally differently: from two rapid wingers and two old-fashioned English centre-backs to an attacking trio of Ronaldo, Rooney and Tevez, and then on to pulling a golden season from Robin van Persie. From a striker's point of view he always let his centre-backs follow you deep into midfield, never dropping off, always up your arse – a nightmare for a forward, but brave from a manager since it can leave holes. Adapt? He won his first Champions League final without Roy Keane and Paul Scholes, arguably his two best players, who were both suspended. He won it by bringing on the right two substitutes at the right time and watching them both score.

Pep Guardiola is a fabulous manager. I love the sort of football he plays. To play for him or for Jürgen Klopp would be both a privilege and enormous fun. I'd also love to set up an experiment where Pep took over at Macclesfield Town for a season, dealing with players who can't pass it, defenders who give goals away and no money to buy replacements. At Manchester City he has full-backs who can play as wingers or midfielders, centre-backs who can bring the ball out and knock it, a goalkeeper who has a touch with his feet like a Premier League outfield player. He's rarely made a duff buy. He plucked Aymeric Laporte from Bilbao, a man yet to play senior international football, and suddenly he's one of the most accomplished defenders in Europe. He improved Raheem Sterling dramatically and made Kyle Walker seem a bargain at £50 million. He found Fernandinho at Shakhtar Donetsk. If he's at Macc and he has to look only at free transfers, if his players can't play like City's can, does he keep the same philosophy or does he go long ball?

In the first part of my career I was selfish, only concerned with what I was doing. I thought of many coaches simply as lackeys. Now I've done my coaching badges, now I've had two decades analysing what the best can do, I'm only about respect.

Managing ages you. Look at the difference in José Mourinho's hair and face in ten years. Watch the close-ups of Graham Taylor during *An Impossible Job*. My mum has always asked me never to try it as she understands what the stress does to you. It's brutal. You get almost no time to turn a club round. Half your players might be sitting around on five-year-contracts, the other half want to be elsewhere. You have a director of football buying players you don't want, you have a chairman who thinks he's a genius yet doesn't know his Arsenal from his Eibar and you have fans who think their club deserves to be in the next division up because they were once there fifteen years before.

It's brutal, yes, but it's also totally engrossing. Could you pull off the miracle that others could not? Could you handle the long hours? As a player, you have a degree of influence on a team. As a manager you have a vision. It's your set-up. Imagine that feeling if you got that team promoted – getting the group together, choosing the formation, dictating the style. Players win matches, but managers win titles. There are so many decisions that have to be made correctly or you will fall short. It's *Championship Manager*, except not on your rubbish computer and without the ability to speed boring matches up by smashing the spacebar.

If I did it, I would take the best of all I have been exposed to. The obsession and organisation of Rafa. The unflappability of Sven. Harry's personality. Pulis's defensive shape and set pieces. Paul Lambert's enthusiasm. Steve McClaren's training sessions. Capello's discipline and art collection. I could do the hard stuff – pulling players off, dropping the wasters. It's the soft stuff I'd struggle with: celebrating on my own rather than with the team, having no one to wind up, no longer being part of a WhatsApp group called No Bells Allowed. If I found out everyone else was going on a night out and I wasn't invited, I might have a little cry.

There are managerial rules. Don't drive the sort of car a player drives. Don't wear trainers with diamond studs on them. Don't work out in the players' gym wearing a sleeveless vest and getting two of the younger lads to spot for you when you're bench-pressing. Become a master at PowerPoint: you'll only use it once at each club, when you have your interview, but it can blow the mind of an impressionable chief executive.

The assistant manager is almost a manager. Harry had Jim Smith; we used to call them the Flat Cap Combo. Jim's exact responsibilities were never that clear to us players. He used to organise chip-the-crossbar contests for a tenner a pop and then go inside when the actual training started. Still wearing his cap.

It's a position one arse-width from power. The assistant gets much of the good stuff without the bad: he can still share a joke with the players, has a tracksuit with his initials on the chest, but he doesn't have to front up to the media. No fan has ever pointed at an assistant manager and started singing, 'You're getting sacked in the morning ...'

And yet some never escape it. Some people are born sidekicks. Phil Neal. Tord Grip. Terry McDermott. John Gorman. Brian Kidd. Most of them get a go as manager somewhere at some stage, but it never ends happily. Bruce Rioch had Stewart Houston as his assistant at Arsenal, then switched and became Houston's assistant when he took over at QPR. It would never have worked. A fundamental law of physics had been broken, and only disaster could follow.

It's the same with coaching staff: fitness coach, goalkeeping coach, analysts. A manager has his loyal lieutenants and they follow him everywhere he goes. He gets a new job and gets the band back together; he gets sacked and they follow him out the door. They have to. They're the mole. They become the final paragraph in the story breaking the news. 'Assistant manager Steve Sidekick has also left club with immediate effect.'

Occasionally, one will be left standing. When the only other option is the chairman's teenage son, this man will become the caretaker manager. And because of another one of football's laws of physics, he will have immediate success, Champions League level success – at least until the moment he is appointed full-time, at which point all form will fall away, and everyone will come to their senses and say, what were we thinking, he was making teas until last month.

We had it at Southampton when Steve Wigley took over from the sacked Paul Sturrock. He got the caretaker role: 'Good old Steve, let's pull together for Steve.' He got the full-time job: 'Hang on, Wigs is our manager?'

A caretaker can find himself typecast. David Pleat did it three times at Spurs. Neil Redfearn has done it four times: Leeds, York and twice at Halifax. Tony Parkes did it six times in eighteen years at Blackburn, and then again at Blackpool. He was caretaker so frequently that no one could remember what his actual job was supposed to be. And yet a player will always fear a manager, temporary or long-term. A manager can make you or break you. When rumours sweep the dressing-room of who might be taking over, footballers think about it in purely selfish terms. Does this bloke rate me? Will I be playing more? Will I be training with the kids?

I was at Southampton and rotting in the reserves when Wigley got sacked. Someone whispered that Harry might be on his way up the road from Portsmouth. I celebrated as if I was already scoring. 'Flipping quality, I'm back in the game …' Stephen Ireland was pied off at Aston Villa by Paul Lambert, so left for Stoke. Shortly afterwards Lambert followed him to Stoke and pied him off there too.

Then there was the case of Dwight Yorke at Manchester United, when Ferguson changed his mind about leaving in 2002 and instead signed a new three-year deal. The players in the dressing-room all looked at Dwight, whose good-times lifestyle was increasingly at odds with the Ferguson way, as the news filtered through. Then one spoke for all. 'Yep, that's you screwed, Yorkie …'

FOOD

Footballers are creatures of habit. Before every game for Spurs, Gareth Bale would always have exactly the same meal: beans on toast. I used to watch him, large plate of plain pasta and chicken in front of me, just like everyone else in the squad, and say to myself: that's not going to give you the energy you need for a game at this level. Two hours later he'd be steaming all over the pitch, running from first minute to last, so much dynamism and strength and speed. The fortieth time he accelerated past me, I'd think, what the hell is in those beans?

It seemed like the sort of meal a seven-year-old might have for tea on a Sunday, when they were still quite full from lunch. Gareth may as well have been eating Numberelli Apaghetti or Alphabites. Yet he was so good, so consistently the outstanding player on the pitch, that I got it in my head it was all down to the beans. They must be magic. If you planted them they'd probably produce a great beanstalk that would take you to a strange land in the sky, inhabited by a giant who wears an Alice band in his hair.

I was jealous. Gareth always wolfed down his beans with obvious enjoyment. Meanwhile, I was forcing my pasta and chicken down, partly because we were allowed no sauce and partly because I'd eaten that dish before every one of my professional matches to that point. There were times, when you had the early Saturday kick-off at 12.30pm, that you'd be attempting to eat it for breakfast. Sitting there in your tracksuit, not really hungry anyway, cup of tea to one side, giant plate of bland nutrition staring at you. On a few rare occasions the team would take pity on you and let you have spag bol instead. Have you ever eaten spag bol before 9am on a Saturday? The best day of the week, and you're starting it in the most spirit-crushingly lacklustre way.

It was Gareth who blew my mind and changed my game. My usual breakfast before a 3pm kick-off was the sort of thing a hungover student might have in their dressing-gown watching *Football Focus*: cereal, toast with Marmite, a pot of tea. Post-Bale I began going bigger early doors – perhaps some eggs, even some fruit – and then a Bale-esque luncheon of magic beans plus yoghurt and banana. He's had seven years at Real Madrid and has won the Champions League four times; the eighth of my many years at Stoke was spent mid-table in the Championship. Some beans are clearly more magic than others.

In my later days I breakfasted on match days with the older gentlemen in the team. Those who are dads are always in the restaurant when it's still dark, your natural alarm clock having been forever rewired. The ones without kids come down for food at 11am and still manage to look more tired. Together we would then tick off one of the most pointless of all footballing traditions, a pre-lunch walk around the hotel car-park, where some dogged autograph hunters tracked us round the coach bays while we tried to avoid eye-contact. It was like a slow-motion game of cat and mouse. Followed by baked beans.

The game moves on in other ways. An increasing number of players are vegan: Jermain Defoe, Chris Smalling, Héctor Bellerín,

Jack Wilshere. I've got a feeling Jermain may be vegan like Pam from *Gavin and Stacey* was vegetarian, with a significant level of non-plant based treats, but he was always about the little advantages and trends – the first player to be constantly in compression tights, a cryotherapy suite installed in his own house, one of the first to have a chef at home.

The chef angle would have been unthinkable a few years ago. There were several in the same building as me in my early days at Aston Villa, but only because I was living in a hotel. Lost for ideas, unable to cook for myself, I'd have a full Belfry carvery most nights. For the single man these days hotel living makes a lot of sense. It's cheaper than eating out, the quality of the food will be excellent and you have someone to talk to you between sessions on the Xbox.

I'm lucky to have Abbey for many reasons, but not least because I can hang on to her healthy coat-tails. She'll do a full green juice in the blender each morning – cucumber, spinach, kale, all things never found at a Belfry carvery – and I'll polish off her remains. The most sophisticated plan I came up with as a single man was bulk-buying from the frozen meals emporium Cook, although at the very start of my first spell at Portsmouth I'd take it in turns making dinner with Shaun Derry and Courtney Pitt, an early prototype of *Come Dine with Me* which, unlike the final television version, usually finished with a penalty shoot-out competition into the inflatable goal which dominated my lounge.

Word gets around about the good chefs. Footballers aren't great at discovering things by themselves. They prefer to be handed things on a plate, not least the identity of people who are going to hand them things on a plate. A few of the canteen staff at training grounds have subsequently developed a lucrative sideline in at-home evening dining. Ask them with sufficient warning, out-bid any team-mate also in the market and they'll be round as required. If you don't mind having the same meal twice in one day and you're capable of putting something in the microwave for three minutes – not a given – you can head home from the training ground after lunch with a plate wrapped in tinfoil. It's the classic signal that someone's partner is away. I've done it many a time. It's like saying goodbye to your mum after Christmas: a kindly woman in her fifties concerned that a well-paid man in his twenties living in a major European city will be unable to find anything edible to keep him alive.

My lunch game changed with Bale and my dinner game was recalibrated by England. It was one of Sven's greatest innovations, along with the post-match jam sessions featuring his assistant Tord Grip on the accordion: a chef travelling with the team at all times, taking over each hotel's kitchens, producing unheard-of culinary wonders like sushi, fresh pasta and a salad bar. It made going away with England feel like a pleasant continental weekend break with a little exercise in the middle.

Sven had his critics but he understood what mattered to players. We are boy-men but we like the illusion of being treated like adults. Juande Ramos at Spurs, by contrast, went the other way and banned tomato ketchup from the players' canteen. If you were seen spreading butter on your toast you were treated as if you'd just sparked up a Benson & Hedges. I could understand if I had moved to an entirely spread-based diet, slamming great golden bricks of it into my mouth. One light smear upon a solitary piece of wholemeal toast, however, did not feel as if it would hinder my performance. Banning ketchup and butter simply antagonised men whose days were spent running around burning excessive amounts of calories; my bodyweight at thirty-seven was within half a kilogram of my bodyweight at QPR aged nineteen, although I'm pleased to say the proportion of muscle had apparently increased. You probably noticed.

What Juande hadn't figured out – and the same goes for Fabio Capello, who briefly tried the same with England – was that the players were having butter on their toast for breakfast at home and ketchup with their evening meals. For all the resentment created, he had managed only to marginally decrease the intake of something his players were eating anyway. I say all this without even being a huge ketchup fan. I have some sympathy with Gianfranco Zola and Thierry Henry when they arrived in England from Serie A and could not work out what this strange red stuff was that people lashed on top of every single meal. In France the flavour comes from the food. You don't need to put a mix of liquidised tomato, spirit vinegar and sugar on it. I would sit next to James McClean at the Stoke training-ground canteen and look on open-mouthed as he poured HP Sauce onto everything he ate – pasta, vegetables, all meats. I've seen him put a blob of it onto his rice pudding. Yet he was one of the fittest players at the club. It worked for him, so why harsh his saucy vibe?

Trends travel with players. In the same way that Sir Walter Raleigh brought potatoes back from the New World, so I like to think David Platt, Paul Gascoigne and Paul Ince introduced fresh pasta and pesto to the Premier League on their return from playing in Italy. It didn't seem to work the other way – I couldn't see Zola or Henry going home with recipes for pie and chips – but for a while it blew the British footballer's mind. Pesto confused me. When I was told it was made with crushed pine nuts my mind was filled instead with images of pine cones. The first time I saw one of the foreign lads at Portsmouth using olive oil I may genuinely have used the word 'wow'. Our canteen had been on the naval base at HMS *Collingwood*. You were served food with ladles onto a metal tray. Among career sailors the phrase 'extra virgin' had very different connotations.

Football canteens now are unrecognisable from those rough old days. The best are like real restaurants. You would happily book ahead and pay to eat there. The Spurs set-up on Hotspur Way in Enfield is a marvel. You go back for seconds whenever you can, although you should always expect stick from your fellow players when you do so, more so if you're one of the coaching staff. Yet still the majority of the overseas players will spurn the best of what Britain has to offer in favour of something their partners have knocked up for them at home. They will be flouncing out with a dismissive, 'I can't eat this!' around the same point as I'm tucking into my second helping. 'Carol, I absolutely adore what you've done with this dry chicken ...'

Creatures of habit, there are certain restaurants in each major British city that all footballers will frequent. There is San Carlo on King Street in Manchester and another branch on Temple Street in Birmingham; there is a Chinese called Wings on Lincoln Square in Manchester where they must have an unspoken rule that at least one Premier League footballer is always dining. It's run by Mr Wing, a lovely fella who will always look after you. Wayne Rooney hired the whole thing out for his birthday one year. At some stage in proceedings he and I did a karaoke turn bolstered by Gareth Barry and Joe Hart. We did Westlife's 'Flying Without Wings', despite being literally within Wings, which tells you something else about the mentality of footballers.

Where once a footballer's favourite meal out was steak and chips (protein plus carbohydrate, perhaps a token pea garnish for appearances) we are now truly global in our culinary tastes. Rio Ferdinand has an Italian restaurant called Rosso. Clarence Seedorf has Fingers, less an anatomical statement than a chain of Japanese eateries. Pep Guardiola has invested in Tast, a high-end tapas bar in Manchester. The size of the small plates is in proportional contrast to the price – an issue for most civilians but not for footballers trying to catch the eye of the most charismatic manager in the modern game.

There are almost 40,000 places to buy some sort of meal in London. Footballers prefer to eat in one of three: Novikov in Mayfair (Japanese upstairs, Italian downstairs), Sexy Fish on Berkeley Square and Nobu on Berkeley Street. Together with the May Fair Bar they form the Golden Rhombus of Saturday night entertainment for Premier League stars, whether they live in the capital or not. You'll bump into a few of the Liverpool lads. 'I was down in London last week.' 'Oh yeah? Where did you go?' 'Novikov. Top.'

A man can get caught up in the Golden Rhombus and he can forget that anything exists outside it. Through habit, fear, a lack of adventure, it always ends up with the same dish: black cod. I'm not sure who first ordered it, but now everyone has to. It's as if there is nothing else on the menu. Abbey and I can no longer order the dish, despite how delicious it is, because it's become a totem of footballers' herd mentality. I can't even say the words without cringing.

Japanese replaced Italian which replaced the steakhouse. It makes sense. It's healthy, and you can eat a load it while still being capable of movement the next day. The standard of chopstick use is also improving all the time. Where once there was consternation is now a basic level of competency. I'll use chopsticks throughout the starters, albeit with a slight reliance on the lean-low-and-shovel technique, and only abandon them for a fork when the main comes and I realise that I'm eating at such a slow rate that I'm burning more calories in attempting to eat than I'm managing to consume.

A staple of the old haunts was the signed photo of the footballer on the wall, proprietor's arm around his shoulder, empty plate of spaghetti in front of him. Go to Giovanni's in Cardiff and you can still find the faded images of a sated-looking Ian Rush, a light frosting of carbonara sauce on his jet-black moustache. The deal was understood by both parties: you do me a photo, thus attracting easily impressed customers, and your meal is on the house. Thirty years on and the bill is more frequently settled by a game of Credit Card Roulette, where the card of each player present will be placed in a champagne bucket and the waitress asked to pull one out at random. The tension in the room at that moment is on par with a penalty shoot-out in a major cup competition. Will I be eating for free, or will I be walking away with a receipt for eleven black cods?

Our table manners are better than you might think. Much like the cantankerous Fabio Capello ('We have one hour to sit together!') I would often encourage my fellow dining players to place their mobile phones in the middle of the table, with the stipulation that the first one to touch theirs paid for the entire meal. It actively encouraged conversation while at the same time bringing a glorious element of tension to proceedings. You hear your phone ring and see your agent's name flash up. It could be an amazing new deal that he needs to confirm with you right then. Do you risk answering it only to find out he's done a pocket call by accident? Another ringtone. It's your partner. A furious, wounded voicemail versus an £800 bill. And they say there is no atmosphere in football any more.

Goalkeepers tend to be the least messy eaters. They're good with their hands. There will always be one player, often a central defender, who eats instead like a man in a food fight and ends up with diced vegetables in his eyebrows. As a soup connoisseur, I will always eat with a proper soup spoon, tilting the bowl away from me when the level falls sufficiently. It is in such small details that a man defines himself, but I cannot maintain the decorum in other areas. Offered a splash of wine to taste, I'm not even sure what I'm looking for – some sign that it's gone off, or simply that it tastes nice. Just as on a trip to the barber's you are shown the back of your head in the mirror at the end and will say 'Yeah, that's smashing, mate', even if they've shaved in the outline of a cock and balls, so the routine when I'm offered wine is always the same. Nose into glass, frown, double sniff, little pause, nod. 'Yeah, that's fine.'

Before a recent operation I suffered from polyps in my nasal passages, which for a time completely killed my sense of smell and taste. Abbey and I would go out for dinner, the waiter would come over with the wine and I would think back to a Michael McIntyre quote about being selected for the main role in the Bullshit Production. The glass may have had a stinkbomb in it, but unless it was visible to the naked eye I wouldn't have known. And yet I had to go through the whole charade, Abbey trying to keep a straight face. 'What do you think, Pete? Is it corked?' Me going through the whole Production rigmarole when I just wanted to shrug Partridge-style, 'Just flipping pour it, mate ...'

As ever, the overseas stars are ahead of the game. When my old friend Andrés Iniesta signed for Vissel Kobe in Japan, a clause in his deal guaranteed the purchase by the club of a certain number of bottles of Iniesta's own wine label, Bodega Iniesta. His fellow silky passer Andrea Pirlo also has his own vineyard, while the former Manchester United midfielder Anderson has gone one step further into the world of agribusiness and now owns 800 cows. Apparently he used to tell his United team-mates that when he got up to 500 he would retire; it's to the credit of a player sometimes criticised for his work-rate and desire that he pushed on to 800 before sacking the football off. All he ever wanted to do was farm, the Alex James of the Premier League scene.

I've always eaten my evening meal at 6pm, usually with my children. When I mentioned this to Fernando Torres, he told me that he used to go out for dinner at 10pm. Wasn't he starving? The trick was his afternoon kip. He wasn't hungry at 6pm because he'd only just woken up. I liked his thinking, and I liked the scenes when I went to Madrid with Spurs and saw all the kids out with their parents at Torres o'clock. I tried to convert to those sophisticated ways but watching my kids eating tea at 6pm just made me so hungry. By 10pm on a night out I was either knackered or smashed. I once managed to go mental and delay tea until 8pm but it backfired as I'd drunk more on an empty stomach and ended up going home at 9pm.

When an English player transfers to Spain, France or Italy, they must adapt or starve. Go out for dinner at 6pm and nothing in Madrid or Barcelona is open. Wait until 7pm and you're dining by yourself. You start at 10pm and finish at midnight. No wonder continental breakfasts are so small: you've only just eaten. In the UK nothing is ever civilised after 11pm. The only way of having a sit-down meal after midnight is at a bus-stop with chips and pitta.

Abbey and I went away to Paris and neglected to recalibrate our stomachs to French time. We went out for an evening meal at 7pm and ate in silence. We went to a bar and stayed there for two hours, but no one came. We left at 10pm as people started flooding in. We moved on to a club. It was deserted. We sat around for a while, drank on our own until I threw a few shapes on the empty dancefloor and then fell up the stairs at 2am to get a taxi home. Outside was a massive queue of locals waiting to get in. Securing a taxi was the easiest thing in the world because they kept pulling up to drop eager clubbers off. It had been like a sad old wedding: drinking morosely on our own, eating too fast, wanting it all to end so we could go to bed. They say you should dance like there's no one watching. We had no choice. We were two hours off all night.

Parenting changes how you eat as a footballer. The pleasure goes out of a nice restaurant meal. Instead it becomes a race: can you get through your main course before any of your kids has a meltdown? Forget starters or a dessert. You cut your losses where you can and sprint like hell for the bill. If the kids start walking around you're close to the end. You pray it's the sort of place where the menu doubles as a colouring-in sheet, which would also work for some of the football teams I've played for.

The best meal of the year? The Christmas one with all the staff in the canteen. Everyone together, all those you never ordinarily see – the secretaries, the security men, the assistant groundsman. The worst? Anything post-match. You've had caffeine drinks before the game, caffeinated chewing-gum, jelly babies, Gareth Bale's baked beans. Afterwards you smash down a sponsored protein shake, two pizzas and some chicken wings. Your guts are in turmoil. They don't know if it's three at the back or a sweeper.

I think of those canteens and I think of pranks. The easy king of them all being to pass the salt shaker with the top unscrewed. It's so simple but so devastating to the victim's dish. It pains me immensely that Stoke now have non-screwable tops to the salt and pepper pots. I think of canteens and I think of nerves, too: how I used to go to the old Spurs training pitches at Mill Hill as a schoolboy and be so anxious in front of the older youth players that

I would sit frozen to my seat. I have an abiding memory of Gary Barlow singing on the radio about lipstick marks on his coffee cup, and me being so nervous I couldn't even pick my own coffee cup up. I would sit there waiting to be told what to do, unable to eat, unable to stand in line to get food to eat.

I think too about Bruno Martins Indi at Stoke, bringing in his own tub of coffee and hiding it behind the coffee machine in the players' lounge. He put his name on it with a Post-it note, like a money-conscious student. It wasn't even posh coffee, nothing ground or even partial-bean, just an absolute standard Douwe Egberts. Obviously we demolished it. I stuck it on the table and we piled in. Even the lads who don't like coffee were throwing it back. All the time the little yellow note lying balefully on the floor, its solitary word both a cry of dismay and a warning that carried no threat whatsoever: 'Bruno's.'

RED MISTS

I'm not by nature an angry man. I don't swear at the television. I don't rant on social media. I almost always wake up in a good mood. I got to play football every day, except on the days I got to rest because I'd been playing too much football. Much in my life still makes me very happy indeed.

And yet on the pitch I got angrier. Far from mellowing with age, I Meldrewed with age. I was grumpier than ever before. There were times when I disgraced myself with tackles so bad they required public apologies, when I've behaved as if I have no control over my actions. I'm not alone in that. In every team there is at least one player with a hair trigger. Inside most professionals is a beast ready to roar. All that's needed is the right provocation to set them loose.

Mill Hill, north London. I'm training with the Spurs youth team. We have a kid playing up front who can do it all. He has already played for England at his age level and most wise observers are expecting him to one day make the senior side too. He's strong in the air, good off either foot and he's fast. But he's also a lunatic. He loses his temper as often as he loses his marker. He kicks people. He is to referees what meerkats are to snakes: up in their faces, insolent, always on the attack.

The coaches know this. They know too that it's holding him back. It limits what you can do on the pitch when you're sent from it so frequently. So the hard man of a manager decides to school him in training by playing sneaky centre-half to his centre-forward, getting right up his backside, standing on his heels, pushing him. Son, this is what defenders will do to you. Let's practise not reacting. Let's be calm. Let's stay on the pitch.

It was a noble plan but a flawed one. The first time the lad was kicked you could see him twitch. The second time his eyes went. The third time all of him went. A characteristically quicksilver turn, one punch. Smack. The coach went down like George Groves to Carl Froch. Out like a light. The lad just walked off. Straight to the changing-room. That's the last we'll ever see of him, we all thought. Remarkably, he was back in the very next morning, although it didn't last long. Beating up the youth team manager is never going to advance your career. It's not quite what potential suitors are looking for in a young player.

When the red mist descends, logic and sense go out of the window. You think of Joey Barton elbowing Carlos Tevez, kicking Sergio Agüero and then trying to headbutt Vincent Kompany in the space of about three minutes in May 2012. Paulo Di Canio, shoving referee Paul Alcock and then, as a manager a decade later, fighting one of his own players. Gennaro Gattuso, as an unhinged Italian midfielder an unholy combination of those previous two, deciding in 2011 that nutting then Tottenham coach Joe Jordan might somehow be sensible. Joe Jordan was one of the most frightening footballers of the twentieth century. He was nicknamed Jaws in Britain and *Lo Squalo* ('The Shark') in Italy. Gattuso may as well have tried to French-kiss a crocodile. He still did it, because his mind had gone. You can see the horror on the faces of his

Milan team-mates as they try to pull him away. 'Mate! You've got an ageing Harry Redknapp there, Kevin Bond if it has to be an assistant coach. Oh no, Joe's taken his glasses off. Run!'

I've never known an angrier player on the pitch than the young Wayne Rooney. He was the same in training as he was in those early big games for Everton and England: a crew-cut bull of a boy, smashing opponents and then getting up to smash in shots with equal ferocity. It was essential to the threat that he was, and his team-mates and teams' supporters loved him for it. My dad loved it; he had idolised the Chelsea of Ron Harris and Micky Droy, and used to repeatedly make me watch his video of the 1970 FA Cup final replay, an absolute bloodbath of a game where they spent more time kicking chunks out of each than kicking the ball. Twenty-five years on, referee David Elleray watched it again and claimed that by the standards of the 1990s, it merited six red cards and twenty yellow. By the standards of 2019 it would have been a three-a-side. That all twenty-two players who began the game lived to see the trophy raised by Harris was one of the great medical miracles of its time.

I think Dad wanted to toughen me up. A lot of the lads I was coming up against were from rough old backgrounds, and they could handle themselves. Perhaps it's a good thing he hadn't seen me in the school playground, where I was a terrible wind-up merchant, very much the Craig Bellamy of the west London under-11s' scene.

Badminton is by no means the sport of the streets, but if you refuse to let anyone else play then you pay the price. It was my mate Rob who snapped, snatching away the racquet and smacking me across the back with it. I went down like Willem Defoe in *Platoon* – onto my knees, arms outstretched, head thrown back, face twisted in agony. A few weeks later, playing for North Ealing Primary in the big clash away at Northolt, Rob's brother Ed was having a nightmare, and I kept telling him so. Just like his twin, Ed snapped. He ran over, kicked me, and was instantly sent off. As he left the pitch I carried on. 'Not only are you rubbish, but you've got yourself sent off too. Useless!'

Those demons have stayed with me. In my debut season at QPR I was sent off at Crewe for two pointless yellow cards – one for a stroppy tackle, the other for a stroppier refusal to retreat ten yards from the subsequent free-kick. Against Chelsea for Liverpool a few years later, I behaved even worse. John Obi Mikel was playing the role of that Spurs youth team coach, standing on my toes every time Pepe Reina hit a long goal-kick towards me. Every time I tried to control the ball I'd find my foot nailed to the floor by his studs, yet the referee was giving me nothing. I tried to chest one down. Mikel stood on me again. The ball rolled away towards the touchline, him trying to shield it from me, and I lost the plot. I don't even properly remember, but it was horrific, a two-footed scissored lunge. It didn't look like I was trying to break Mikel's leg. It looked like I was trying to break both his legs.

Thankfully I partly missed him. He was sensible and nimble enough to jump out of the way. I was still so angry that I accused him of diving, which was laughable when the only one doing any diving was me. I told another Chelsea player to fuck off. I then delivered a lecture to the media afterwards along the lines of foreign players bringing so many good things to the English game but diving not being one of them.

Only when I watched it back did I realise quite what I'd done. Was that me? It was like my body was no longer my own. I spoke to Ben Thatcher once about his infamous elbow to the face of Pedro Mendes. He couldn't explain it. He thought Mendes was a really nice bloke, and yet he knocked him unconscious into the advertising hoardings. He described it as almost an out-of-body experience. He genuinely didn't think it was that bad until he watched it back, which was around the same time he was banned by Manchester City for six matches and the FA for eight more.

Sometimes it's purely your own fault. When you miscontrol a pass and the ball bounces away from you, you're both angry at your own mistake and convinced you must now win the ball back, a combination that leads to all manner of brutal lunges and studs-up leaps. Some of my very worst tackles have come like that. You think of Gazza in the World Cup semi-final of 1990, diving in on Thomas Berthold, lunging again at Gary Charles in the 1991 FA Cup final, chasing a ball that was never really his, going in at waist height. Classic red mist.

Sometimes it's because of what is happening elsewhere in your life, but not the way you might think. If you're having a difficult time at home it can produce your most focused football. The game is your release, your escape from it all, and so your concentration is total. You relish the physical challenge but you're getting it all out of your system. It's when everything else is too easy that you're likely to snap. If your days have been spent playing Ludo with your daughters then you've forgotten what it's like to take an elbow in the chops and roll with it, depending on how competitive your daughters might be. It's why retired footballers often throw themselves into something equally as physical when their first careers come to an end. Jamie Carragher drops his kids off at school each day and then drives straight to a boxing gym in Liverpool for a two-hour training session. He's replicating exactly what he had for the previous twenty years: knockabout banter in the changing-rooms with some proper characters, some shouting and barging, running around in a restricted area waving his arms about and then a quick shower followed by some lunch. He's not so much retired as done a job swap.

Red mists descend where you see them and where you don't. To be in a dressing-room at half-time in a big match is to watch eleven pans of steaming water all ready to boil over. Someone hasn't tracked a runner. Another has had a shot when there was an easy pass on for an unmarked team-mate. Now it all comes out – fingers jabbed in chests, shoving and shouting, punches swung. I've seen proper fist-fights, and it's actually a good thing. It shows you care. It shows that you have standards. The dressing-rooms to worry about are the ones free of red mists. How can you be calm if you're 2–0 down and sinking like stones?

Nothing makes players angrier than a spit. It's considered the lowest of the low, far worse than a simple brutal tackle, partly because it's sly and sneaky, partly because it's bodily fluid. Some fine players have been caught out – Francesco Totti gobbing all over Christian Poulsen at Euro 2004, Patrick Vieira landing one on the torso of Neil Ruddock for Arsenal against West Ham (a decent-sized target, to be fair), Cristiano Ronaldo getting chopped by Robbie Savage and, from his knees, spitting at Savage's unmentionables. It always causes a mass pile-in, and usually at least one red card.

There is no more memorable example than Frank Rijkaard's mouthful into the back of Rudi Völler's hair at the 1990 World Cup. It's a miracle of technique – Rijkaard absolutely pinged it – and accuracy, nestling deep in the springy curls of the German striker's mullet. I always thought the perm should have cushioned the impact, absorbing all the kinetic energy, but Völler knew exactly what had happened, as if his hair was alive, like that of Medusa. The intricate structure held the string of saliva there for all to see, one of the defining images of that marvellous tournament.

For defenders it's the relentless pacy forward who will most wind them up – accelerating past them as if they're an overweight spectator rather than a professional athlete, ghosting round their outside as if they're a cone on the training pitch. They take their revenge with what we might call a delay tackle, when they size up what should be a 70–30 challenge in their favour, hold off for a fraction of a second until it's a 50–50, hold off a fraction more until it's a 30–70 and then absolutely launch into it. The referee sees a man in control winning the ball. The defender sees sweet revenge. The striker sees sky and then an extreme close-up of grass.

Revenge comes soon. The defender has the ball deep in his half, about to clear it down the line. The striker comes sliding in, ostensibly to block it, more accurately to let the ball fly past him and then keep sliding into the defender's standing leg. It looks like you're simply trying to close him down, beavering away diligently for your team, but the ball was never in your thoughts.

And so it rolls on. The centre-half is shepherding the ball out for a goal-kick. You're chasing him down. He's holding you off, making you look silly. You've got two options: continuing to be mugged off, waving your outstretched leg at the ball while he sticks his backside into you and keeps you at bay with all the ease of a man against a child, or launching into him, chopping him down and taking the inevitable card. Being so publically belittled is humiliating and makes you lose your rag. You dive in. You bounce off his massive thighs. You lie there in the mud, the crowd laughing, and as the ref shows you a yellow card the defender picks the ball up, pops it down casually for the free-kick and trots past you, trying not to laugh too obviously.

The best players do play on the edge. They need that fire, that overwhelming desire, to seize control of the big games. Steven

Gerrard had it: sent off in the Merseyside derby as a nineteen-year-old and then again after only 18 minutes in March 2006; a red card against Manchester United in the FA Cup in 2011, another after only thirty-eight seconds in his last match against them in 2015. Rooney had it. Gazza had it. Dele Alli has it now. There is such a fine line between having the best game anyone has ever seen, and momentarily going too far and ruining it for the entire team.

There are also the plain dirty, the ones for whom it is less mist and more lifestyle choice. Sergio Ramos has won the World Cup, the European Championship and multiple European Cups. He's also the most carded player in the history of La Liga, the Champions League, and the Spanish national team. He's the most booked player in the history of any of the major European leagues. Despite that he always looks surprised to be sent off, astonishment on his face, his eyes innocent and his arms out in supplication. It's why Eric Dier's tackle on him for England against Spain in October 2018 brought such a smile to so many faces. Ball won. Man taken. Is there a problem, Sergio?

And yet, for those who do not make it a lifestyle choice, the red mist can part as quickly as it descends. When you see the referee reaching for his back pocket, you know. You see the red card and your heart sinks. Look at Rooney against Portugal in the 2006 World Cup, head going back, then hands on knees. Or David Beckham after his kick at Argentina's Diego Simeone eight years earlier, face as white as his shirt, trudging off without daring to look at his team-mates. Even those who keep the rant going as they are ushered off – the Bartons and Di Canios of this world – are doing it because they know what they've done. Angry at themselves, angrier at the world.

STRIKERS

There are some things you can be certain of, on the basis of first-hand experience, and this is one: strikers are most selfish human beings of all time.

We are. Any striker who pretends otherwise is not really a striker. They're an attacking midfielder, or a winger who's cutting in too much. A striker is selfish because it's wired into us from an early age. As a kid I used to hog the ball. Other kids often weren't that keen on being in my team because they knew I wouldn't pass. I wouldn't pass because I wanted the glory. I wanted the adoration that comes with scoring goals. Off the pitch I've always been relaxed, generous, chatty. On the pitch I'm a shit. I'm a striker.

Scoring goals is the best feeling in the world. You realise that when you're playing five-a-sides aged nine and you're banging them in for fun, and all the parents on the touchline are cheering you and all your team-mates want to hug you. You knew you were good and so, it seemed, did everyone else. I loved it. I would stand there being mobbed and think: 'I am absolutely all over this. It's all I ever want to do.'

Thirty years on I was still chasing that feeling. It doesn't actually matter whether you're scoring for England at Wembley or in your local park. The joy is the same, it's just the noise levels that change. When I was about twelve I used to join in park kickabouts with the kebab-shop men from down the road. These were real intense games played by real intense Turks. I'd bang in a goal and they would be lobbing me up in the air, piling on, me sticking an arm out of the melee and giving it loads with them. 'Yes, fucking right!'

The striker is the lead singer in the band. You have to enjoy the attention and you have to be able to handle it. It's why strikers usually have the most extravagant haircuts and the most colourful boots. We're prima donnas. We're frequently petulant. The posters in *Match* and *Shoot!* when we were kids were all strikers, and we still think of ourselves as the pin-up boys.

Strikers are selfish in ways you can see and in ways you might not. Jermain Defoe and I had a good record playing together, but there would genuinely be times when he had the chance to play me in but would instead push the pass a little wide, so I'd have to cross it back to him instead. The first time it would happen in a match you'd give him a mouthful afterwards – 'J! For fuck's sake!' – and you'd get an apologetic raised hand and a shout back – 'Sorry mate, next time yeah?' Then it would happen again. And then again. In the end I realised I couldn't say any more. He was always going to do it, and he scored enough himself to justify it. We were mates. We were partners. But we were also in competition.

Someone told me as a kid that I'd end up at centre-back. You're big, they said. You're not about pace, you could pass it out from the back. Quite a few expected it as my career went long. You end up moving backwards the older you get: my mate Dion Dublin went to Manchester United as a striker and finished at Norwich at centre-half. But I never wanted to move, and so I worked on my technique and my heading and I made the case, every single week, that I should remain the glory-boy. Had I become a defender, there's no way I would still have been playing aged thirty-eight. I love the game, but where would the adrenaline come from? Being a striker, you are chasing a fix. The more goals you score, the more goals you want. Look at Mo Salah in his second season at Liverpool. You get big numbers one year, you get golden boots and glittering accolades, and you want them all the next. Give me the penalties. Get me chances because I need to keep up with Harry Kane.

Leo Messi is the exception because he scores so many and yet lays on goals for team-mates too, but pure strikers don't have that generosity in them. Strikers are about themselves. Defenders want the team to do well, but strikers are happy if the team loses yet they've scored. It sounds ruthless, but your job is to score goals. Nothing else. Without that greedy streak you'll never make it, and without that self-obsession you won't be able to give to the team either. My first thought when I was relegated with Stoke was that I could be the one who scored the goal in the play-off final that got us back up. A selfish thought with a benevolent effect.

The hit a goal gives you never dies off. You can see it in the face of a striker who hasn't scored for ten games, or who has been out with injury for months. The emotional release when they finally score almost breaks them apart. All the doubts and pain and worry explode out of you in one moment. It's the most intense explosion of passion you'll ever see from many British men. Forget the Messi and Cristiano Ronaldo numbers; they're chasing hat-tricks, not individual goals, and a solitary strike in every game would feel like a disappointment to them. For the rest of us, the kick goes on. I scored just over 200 goals in my professional career, and every single one made me feel amazing.

Ronaldo and Messi are so good in so many areas that they've almost driven to extinction one of the great beasts of the old football world: the goal-hanger. The goal-hanger, who will more often self-identify as a poacher, was defined by his gloriously one-dimensional nature. Always in the six-yard box, at least half his goals per season scored from less than five yards out. Messy goals, shinny goals, tap-ins and steals off others. They would still be the most important player in the team and the one with all the awards come the end. The great poachers were all artists in their own right. Gerd Müller. Gary Lineker. Filippo Inzaghi. Emilio Butragueño. All that feeding off scraps made them kings at the top table: a World Cup winner, a World Cup golden boot, six La Liga titles, three Champions League trophies. You could sum them all up with Johan Cruyff's magnificently snooty comment about Inzaghi: 'Look, the thing about Inzahgi is he can't actually play football at all. He's just always in the right position.'

Striking started to change in the early 2000s. In many ways Ruud van Nistelrooy was born to be a poacher; he scored 150 goals for Manchester United, and only one of them came from outside the box. He was certainly selfish. A goal in a defeat was a win for him. But he could do too much else to be a true goal-hanger. His link-up play was excellent, and he scored one goal, against Fulham in 2003, that would have delighted Ryan Giggs: a solo spin, turn and dribble from the halfway line with a cheeky early finish to boot.

These days, being a poacher just isn't enough. You need to drive the pheasants onto your friends' guns as well as stealing them yourself. A couple of seasons ago Pep Guardiola was definitely looking to phase Sergio Agüero out of his first XI. Gabriel Jesus was the coming man. Pep knew Agüero was a magnificent finisher, but he wanted more, and his one-dimensional beauty had to do more as a result –

drop deeper, press defenders, play others in. To consider dropping your club's all-time record goal-scorer appeared to be madness, but Agüero responded magnificently. The fact that Pep even thought about dropping him shows how managers now demand more.

Even so, there is something about the poacher's art that should endure. There is nothing wrong with a goal off your knee from two yards out. You don't get double points for one smashed in on the volley from the 'D'. I played with one troubled young striker who spent too much time trying to score the perfect goal. He would hang around on the edge of the box waiting for a cut-back so he could curl one in, rather than getting between the two posts where a loose ball might hand him a goal on a silver salver.

Timing is critical to a striker. So too is movement – judging where the pass or cross is going to come and being there first. You can get five or six Premier League goals a season just from hanging around between the penalty spot and the goal line, looking for ricochets to slam in. I would pride myself on being in the penalty box 100 per cent of the time the ball was coming in, even if I had just been linking up play deep in our own half. The moment the ball goes wide is the moment I hit top speed, which may be popping-to-the-shops speed for most players and reversing-off-the-drive speed for Gareth Bale but reflects too my entire strategy. And I would constantly be moving to get a chance. The stats we get from the GPS units in our shirts would indicate, season after season, that I was in the top three for distance run in almost every game. No wonder I've struggled to put on weight. I'd cover around twelve kilometres a match, which for a striker is a notable amount, and I did it all in pursuit of goals.

I was still learning aged thirty-eight. At matches, sitting on the bench, I'd watch the forwards and log their movement – going in behind, down the sides, the things I could never do because I didn't have the raw pace. I'd have given almost anything to be flat-out fast and be able to latch onto a ball over the top, but the fact I couldn't meant I had to rely on developing other attributes, and unlike pace, those don't fade in your late thirties. I'd watch the forwards because I used to do it when I went to games as a teenager with my dad, sitting in the Matthew Harding Upper at Stamford Bridge. Andy Cole, always on the shoulder of the last defender, never back in his own half at any point in the game, all little darts into space. Gianfranco Zola, a very different player, a man with so much vision it was like he had watched an advance screening of the game the week before. Les Ferdinand, the tallest five foot eleven man of all time, owning the penalty area and the zone in front of it, out-jumping defenders six inches bigger than him. For a kid who wants to be striker you cannot beat watching the game in the flesh, the complete picture widescreen in front you, your attention zooming in like a camera never could. I used to watch the strikers so intently I'd sometimes leave not knowing the score.

Then I began to do it for a living, and I discovered that it was less a union of brothers than a constant battle for supremacy. Roman Pavlyuchenko was always outwardly civil to me when were together at Spurs, but I got the genuine impression he didn't like me, purely because I played the same position as him. A lot of strikers feel that way about other strikers, but they usually manage to disguise it a little better. Pav was not a man given to great personal warmth, but even bearing in mind his natural temperament there was a constant vibe whenever he looked at me. Being a striker, I tried to use it to my own advantage, and when he was on the bench and I was starting I would run about the pitch thinking, I really hope I play well today so I can stick it to that misery guts.

It must have worked, because I'd always seem to get picked for the big Champions League games ahead of him, even when we were playing one up front with Rafael van der Vaart in behind. And it made me feel rather good about myself, just as it had been testing being in the England set-up and getting the distinct impression that Dean Ashton had me in his sights. Dean was good – strong in the air, capable of striking with either foot, very good at rolling defenders. Had he not been so unlucky with injury he may have played instead of me a lot more.

You win some of these battles but those other strikers are always at your heels. You may think yourself a footballing pin-up but there is always someone younger and prettier waiting to replace you. When you get past thirty your manager starts looking at you like you're ready for a retirement bungalow in Bognor, and the pretenders queue up. At Stoke it kept happening and I had to keep trying to fight them off. Wilfried Bony. Peter Odemwingie. John Guidetti. Mame Biram Diouf. Saido Berahino. Ivory Coast, Nigeria, Sweden, Senegal, Burundi: it was difficult not to be paranoid and think the world was out to get me. It was cut-throat and it was cruel but I saw them all off, at least until Stoke decided Sam Vokes was the answer and sent me to Burnley with minimal warning. All those distant rivals and it was a Welshman from the New Forest who saw me off. I couldn't complain. I knew how the game worked.

There is also that strangest of creature: the unselfish striker. You know they're an unselfish striker because they never score any goals. No, I'm being unfair. You know they're an unselfish striker because everyone refers to them as an unselfish striker. It becomes their identity, and it's a compliment and an insult rolled into one. Unselfishness is an attribute most parents would love their children to show. But their children are not Premier League strikers.

Shane Long. Emile Heskey. Paul Dickov. Peter Beardsley. All of them scored goals, but they set up heaps for others too. There's a reason why Michael Owen rated Heskey as his favourite strike partner. One of them kicked the door down before subduing the guards and the other strolled in for the crown jewels. Heskey had four seasons at Liverpool. During that time Owen scored more goals – 99 in 181 appearances – than he managed before or after. He helped Liverpool win a famous treble in 2001, won European Player of the Year and got a move to Real Madrid. Emile went to Birmingham, and then Wigan. And they say karma pays you back.

Shane Long went twenty-three games without a goal up to December 2016. The following year he had a fresh drought that lasted 325 days. Four months after that he went another 279 days scoreless. Even typing those words makes me feel slightly sick. The non-footballer might ask why he's had such a decent Premier League career. I can tell you: he runs his arse off. He runs short. He runs decoys. He runs into the corners, and no striker naturally wants to go anywhere near the corners. I admire him all the more for the fact I know I could never follow suit. You're a striker, not a charity worker. Benítez was delighted with my work when I went eighteen games without a goal for Liverpool, and made a point of telling me. It made no difference. There was still a part of me that was dying inside. There is a pleasure that comes in laying on a goal for someone else but compared to scoring one yourself it doesn't touch the sides. It's like meeting the most funny, beautiful woman you've ever seen and you reacting to her leaning in for a kiss by offering up your mate's mobile number.

The true striker will ignore old friends to celebrate a goal. I scored for Stoke away at West Ham towards the end of the 2017–18 season. It was a tap-in from four yards. Because I thought it was the goal that would keep us in the Premier League, I went bananas and made for the Stoke fans. Joe Allen tried to congratulate me. I elbowed him in the face. I had no recollection of it whatsoever. It was only when Joe came up to me afterwards and complained that his jaw was in bits that I realised what I had done. Having scored a goal notable only for its simplicity I had clattered an old mate to celebrate with a load of people I had never met before. To put it another way, I had seriously injured a great pal just so that I could be adored. Classic striker. I watched it on *Match of the Day* on catch-up later that night. My behaviour was so reprehensible that I had to keep rewinding it to convince myself I could truly have done such a thing. I then sent him a 3am text full of remorse and shame. 'Sorry mate hahaha smiley-face emoji.'

Your manners as a striker are seldom acceptable. You can do nothing for a goal and yet celebrate it like you have dribbled it past five. You can watch someone else dribble it past five, nudge their pass in from a yard out and then wheel away to take all the credit.

Playing away in Milan for Spurs in the Champions League, Aaron Lennon broke from inside our own half, burned two defenders on the outside and then cut it back with the goalkeeper stranded. I brushed it in and then ran off in the opposite direction. I blew kisses to the crowd. I raised my arms like a boxer who has just won a split-decision after twelve brutal rounds.

Looking back at it now I'm embarrassed. You can see the moment it's clicked and I've thought, I've done nothing to warrant this goal, but that moment comes after I've celebrated with several players who hadn't touched the ball at all. It's shameful how long it takes me to remember Aaron is out there somewhere, and disgusting how I then give him an exaggerated point as if to say, you cheeky little scamp . . Thankfully he jumped up and embraced me, and I was able to whisper a half-arsed apology in his ear. 'You did that. Oh – you know.'

You can try to pretend that pointing at the goal's creator makes it all better, but it's always too late. One of my first Robots came when David Beckham and Jamie Carragher did all the donkey-work down the right and I tapped it in with my nose under the crossbar. I then made Joe Cole wait with his congratulatory hand out so I could milk it. It's like a wicketkeeper in a Test match taking a simple catch and running away waving the ball in the air while the bowler whose skill induced the outside edge stands there on his own. Everyone else in the team mobbing the keeper, and eventually he climbs out of the embrace of strangers in the crowd and jogs over to pat the bowler on the arse.

I've said I'm not a selfish person, but these are the acts of a selfish man. It feels like I'm a different person. I bin off my mates to celebrate. Sometimes I want to hurt someone. I don't think I'm that man, but it appears I am. I'm a striker. I'm a shit.

There is a price we pay for these shameful actions, though, and it is called the miss. If you miss a simple chance it's always your fault. If you miss a chance you conversely make everyone in the crowd a natural-born assassin. Nothing makes the spectator inflate their own footballing abilities like seeing a professional mess up. When Harry Redknapp famously remarked that his wife Sandra could have converted a chance that had been spurned by Darren Bent, you knew that Darren was done for at Spurs.

Misses stay with you. If you're an Arsenal fan, you will adore Thierry Henry but be haunted by the straightforward chances he failed to bury in the Champions League final of 2006 that they went on to lose. Manchester United supporters have every reason to appreciate Andy Cole but will also never forget the chance against

West Ham on the final day of the 1994–5 season that, had he taken rather than seen well saved by Luděk Mikloško, would have won United the Premier League title at the expense of Blackburn. I still think about Chris Waddle hitting the inside of the post against West Germany in the semis of Italia 90 and Gazza stretching and not quite reaching that cross from Alan Shearer against Germany at Euro 96. Each time I see the Gazza golden goal chance I subconsciously stretch out my own right leg as if I can rewind history and poke it in, which ironically had I been playing aged sixteen I could easily have done, as my legs were already twice as long as Gazza's.

How many punters who aren't Wolves, Charlton or Burnley fans could describe a Chris Iwelumo goal? But everyone can picture his miss from two yards out for Scotland against Norway, when the keeper was out on his feet and the goal was wide open. Had Chris banged in the winner minutes later, or Scotland won that game some other way rather than drawing 0–0, and with it ruining their chances of qualifying for the 2010 World Cup, then it would never had maintained its grisly allure. I missed a bad one against Trinidad in the 2006 World Cup but it was erased by my headed goal shortly afterwards. You can't find it clipped up on its own on YouTube, whereas simply starting to type 'Iwelumo' auto-completes to produce his lowest ebb. In the warm-up game against Jamaica no one remembers my rubbish dinked penalty miss because I completed my hat-trick a couple of minutes later.

But if nothing follows the miss except disappointment and defeat, you're done for. The worst feeling a striker can have is to miss a sitter and then watch the opposition breaking away down the other end at pace. If you were in defence you'd suddenly become the best centre-back in the world, but you aren't, so you're instead powerless and scared, watching the three sides of the ground jumping to their feet and thinking, 'Please don't score, please don't score …'

Miss and win and the miss never gets shown on *Match of the Day*. Miss and lose and everything bad stems from you. The pundit will talk over your aberration from multiple angles, grimace and say, 'If only they'd taken their chances …', and you're slumped on your sofa, weeping into the throw-cushions. 'Yeah, that was me …'

It takes a striker to appreciate all the tiny nuances that make up a striker's game. I know if I'm going to have a good game from my very first touch of the match. If you receive the ball with your back to goal and you kill it and hold the defender off, you feel like you will bury any chance that comes your way. You lay it off and the thought sneaks into your head: I'm on it here, it's happening today. You're also thinking, I don't really want to be on this part of the pitch, far from goal, with a defender's knee going into the back of my thigh, but I'm doing it to be ready for the penalty-box good stuff that will follow. If the defender is a meat-head and he comes through the back of you, the doubts kick up instead. If he takes the ball and strolls off, he's owned you. You've been dominated. This could be a long, bad day.

You have your own mental map of the penalty area. You take the smallest of subconscious clues – the angle of a whitewashed line glimpsed in the corner of an eye, whether it's the right-sided centre-back or the left-sided one who is clambering all over you – and you know exactly where the goalposts are and what shot you need to get away to have the highest percentage chance of scoring. Most of the time you don't look up to see where the goal or the goalkeeper is. You just know. I'm beyond the right edge of the 'D' – okay, the near-post shot probably isn't on. I can see the penalty spot in my peripheral vision – good, I could go either way here.

You practise it so much as a kid and then a fully formed adult that you barely consider what you're doing. You always start at the back post if a cross is coming in, because if you start front you can't get back if the cross is hit long. If the winger is struggling to get the ball in, you dart across to the front post because it's not reaching you at the back. When you do your work outside the box, you work out which of the centre-halves is the weak link, and pull onto them when you are in the box.

Be patient. When you see the winger breaking free down the flank or your full-back overlapping him, it's too easy to let the excitement rush over you – we're in! we're in! – and to make your run too early. Instead you have to wait – we're in … pause … pause … go! – so that you don't overrun the pull-back that's coming.

If you go past the near post, it might be the best run to get away from your marker, but nine times out of ten you won't be able to get the right touch to score. The only option to you there is the glancing header or flick, which is not only one of the hardest skills to pull off but can leave you looking like an idiot if it fails to come off. 'Ah, if only they'd taken their chances …' If you wait, you have less chance of receiving the ball but a much greater chance of scoring. Wait, and you have the whole goal to aim at. Drive the ball, clip it, curl it. All options are now open to you.

The margins are so fine. Start your run a second too early and you'll overrun the cross by two or three metres. Get the angle of your dart even a few degrees off and you'll be in the wrong place again. It's why it's such a great feeling when it comes off. So much goes into it. They say footballers are stupid, but if you set up a university course based around the art of striking, you would have otherwise brilliant mathematicians totally baffled by the complexity and speed of the calculations required.

Imagine the equation required for even a straightforward volley off a cross. 'Take a spherical object travelling at 72 miles an hour, on a trajectory of 18.6 degrees, with a cross-wind of 12 miles an hour that will drop to 2 miles an hour where the main stand blocks it off. At what exact point must the outside of your foot make contact with a small area of this spherical object to send it on a controlled curve into an area 14 feet away that is less than a square foot in size? You will also have someone else pushing you as you attempt to make this contact, while your stabilising leg will be in uneven turf made slippery by rain and watering.'

That's looking merely at the cross and shot, as if they operate in isolation to the other twenty players. For that ball to get to the winger it's been slotted at the perfect pace and direction to the feet of multiple other players, all of different height and pace, travelling at varying speeds on a surface that is anything but uniform. And every single action will have an opposing figure attempting to make that action as difficult as possible.

Chess grandmasters are referred to as geniuses. Chess pieces can only move in set directions. No winger is limited to the diagonal runs of a bishop and no full-back the straight bursts of the rook, even if Tony Pulis sometimes tried to make it that way. One chess player controls all sixteen pieces. He is up against one other chess player. A football team is eleven brains controlling eleven independent players, battling eleven other brains and bodies, sometimes with Tony Pulis screaming at them from the touchline too.

David Silva sees passes and movement and angles that ordinary people don't see. That is a rare and special form of intelligence. He is constantly plotting graphs and speed and trajectories and doing it while running around with his heart racing in front of 40,000 screaming people. Wayne Rooney knew how to find almost invisible pockets of space, when to turn, how much weight to put on a pass, where to run, how to launch himself into the air to make perfect contact with a ball travelling across him too fast for most people to even lay a finger on.

These are all constant mathematical equations. If black cab drivers in London are virtuoso braniacs for being able to pilot you anywhere in town without recourse to a map or satnav, footballers are masterminds of their own surroundings too. That's why we fancy ourselves. That's why we're show-ponies and divas. We know what we do. There is such a thing as the strikers' striker, in the same way there is a guitarists' guitarist. We don't really include Ronaldo and Messi as nines; they don't hold the ball up, move it wide and then get in the box, mainly because they're too busy doing loads of other mind-blowing revolutionary things, but still. The strikers' strikers are Shearer, Ferdinand, Jürgen Klinsmann. My all-time favourite number nine is early Ronaldo, the Brazilian one. What he did at PSV, at Barcelona ... I used to tape his Inter Milan games when they were on Channel 4's *Football Italia* just to watch his runs and finishing. I don't care how fat he is now. He can get as fat as he wants. He's earned it.

I also loved early Robbie Fowler – the relish he took in scoring goals, the happy celebrations that followed. What Harry Kane is doing at the moment is frightening. He's not like thin-era Ronaldo, slicing teams open with his pace, and he doesn't have one other attribute that is better than anyone else in the world, but he's nine out of ten at everything. Luis Suárez blows my mind: I remember Rio Ferdinand telling me that he had this trick where he dribbled the ball at your legs, just to pick up the rebound and be away. You'd feel the ball against your foot, stop because you had it, and then look up to see him away and gone. Suárez looks lucky. He scores a lot of goals after appearing to bumble his way through, or off what appear to be ricochets. They're not ricochets. He's played for them. He's turned you into an inadvertent team-mate. You've given him an assist.

The definition of a good goal changes with the passing years. You watch back online compilations of the old masters and it can all seem unfairly easy. The old goal of the season clips can be slightly underwhelming. 'What. A. Goal!' screams the commentator. 'See. That. Every week!' you think.

My most pleasing goals from a technical perspective are the flick-up-and-volley for Stoke against Manchester City and the overhead kick for Liverpool against Galatasaray in the Champions League. The greatest buzz came from the one I scored for Spurs away at City. I was five yards out and the net was gaping but it got us into Europe ahead of them and the Spurs fans were going ripe bananas.

But I've loved every one. There are no unwanted goals as a striker. They're all your babies, and they are all beautiful.

HOLIDAYS

There is a place up in the north of Sardinia near Porto Cervo that is close to holiday heaven. Deep blue sea, little pale-sand beach, headlands and coves. David Platt was the first British explorer to make land there; he had a place in the area during his long spell in Serie A, and he took us lads in the England under-21 squad along one lucky summer. There are football pitches, a golf course, multiple swimming pools, villas. I went back there as a fully grown footballer with Abbey. As we walked in we saw Gianluca Vialli by the pool, looking stylish in the heat in a way that no British man can manage: blue cotton shirt unbuttoned extravagantly low, arse-hugging tailored chino shorts, muscular tanned legs. There was nothing about the look that I could replicate, and I hurried Abbey along with a firm hand in the small of her back.

Still, I thought. I've arrived. I'm a Premier League footballer and I'm going to act with class. Down at the quayside were small motor boats that you could take out for the day. No need for a licence, but the romantic man could easily order a luncheon hamper and a bottle of champagne on ice to take his gorgeous wife for a spin along the coast, stopping in a secluded bay to drop anchor, eat a little seafood, catch a few Mediterranean rays. Get a load of that, Gianluca.

The boat trip all began so well: chugging gently away from the jetty; me at the wheel feeling like the captain and king of all I could survey; dropping anchor in a beautiful spot. Cracking open the hamper and the champers, Abbey gave me you're-my-hero vibes. I am on absolute fire here, I thought, as we lay back on the cushions and had a little woozy doze as the boat bobbed about.

Suddenly I felt colder. A great shadow had come over us. Had the sun gone behind a rogue cloud? I opened my eyes to see an enormous yacht gliding to a stop directly next to us. It was gigantic – sixty-odd metres long, three levels of decking, enough cabins to house a football team. Which made sense, because I then spotted Flavio Briatore strolling along the deck. At the time Flavio was spending some of his many millions as joint owner of QPR, although he didn't seem to have brought Peter Ramage or Ákos Buzsáky along with him for the ride.

Our motor launch suddenly looked like a child's inflatable dinghy in comparison. It looked like something Flavio might store on the poop-deck to send ashore for supplies. Abbey looked up at this floating palace and put her hands on her hips. 'Why are we on this boat? I want to be up there!' Flavio had not only taken away the sun, he had stolen my thunder as well. I have never felt more comprehensively gazumped.

Flavio and his supermodel wife eventually got off, intimidated I like to think by the presence of QPR's player of the season 2000–2001. 'I signed for your club for a mere £60,000 and was sold less than 12 months later for £1.5 million, making a tidy profit of almost a million and a half quid!' I wanted to shout after him. 'That represents an excellent return on an investment that you, as a successful multi-millionaire entrepreneur, may well appreciate! Flavio? FLAVIO!'

Alas, my pithy words would have been lost in the vast swell left by his departure. It was then that I realised the wind had picked up while he had been moored next to us. Flavio had actually been inadvertently protecting us from some serious weather that was blowing in from the ocean. Time to be off too, I thought, and grabbed hold of the rope to haul in the anchor.

It didn't budge. The anchor was snagged on something. No problem, I thought. I'll just pull harder.

Nothing.

Okay. Let's stick her in reverse, free the anchor from whatever it's trapped under and heave it up.

Nothing again.

It was now that we started to panic. The wind was sending waves thumping against the hull, spinning us round on our accidental mooring, sending us swinging towards a shoreline that on closer inspection seemed to be made entirely of large jagged rocks.

A yacht came zipping past us, the crew shouting at us in Italian, gesticulating at us to get out of the way. I don't speak nautical Italian but it was quite clear that one of them had questioned my seafaring abilities and additionally called me a fucking idiot. It gave me fresh impetus, and together Abbey and I gave the rope everything we had.

We may as well have been trying to tow Flavio's palace. I looked around, spotted the corkscrew in the hamper and started sawing manically at the rope. There is a reason why no saw is corkscrew-shaped. Soon there were more holes in my fingers than the ropes. Blood on the deck, panic in our throats. What had begun as a romantic gesture was running into a horror movie. The rocks were getting closer. Abbey was readying the life-ring. With one more desperate stab with the point of the corkscrew the rope suddenly snapped. I whacked the throttle forward and we roared away, freezing, exhausted, covered in salt and dried blood like sailors cut adrift for days.

Back at the jetty, overjoyed to be back, I realised that we had no anchor and thus might be in serious trouble. The sensible thing to do, I knew – the adult thing, the responsible thing – would be to inform the staff immediately, and give them my credit card details so I could pay for the damage inflicted. Characteristically, I pied off that approach in favour of hiding the severed rope in a box, tying the boat up quickly and striding off with only a cursory word for the chap in charge. 'Everything alright sir?' 'Spot on mate, loved it.'

By dinner time, our panic had subsided and the whole episode had taken on a comical knockabout air. Abbey and I were laughing about it, waving the corkscrew on our table about. We saw Jermaine Jenas down by the pool and gave him a wave.

The next evening we bumped into Jermaine again.

'Good day, mate?'

'It was for a bit. You know those motor launches? We took one of them out for a spin. We were in the middle of nowhere and went to park up, but there was no bloody anchor!'

Me and Abbey looked at each other.

'That's a disgrace,' muttered Abbey.

'I'm absolutely fuming,' I agreed. 'I would give the fella down by the jetty dog's abuse. You can't be sending boats out without an anchor. What sort of place is this?'

To think my holidays as a footballer began in such contrasting style. As a young player you just go where the footballers two years older than you are going, which in my case was Tenerife and Ayia Napa. I wanted to go to neither, which mattered less than the fact that everyone else was going and that it was three hundred quid all in for return flights and a week's accommodation.

Every youth team in the Premier League seemed to be there. The big hitters of the scene were the brash young talents who had already broken into the first teams: Rio Ferdinand, Frank Lampard, Jason Euell; Frank Sinclair, Andy Myers, Michael Duberry. The look was sleeveless tops and Maharishi trousers, the sounds UK garage, the transport of choice a rented moped. Maharishi trousers worked for me – they were long and baggy, and hinted at a girth of thigh that I did not possess. I tried my best with garage, and actually enjoyed it for a time, but my arms were poorly showcased in a sleeveless top. I used to look at the chiselled biceps of Rio and of Frank Sinclair and think, bloody hell. I'd then look at my own thin, pale arms and see only linguine. Possibly as a result I had no luck with the girls whatsoever. I can't wait until I get in the first team, I thought. I'm going to come back here and clean up. Then I got in the first team and was desperate not to go back.

I was still finding myself, let alone a more fitting holiday destination. A few years later, playing well at Portsmouth, I was given a week off training by the manager Graham Rix. I went to Gran Canaria with my mum. A few years on I tried Cancún, which in spring may be amazing but in June is just hot. I then fell back into the rhythm established by those two years older than me: Portugal first, and then a few years later, Florida.

It's now all about Dubai. When I started out at QPR no one in the UK had heard of the place, unless they sailed a dhow and dealt in spices. Twenty years of frantic building-boom later, it's the go-to destination. I'm not actually a huge fan but I'm trapped by the practicality of it all: guaranteed weather during the league's international midweek break, a flight of just five hours, good hotels and rather nice restaurants.

Managers go to different places. Managers go to Barbados and an all-inclusive resort. You do not want to bump into your manager on your holidays any more than you want to stay in the same hotel as your teacher when you're at school. But you will always bump into another footballer. It can be awkward when you first spot them in the hotel; you've never been formally introduced before, but you once spent ninety minutes trying to elbow each other, and now you're self-consciously standing next to each other in the queue for the egg station. I cannot be arsed with this, you think, smiling and nodding, asking how his new manager is, trying to read his eyes to see if he's going to give you one more sly dig in the ribs as you lean forward to request a cheese and tomato omelette. Two days later you're playing golf with him, absolute best mates, because you've realised you have so much in common. It's like a footballer holiday romance. 'Tell me more about the 3G surface at the training ground.' 'I will if you explain the story behind that charming new tattoo you've got down your shin.' 'You first.' 'No you …'

I've seen players go on holiday with a team-mate. It always looks a bit weird, as if they have no other friends. I saw it once at a family resort. The two of them had clearly followed the wrong bit of advice. They wanted buckets of cocktails and a wet T-shirt competition and instead had a pirate-themed play-club and actors bowling about dressed as the cast of *Frozen*.

I took Abbey to Crete a few years ago. En route to our villa we passed through Malia, site of regrettable holidays of the past. I felt the bad memories come back to haunt me as I watched the streets and bars go by. Then, suddenly – 'Hang on Abs, is that David Bentley?' We ended up having a night out with him of spectacular size. At one point all three of us were dancing on a table, at least until Abbey busted a move bigger than the surface area beneath us, disappeared backwards and crash-landed on the tiled floor. We took her back to the villa, called a doctor and were told that she had broken her coccyx. I'll never forget the image on her lying face down on the bed, the female doctor massaging cream into Abbey's naked arse as she repeatedly threw up into a bucket. None of that would have happened without David Bentley. Don't tell me he didn't fulfil his potential.

There's a new one that's cropped up on the scene in the last few years, as showcased by Paul Pogba and Romelu Lukaku: the rented house in the Los Angeles hills, private party in permanent swing. With it comes a new standard Instagram shot: player on the steps on a private jet, or kicking back inside with a champagne flute, accompanied by a cheeky hashtag. #nitetimeflitetime #cristalairbaby.

I don't know much it costs to fly to LA on a private jet. I know London to Mallorca is about £10,000, so you can probably work it out. Is it worth it? A commercial flight is the trickiest part of a footballer's holiday. You're there to be abused by anyone who spots you, and the clever disguise I use on other forms of mass transit – a device I call my Train Hat, which is a hat I wear when on the train – does not have the same power when you're a sitting duck in the departure lounge for two hours beforehand. Catch the wrong flight and 30 lads on a stag-do from Manchester will spend all three hours of an EasyJet flight singing abusive songs at you and your partner. Sometimes the only option is to commit to it. On a flight from Paris to Nice during the 2016 European Championship I had my Train Hat removed early by the sixty Northern Ireland fans on board and realised I had no choice but to join them in 900 kilometres of the song about Will Grigg being on fire.

On a private jet there's no security queues, no checking in, no baggage limit. You don't bother with the usual rammed airports.

Instead you take off from the old World War II RAF ones – Biggin Hill, Northolt, Farnborough – like Bling Command, as though you're on a critical mission to Dresden rather than a knees-up at an exclusive Portuguese golf resort. There's seldom even a scheduled departure time. You're on board with a cold beer, and someone will look around, shrug, and say, 'Shall we go now?'

I've been lucky sometimes. Abbey was on the *Strictly Come Dancing* show in Blackpool one Saturday and I was on a solemn pledge to come and watch. Which was fine until I overplayed my hand in the pub the night before and woke up at one in the afternoon. I was supposed to be there at five. I had no car, even if it had been advisable to drive the 250 miles north.

Sophie Ellis-Bextor was also on the show. About twenty minutes after I woke up, I got a call from her husband Richard, the bass player in The Feeling. Crouchie old boy, I'm flying up to Blackpool in a couple of hours, can I offer you a lift? Turns out he was a pilot. Turns out his mate had lent him his plane. He was leaving at 3pm I went back to bed for an hour, got a cab to the private airfield, chilled in the back of the plane while he drove it – I mean flew it – and arrived in Blackpool slightly ahead of schedule.

Abbey was beside herself. 'Oh Pete, I knew you'd make it.' 'Wouldn't have missed this for the world, babe ...'

You have your mavericks. If you've read my first book you'll be familiar with the unusual behaviour of Rob Green, a man so incomprehensible he would read books on the team bus or go to his local pub and have a cup of tea by the fire. He's the same with his holidays. The rest of the lads will be comparing Dubai tans when Rob bowls in and announces he's been to the Great Wall of China. Another goalkeeper, Loris Karius, posed for pictures by his poolside rented villa in Beverly Hills. Rob had a snap at the summit of Mount Kilimanjaro having trekked it with an old school chum.

I was always slightly envious when he told me about his expeditions. Had I missed out? Had I not been brave enough? In my England days your summer was eaten into by international tournaments, except when you got beaten at home by Croatia and don't qualify. It made you risk-averse. You just wanted to go somewhere that did a job. Playing away from home you get to travel to some amazing places, and you see absolutely nothing of them. The stamps in my passport are extraordinary yet the memories are all of bland hotels and Theo Walcott in official Football Association lounge-wear.

Word of mouth has been a help. I never fancied Ibiza – too much banging house music for me, too many memories of smashed-up Brits abroad from my trips at a younger age as a smashed-up Brit abroad. Then I spoke to Fernando Torres, and Luis García, and Pepe Reina. All of them spent their summers in Ibiza. 'Is it not all English lunatics?' 'No, just don't go to San Antonio.' I tried it one summer, a villa in the sticks, and loved it. Being a footballer, I then went back to the same place five years on the spin.

Xabi Alonso was great for tips of where to go in Madrid. At Stoke, Bojan Krkić gave me the inside line on Barcelona. In return, I told them all about the Samrat Indian restaurant in Ealing. Former Middlesbrough striker Mido kept the farm he bought in Yarm long after his time at the Riverside was up. It's his kids' favourite holiday destination. They would much rather be on a rope-swing or wading through a tributary of the Tees than snorkelling off Sharm El Sheikh. 'Daddy, please can we go to Middlesbrough? Please?'

Most of us use the same travel agents, in the same way that no footballer can have their house done up without using the same interior decorator as four of their team-mates. The travel agent is usually the same one that the club employ to organise the pre-season training trip, because if you can sort out flights, accommodation, training kit and very specific dietary requirements for twenty-eight players and fifteen staff, you can probably handle a family weekend in Dubai. You always wonder what the mark-up might be, but you're prepared to pay it because the idea of having to read TripAdvisor reviews and make a quick, safe online reservation intimidates the hell out of you.

No one ever learns the local language. Only on the rarest of occasions will you even try a *por favor* or *obrigado*. No one ever comes back with a charming local recipe or a clay pot for making tagine. So frequently do players forget their passports for overseas games that most clubs ask you to hand them in at the club the day before departure, where they can be looked after by a responsible adult and only handed out briefly when required. We can't do things for ourselves. Many will have literally no idea what country they're in. You could show them a map of Europe and they would struggle to get within three national borders of their current location.

Everywhere are Louis Vuitton cases with accessorised man-bags, except for one player I know who insisted on a transparent suitcase. You could see his underwear, his crumpled shirts, his washbag. The inside of my suitcase is one of the things I'd least like strangers to see. It's like wearing transparent trousers.

You are expected to keep fit on your holidays. In summer the club will fat-test us before we leave and fat-test us when we return. You're then fined for every percentage point that you might gain. I tend to tick over with some light swimming and tennis, although one year Abbey persuaded me to try a yoga class that the resort was offering. I was stretched out in Downward Dog, surrounded only by women, acutely conscious of not letting my long limbs interfere with anyone else's personal space, when I glanced up to see Graeme Souness at the studio door, just back from a punishing heavy metal workout in the gym. He was staring at me in disgust. 'What the hell do you think you're doing?'

And still we have never cracked what we might call the Vialli Code, the correct way to dress when away. Phil Jones represented all that goes wrong when he was pictured the other year in a tight-fitting vest, shorts that were too short and a generic baseball cap. We spent years persisting with budgie-smuggler trunks when the rest of the world was in bermudas, and then hammered board shorts even when the wheel had turned full circle and Cristiano Ronaldo was wearing a thong so brief you could see his breakfast. Through all this my dad Bruce has resolutely stuck with the Speedo. He's in his late fifties but still feels happiest on holiday in something last seen on Mark Spitz at the 1976 Olympics. My sister would refuse to go the beach with him.

His excuse? I'm a serious swimmer. These things make a difference. I used to enjoy asking how many milliseconds he was looking to shave off his time from the sun-lounger to the buoy and back, and then ask him if he was that bothered why he wasn't shaving other areas too. Dad, Michael Phelps is the most decorated swimmer of all time. He has won more Olympic medals than 161 individual countries. And yet even he prefers a knee-length costume. Might he just be on to something?

SHIRTS

For some people, hearing a particular song will instantly transport them back to a different time. The melody and beat kick in and you're at the school disco or in your mate's bedroom or on holiday with the boys. For others it's the merest whiff of a certain smell. Suddenly the memories come flooding back – of an old flame, a trip away, a more innocent time.

For me it's football shirts. I see the blue Chelsea one with red trim and Amiga across the chest and suddenly my head is full of Gareth Hall and Erland Johnsen. You show me a QPR home kit with Compaq picked out in large white letters over one of the blue hoops and once again I'm happily skipping along in the company of Andy Impey and Clive Wilson.

I love football shirts. I always have. I always will. I don't mind an album cover, and band posters are fine, but there's nothing like a shiny bit of ill-fitting polyester mass-produced in China with a label inside that says KEEP AWAY FROM NAKED FLAMES to truly get the heart racing.

I was lucky. I have always had football shirts in my life. The first time I was ever really conscious of owning something special was when I was given the Chelsea drill-top from about 1988 which had a diagonal stripe across the chest. This was the same era that Chelsea's away shirt was a delightful shade of jade, not dissimilar to the Barcelona change kit of a few years back. In my mind's eye I can see the original Hazard of Stamford Bridge, Micky, strolling about in midfield like a prototype Andrés Iniesta, although the similarities between the clubs at that point probably ended there; Chelsea's big trophy win of that period was the Full Members' Cup, and they would shortly be relegated to the Second Division. And if you think there is something funny about John Bumstead's name, you need to show some respect.

Kits in 1980s were so shiny and smooth. It felt like a giant leap forward from the scratchy weave that had dominated the late 1970s, and the designs marched forward hand in hand with the technology. There's an argument that shirts peaked at the end of that decade, the season that ended with Italia 90. The England shirt that will forever be associated with Gazza mopping his eyes with its front and Keith Allen wandering around in the background on the video for 'World in Motion' is maybe my favourite one of all time, including all the versions I got to wear many years later.

I was nine years old during that World Cup. The tea-time kick-offs were the only thing that got me inside. As soon as they finished I'd be back in the garden or down the road to Pitshanger Park for more games in my replica kits. The Italian one is always a beauty. They never get it wrong. But that edition, the shirt worn so beautifully by Totò Schillaci, by Roberto Baggio, by Guiseppe 'The Prince' Giannini pinging passes around with nonchalant ease … The blue of the blue! The contrasting white of the shorts! Watching Baggio's ponytail swishing, Franco Baresi strolling about and Giannini's dark locks bobbing as he ran – that was as good as the opening credits of *Baywatch* for me. Even the goalie shirt was a thing of beauty: a fantastic silver, strangely almost bat-wing under the armpits, modelled with typical Italian style by Walter Zenga or Gianluca Pagliuca.

I was a full-kit wanker in the Brazil shirt from that same World Cup. I wore it to training with Northolt Hotspurs. In my head I thought I was Careca; on the field I was an obvious target for anyone who'd had a bad day at school. It was a golden shirt, and the start of a golden period for me and shirts. The best shop in the world as far as I was concerned was Soccer Scene on Carnaby Street. It wasn't big but it had shirts that you could only dream of. It was football porn. Dad would take me up there on the Central Line from Hanger Lane to Oxford Circus for a birthday treat or if I'd been playing really well. I'd stand and stare and desperately hope they had my unusual size.

My Italian obsession continued after the World Cup in the shape of James Richardson and Channel 4's *Football Italia*. I'd watch the Saturday magazine show, when he'd be sitting on a sunny café terrace with an espresso and the *Corriere dello Sport* and the pink of *La Gazzetta*, and then I'd follow it with the live match on the Sunday afternoon. I loved that Sampdoria team of Vialli, Mancini and Lombardo and I loved both the iconic blue home shirt with the white, red and black band around the chest and the white away kit. The sponsors were ERG. I've got no idea what they did. Perhaps they were Erg. But I've remembered them, so their endorsement clearly paid off.

I had the Chris Waddle Marseille kit, the white with pale blue stripes across the shoulders. If that didn't make me privileged enough, I had it in long sleeves. It was so rare that it used to stop rival kids dead in Pitshanger Park. 'Wow! You've got a long-sleeved foreign shirt!' While wearing it I'd try to run in languid fashion like

Waddle himself, just as when I wore my Italia 90 England one I'd bustle like Gazza, or attempt to bob and weave like Roy Wegerle in my QPR top.

If I sound spoiled I did try to share the love. I'd lend them out to mates so we could have All-Star five-a-sides. One mate would be in the long-sleeved Marseille shirt, another in the Sampdoria away one and I'd be in the QPR Classic FM number pretending to be Les Ferdinand. When I later got to play with Sir Les in my earliest days at Spurs it almost blew my mind, although whereas I loved the long sleeve he would never be seen in anything but a short sleeve. He was too hard to have his wrists covered, although he was also an absolute gentleman.

Sometimes you ended up in kits that had no relation to your leanings. I was at a five-a-side tournament one summer, possibly in 1993, when the kit stall was doing a special offer on Liverpool's Adidas green away kit – the one with the three stripes in white over the right shoulder that you might associate with Mike Marsh and Torben Piechnik. The shorts were the reverse – the three stripes coming up over the left thigh – and it was these that the stall was knocking out, for a remarkable £2 a pair. All the lads were piling in. At that point I had no affiliation with Liverpool, but an official pair of shorts was an official pair of shorts. I used to wear them as pyjama bottoms. I had them for years, certainly longer than Mike Marsh or Torben Piechnik.

As I got older and started training with QPR, my Chelsea allegiances weakened and my interest in other British kits grew. I loved the Rangers one of Brian Laudrup's era, particularly the one with white and red hoops around the shoulders which had something of France about it, had it not been for McEwan's Lager being the sponsors. Aston Villa's retro-inspired lace-up neck of 1993 rocked my world, worn so well by Dalian Atkinson when he scored that worldie against Wimbledon at Plough Lane, and actually laced up properly by his strike partner Dean Saunders. I liked Newcastle's claret and blue hooped away shirt of 1996, showcased so stylishly by David Ginola, and the tight-fitting one that Kappa made for Wales, even if it made John Hartson look like a portly flanker.

There are so many reasons why I would have loved to have played in Italy – the food, the culture, the weather, even the football – but they could have sold me any move based on the shirts. There's barely a bad one in there. Juve's stripes. Udinese's homage. The simplicity and distinctiveness of both Milan and Inter; the unique colour of Roma; the dreaminess of the Napoli blue. In the same way, any player who makes the France national side knows that they are blessed. They get it bang on every single time: the 1984 European Championship-winning shirt of Platini, Giresse and Tigana; the three-stripes sleeves of the World Cup 1998; the paler blue body and darker blue sleeves of Russia 2018.

A good shirt sponsor can make the shirt sing. I could go through a list of sponsors and we'd all instantly see the shirts they decorated. Crown Paints. Sharp. Coors. The 1984 Juventus one with Ariston on the front – just as memorable as Michel Platini, easier to spell than Zbigniew Boniek. It was made by Kappa, the Gieves & Hawkes of Italian football shirts. Inter Milan and Pirelli, both the logo and the font a perfect fit for the blue and black vertical stripes.

Sponsors garnish a kit and they tell their own tale of passing time too. Once it was all local car dealerships and kitchen shops. Then you had the VHS video era – Sharp, Hitachi, JVC – and console time: Arsenal and Dreamcast, spot on for a team that was dreamy too.

Now it's all betting companies. But the first year of the Premier League back in 1992 had some belters. Draper Tools for Southampton (Hampshire-based family business). Laver for Sheffield United (Yorkshire timber). Manchester City had Brother (sewing-machines from Singapore, since you ask). Aston Villa had Mita (photocopiers). It's like a time capsule. I've never bought a precision tool, a sewing-machine, a copier or a bulk load of hardwood. But I can see all those shirts now. Ipswich had Fisons, the fertiliser lot. Of course they did.

I miss the old one to eleven numbering system, if I'm honest, There was something magical about it. Seven a right winger, eleven a left winger, ten for the flamboyant playmaker. Two and three standard full-backs, eight central mid, your main man. Six was controversial. Was it a deep-lying midfielder or a centre-half? Numbers matter. If you swap shirts with the Barcelona ten and it's not Messi, it doesn't mean anything. They also matter only on the pitch. I did all my shirt numbers in the casinos of Vegas one year. It doesn't work.

A horrible shirt can be made beautiful by the season that it was worn, in the same way that you can have bands with terrible names but hugely popular back catalogues. Oasis is no sort of name for a band. What is a coldplay? Norwich's kit of 1993 was in theory a shocker – a washed-out yellow covered in green scribbles. But because it is associated with the Canaries charging through the UEFA Cup, with Jeremy Goss smashing in wonder-volleys against Bayern Munich and Leeds, it will forever have a special place in Norfolk hearts. The Norwich and Peterborough Building Society. Another classic sponsor of its time.

If I were to start a club from scratch now, I'd design a shirt around the one I wore with West Middlesex Colts. Green and black vertical stripes. Different, nostalgic. Although a vertical stripe makes me look even taller, so I would have to be manager rather than on the pitch. A hooped shirt makes me look fatter, which is much better. Xherdan Shaqiri needs a vertical stripe. I've said too much.

It would have to be long-sleeved. I also like a collar; the only round neck that has ever worked was the deliberately high one on the Newcastle home shirt of 1998, as seen on Warren Barton and Stéphane Guivarc'h. The shorts would have to be long too for obvious reasons. Ian Ormondroyd was the Crouch of his day, and in the tiny shorts of 1989 I would have looked as exposed as he and his Aston Villa team-mate Kent Nielsen did back then, with no discernible change in leg girth from ankle to upper thigh. The shorts would be black, the socks black with green tops.

I do wonder if I will still be able to wear football shirts when I'm fifty. They don't look great on an older man, and I've spent so much of my childhood and adult life in them that perhaps I've burned all my matches. I may have to try a retro one, and then gradually move towards the posh club scarf, like Mancini at City. Maybe a bobble hat. The rosette is now out of the game.

There is one ageing man still rocking the kit look. You get so much of it as a player that you end up giving half of it away, and my dad is a hoarder. He's hung onto to everything I've passed on, which means he'll come down for breakfast in a QPR top with the number 28 on the back and then pop a Villa anorak on to walk the dog. If it's not raining and he needs a pint of milk it's an England World Cup 2006 tracksuit. Like father, like son.

REFEREES

There we were in the park, early teens, all of us in the kits we'd asked for that Christmas. Me in the blue of Vialli's Sampdoria, one mate in the red and white of Arsenal, a lad in the QPR home shirt and another in the white of England. In the distance we see one of the other lads jogging towards us. There were a few frowns and murmurs of confusion. What was he wearing? It looked different – was it a previously undiscovered third kit, or something from a hipster Italian club in the bottom reaches of Serie B?

It was only as he approached that we realised the truth, and we almost staggered under the shock. He'd come in a brand new referee's kit. Black jersey with white badge, black shorts, black socks with white tops. What we might call the full Roger Milford.

Our minds were blown. Under questioning he revealed that this was no heinous parental error. He'd specifically requested it on his Christmas list. Under match conditions he then revealed a perverse side to his character that none of us had ever imagined. He didn't attempt to referee our game, as you might now expect, but was instead caught between the player he had once been and the official he appeared to want to become. He was good on the ball. He was still throwing in his step overs and feints. But he couldn't reconcile himself to their end product. I'd bang one in the top corner and run off pretending to be Gazza. He'd smash a volley home, run off, remember he wanted to be David Elleray and book himself for over-celebrating.

It stunned us because it was all so far outside our experience. None of us had ever met anyone who actively wanted to be a ref. There had never even been a whisper along the lines of, 'That might be fun …' There are no posters of superstar officials in *Match* or *Shoot!* No one had Jeff Winter dishing out a red card on their bedroom wall.

All these years on I still have the same computational issue. It's not even close to the spectrum of my understanding. Kids want to be footballers, astronauts, dolphin trainers. They want to be liked. They enjoy having friends over for tea. Referees are never liked. Make any decision and half the other men on the pitch instantly hate you. No one invites referees up to the players' lounge afterwards, any more than a kid would ask the headteacher to come to their birthday party. You don't have obvious friends. The linesmen? They're not your mates. They're assistant referees. They're rivals. They want to bin you off. They want your job.

Referees are now relatively fit. Put them in the general population and they will actually look quite trim: defined calves, strong thighs, possibly the outline of modest pectoral muscles. Put them on a pitch surrounded by professional athletes and instead they are ruined by the contrast. They appear to lack strength, to have arms that are too skinny and legs that look the wrong shape. They look narrow-shouldered and incapable of running with anywhere near the same pace or easy coordination. I can sympathise; it's something I've had to deal with throughout my own career.

They can't have cool haircuts. Imagine a ref running about with a man-bun and hipster beard. You can't. Neither can you have referees with bleached highlights or corn-rows. They are doomed by profession to walking into a barber's and asking for a little bit off all over. There are no Premier League footballers who look like Mike Dean.

There is a reason all match officials arrive together in a Viano people-carrier. Get seen driving into a ground in a nice car and everyone who spots you will resent it. Not for the referee a Ferrari or pimped-up Range Rover with personalised plates. The people-carrier is anonymous. They're not on their own. Someone else is driving so they can duck down pretending to be picking something up off the floor when they go past curious spectators. When they get into the stadium they have to get changed in the pokiest dressing-room in the building. There's insufficient room for four men to simultaneously be naked. Things winking everywhere. Rapid reassessments being made. You get changed first Dave, I'll go for a walk.

As a retired player you look back fondly at your career stats. They're who you are. They're what you did. They're a benchmark and comparison point. As a referee no one gives a shit. Did you know Mark Clattenburg finished with 292 Premier League games, dishing out 48 red cards? Of course not.

Do referees frame their shirts from big games? There is seldom anything memorable about a ref's shirt and there is never an iconic number. There is no 'Dean 10' or 'Atkinson 11'. No one ever says, woah, remember that 2001 Premier League ref's kit? Ooh yeah, what a beauty that was ...

As a referee you finish your day's work, and the best possible scenario is that no one remembers you were involved in the game. No contentious decisions, no sendings-off, everyone enjoyed it. At your absolute best you're invisible. The only one who knows is the head of referees, and all he might do is file a report to some computer system somewhere that marks you out of ten in various arcane categories, like you're a pedigree hound at Crufts.

You get home. You're enjoying some tea with the family. How was school, kids? Great, Dad. How was your day? Yeah triffic. Only 40,000 people called me a wanker.

And yet. You have no discernible football ability, but you're running around on the pitch at Wembley, watching the finest players of their generation at such close quarters that you could almost touch them, if you had the pace to keep up. You're in the centre-circle at Old Trafford, or Anfield, jogging round in the middle of it all, as if you had a virtual reality headset on. You can hear the players' breathe. You can see the effort on their faces. And you are getting paid, quite a significant amount if you're at the top. Refs employed by PGMOL (Professional Game Match Officials Limited) are on a yearly retainer of around £42,000 in the Premier League. Each match you ref you'll get another grand or so on top. Make it to the Champions League and it's almost £6,000 per game. You can be on £70,000 a year without being able to trap a bag of cement. Unlike an outfield player you can keep doing it into your mid-forties. It's decent.

Referees are changing. Mark Clattenburg has tattoos. One of them depicts the European Cup, as if he'd won it rather than blowing a whistle during it. They have egos, because strange individuals struck by some unholy compulsion now occasionally request selfies and autographs. They relish the limelight. Look at Mike Dean and his dramatic points at the penalty spot, as if he were conducting an orchestra rather than turning the pages for the pianist. You think of Jeff Winter, not only writing an autobiography but including a passage where he speculated that the applause at the end of his final game was in part directed at him rather than the victorious home side. If you do think of Jeff Winter, try not to visit his website, where he is selling T-shirts and doing so by modelling one in front of a mirror that inadvertently indicates that below the waist he is not wearing anything at all.

Because some referees have egos, some players can boss games by controlling them. Where once a player only referred to an official by shouting 'ref', it's now 'Mike' and 'Phil' and 'Andre'. John Terry was the first I heard doing it, and initially I had no idea who he was talking to. There was no Mike playing for Chelsea. When I realised it was the ref I began to see who was the puppet and who was the puppeteer. Every decision got a shout. 'Cracking decision, Mike.' 'Yes, bang on, Mike.' Before you know it the ref's calling him JT. Now if Terry clatters someone it's like yellow-carding your mate. Are you going to be as hard on him when you're ready to start sending each other Christmas cards?

When Ashley Williams came to Stoke on loan one of the first things he did was buttonhole Darren Fletcher. 'I used to hate you, Fletch. When I played you with Swansea and Everton I used to watch you reffing it from the centre-circle, always in his ear, always giving him a steer, and it wound me up something special. I waited in the tunnel once to knock you out. But it turns out you're actually alright.'

There have been times when I've struggled with referees. Before the 2006 World Cup, Graham Poll said that the tournament officials had been in a meeting where they were specifically warned about me. He uses his arms when he's jumping for headers, that Crouch. Watch him. They can't have been watching that carefully, because they missed me pulling Brent Sancho's dreadlocks as I headed England in front against Trinidad.

But I was giving too many fouls away with England and in the Champions League with Liverpool, so I had to change my style. Even after that, I got fewer decisions than I should. They were fouls on me that you couldn't see because the defender was hidden behind me. Within fifteen minutes of a game starting I'd know whether I'd got a fair ref or one who wouldn't give me a bean, and there was nothing you can do about it. All that changed was my dad's attitude afterwards. When as a kid I would blame referees for my bad performances he would absolutely hammer me. No excuses, son. That centre-half owned you. Having had twenty years as a professional he no longer thought I needed toughening up, and went the other way. Come on Dad, I played badly. Badly? That idiot never gave you a chance …

I do occasionally wonder what sort of official I might be if given the chance. Sunday league players know because they'll often have to run the line for a half. As I haven't I've got a feeling I'd still be a player in a ref's body. If a mouthy striker gave me stick I'd give it right back. 'I'm crap, am I? You're worse. You've just missed a sitter, I'm the fourth official in the Europa League semi-final next week.' I'd rather that than the false brown-nosing of rugby, where the players have to call the referee 'sir' but can then mete out acts of casual brutality upon each other. Footballers aren't all animals simply because they don't treat the officials like the head prefect. Not all rugby players are stand up guys.

The showing of cards fascinates me – not the decision to do so, but the manner in which it's done. I knew a lad who used to randomly two-foot tackle his mates as they were stood at the bar ordering drinks. Another one of the group played the ref. He'd decide whether the tackle had been filthy or milked and show an actual card as appropriate – red for studs up, yellow for a dive. On the pitch I think I'd have been flamboyant. I'd be delighted the opportunity had arisen. Card out. Bang. Have that.

Having been a player, neither would I fall for the sly tricks we use to get referees to change their minds. The making-a-ball shape with our hands when to be accurate we should be miming a set of studs raking down someone's Achilles. The hands pressed together in prayer, usually with the fingers wagging slightly in supplication: surely you can't book me for that, I beg of you ... The team-mate coming over with his hands ostentatiously clasped behind his back as all his mates rage at the referees. Talk to me, I'm the good cop. The fake card is horrible – waving an imaginary yellow at the ref to get an opposition player in trouble – but so too is the Italian-style gesticulating with fingertips on each hand, as if you're milking your own nipples. Joe Cole started doing it towards the end of his career. Joe, I used to think, you're from Camden, not Lake Como.

No one likes the slow reveal, where you see the card coming as the ref reaches leisurely for his pocket, takes the yellow out and then holds it casually at navel height before reluctantly holding it up. It sucks all the drama out of it. The yellow card now seems to always be stowed in the breast pocket, the red in the rear of the shorts. I wouldn't be adverse to the officials swapping it around randomly to keep the jeopardy up – the ref running over, the fingers reaching towards his arse-cheeks, the crowd gasping ... The back pocket gives more of a flourish. The arm has to travel further and at greater speed. It's like producing a bunch of flowers from behind your back rather than cradling them in front of you. Drama. Surprise.

There are referees who can't wait to whip out a card. The ones who like to do it as they're still running, almost falling over their own words in the excitement. You see them canter to a halt and then think, oops, better write down their name and number before I forget. The alternative is the zen master, carefully noting all the details with his tiny little referee's pen before finally raising the card like a man offering his mate a cigarette.

I genuinely think a red card comes as a buzz to a few refs. It's their moment in the sun, the teacher who can finally throw the naughty kid out of their classroom. First the card and then the unnecessary point in the direction of the dressing-rooms, sometimes with the other hand, sometimes with the card itself. These gestures are seldom geographically accurate. Often they're pointing to the family enclosure rather than the tunnel. It doesn't matter. It's a double slap in the face: a sending-off and then the send off. The obvious enjoyment on their face when the decision is a straightforward one rather than contentious. Everyone will praise me for this. I'm the boss among the rabble. I am the sword of justice. I am the law.

As footballers we practise our basic skills again and again – the lay-off, the driven pass, the header. I like to imagine referees doing the same, working on their card-brandishing technique in front of the mirror at home. Yes Mike, liked that one. No, not that one, I've rushed it.

How to do they train? Do they just run, or do they have to practise running while also whistling? Do they work on jogging slowly backwards, as they have to so frequently in a match scenario? The problem I would have as a referee is that I would run like a footballer. I'd go to the ball or charge for the centre of the penalty area. I'd constantly be in the way. A referee has to move like the world's worst defensive midfielder – shuttling about in a small area around the halfway line, never more than fifteen metres from the ball, never closer than five. He has to constantly be where the ball is, but not actually where the ball is.

The saddest thing is watching them warm up before a game. They're not fast by the standards of the other men warming up around them. They don't look good sprinting. They can't go too close to the ends of the pitch because the fans there will shout at them, and they can't go too deep into either half because they'll get in the way of the players. Instead they're left tracking around the centre circle or the touchline closest to the posh seats, the only ones on the pitch who have to bring their own kit, the ones in the worst boots. It's awful, but as a player you just don't take the details of their day into account. I've played more than 500 games as a professional footballer and I still couldn't tell you if referees turn up in shirt and tie or tracksuits.

And then there is the fourth official, the one who gets none of the upsides and all of the downs. The referee is running around on the pitch, immersed in the game. The assistants get to run along the touchline, albeit in a slightly cumbersome fashion. The fourth official gets to stand right next to both benches and be abused throughout the game by both. Any mistake the referee makes is blamed upon them. They are his envoy to the two sets of coaches and substitutes, and so one assistant from each bench will be assigned the job of trying to influence the game through him. I've spent a lot of time on the bench in recent years, and I can tell you that it's relentless. They know the fourth official can speak to the ref via radio mic, so they'll be at him from the start. 'You've had a nightmare!' 'That's never a foul!' 'Hey! Hey! That's the second time he's done that!'

How can they hit back? By telling a manager to stay in his technical area. That's pretty much their only riposte. They are the traffic wardens of football. They are the community officer to the referee's constable. They don't have handcuffs. They don't even have a truncheon. They have to tell a proper policeman if they want to make an arrest. The best case scenario is that they can impose a small on-the-spot fine for littering. 'I warn you, I've got a notepad. If you carry on with this behaviour, I'm going to note it down.'

I say all of that, but football is nothing without its officials. We literally couldn't have a game without them. I couldn't score goals and bask in the adoration of thousands of strangers. We couldn't earn eye-watering amounts of money. Referees are the protectors, the enablers, the hidden hand. And it is such a difficult job. You only have to see what happens at club training grounds when you have a practice match and one of the coaches – highly experienced, quite possibly a former elite player – has to officiate. They're rubbish. They're constantly in the wrong place. They make mistakes. They hate giving decisions. The contest degenerates into a load of hacking and complaints. Full-on square-ups, balls booted away, basic rules no longer adhered to. It's horrible.

So referees deserve our respect. Where do you end up otherwise? And if the Premier League refs should be praised, think too of the teenagers doing it in cold, muddy parks every Sunday morning. No annual retainer, no free trips to games in Europe. Just a lonely few hours being whinged at by hungover cloggers.

Thank you, referees. Thank you.

SET PIECES

There is a view among some in football – the purists, the creatives, a section of those who consider themselves artists – that scoring from a set piece is somehow unfair. It's taking a sledgehammer to a door rather than picking the lock. It's turning the free-flowing choreography of football into the formal line dance of the NFL. It's what you are forced to rely upon when you're not good enough to score any other way.

In February 2005 I scored the equaliser for Southampton against Arsenal from a Jamie Redknapp corner. To Arsène Wenger, fuming that his side's title defence had been undone in such a straightforward manner, it was the final straw. Already upset by Rory Delap's long throw-ins and the somewhat physical approach of David Prutton in our midfield, he referred to me after wards as a 'basketball player', as if I had dunked the ball into Jens Lehmann's net rather than outjumped the defenders he had scouted, signed and coached to head it past a goalkeeper he had selected. The inference was clear: they're not as good as us, they've exploited some inexplicable loophole in the laws of the sport, they have played the game in an underhand manner.

Wenger never really got over it. When he used to bring his Arsenal team to Stoke when I moved north, and his title ambitions were repeatedly Pulised, he would treat our tactics – out-working and out-muscling the opposition, piling big men into the box off every free-kick, corner and throw-in – like the anti-football. It wasn't anti-football; it was anti-Wenger's football, which is why we did it, and why we would have been mad not to. They were miles technically better than us, man for man. Had we tried playing pretty triangles they would have filleted us. So we gave them a problem they couldn't handle, based on set pieces. It worked. I've scored more league goals against Arsenal than any other team. Not bad for someone who plays a different sport.

There's a delicious irony in the set piece being decried at a club where Steve Bould's near-post flick-ons were once a defining and silverware-winning feature. So fearful did some teams become of Stoke's set-piece prowess that panic fed into the initial weakness to create a mad vortex that used to suck goals in. Rattled defenders would be so worried that they would give away penalties. Teams terrified of Delap would concede corners rather than face another of his throw-ins.

We made everything take so long. On every free-kick, even from ones within our own half, we would rumble Shawcross and Robert Huth forward into the opposition penalty box like wrecking-balls. The body language of the opposing defenders would collapse as they trundled up. I remember Reading's Jobi McAnuff sighing as he tried to mark me up on our eleventh corner. 'I've spent twelve seasons trying to get into the Premier League, and now we have, I find out it's like being back in League One ...'

You can work on your formation and your team selection all you like. You can play the most beautiful passing football. If you can't cope with set pieces you will still get beaten. When I was in the under-16s team at Spurs we played our equivalents at

Barcelona. They were amazing. I'd never seen a performance like it. Every single one of them, from the striker to the left-back to the goalkeeper, could play. We were Spurs; we were decent. Against them we looked ordinary. They must have had 90 per cent of the possession and at least five golden chances in each half.

Yet we beat them. We had one set piece, a beautifully weighted free-kick, and I got to it before their keeper: 1–0. They couldn't believe it. They considered it sacrilege, an insult, an outrage. We laughed all the way back to north London. Sometimes at Stoke we used to come off the pitch at the final whistle and say, how the hell have we won that? We had defended for eighty-nine minutes, worked one brilliant free-kick and a cunning corner routine and walked off 2–0 winners. Daylight robbery in stylistic terms, entirely right under the rules of football.

Much like the 50–50 tackle, we love the formal set piece in Britain for exactly this reason. It's a chance for the committed to outwit the gifted. It's something to look forward to. You don't want to rush it, which is why the quick free-kick is greeted with such dismay. In Spain they just want to restart the game as quickly as possible. A five-yard pass sideways, let's crack on. Instead we say, everyone hold on a minute. Let's get the big dogs up. Let's do it all as slowly as possible to ramp up the tension. Few other nations go as berserk for a simple corner as we do. If a cross ricochets off the full-back's leg from a cross and the linesman points to the corner flag we react like it's worth half a goal. 'YES! FUCKING CORNER!' If a pass is played into the winger in exactly the same position that he'd take a corner from, there is barely a murmur. We need the official awarding of the set piece to get us going.

I understand this. When a quick free-kick goes wrong it feels like such a criminal waste that the perpetrators should receive automatic yellow cards. If I were Aymeric Laporte or John Stones, watching David Silva or Kevin De Bruyne taking short corners, it would drive me mad. I'd want it played onto my head as quickly as possible. But I couldn't really complain, because it works. They're winning everything.

Because here's the thing: the quick free-kick is usually a lot better, because no one is marking up and no defensive line has had time to take shape, and short corners can feel the same. Wait for your big men to come up and all the opposition players who were out of position have now taken the chance to get back into position. It's literally the worst time of all to attempt to score.

I set up a goal for Michael Owen on my England debut by taking a quck free-kick. Looked up, saw a gap, sent him through, international career up and running. The only issue I have with the quick one is when you're still on the ground having been fouled, and in your keenness to take it you end up trying to kick the ball while you have one hand on it to stop it rolling and one knee still on the ground. For a man of six foot seven it's not very becoming.

Even a kick-off is a set piece, and it used to be one of my favourites. When you had a strike partner it was an opportunity to be bullish at the start of a match – I'm feeling good today mate, make sure you play me in, yeah? – and to cane your defence when they had just conceded. As you waited for the goalkeeper to pick the ball out of his net and hoof it back to you, opposition players all smiles as they jogged back past still celebrating, the two of you used to whinge like a pair of cantankerous old pensioners.

'What the hell are we playing with here?'

'We're running around like idiots, and these fucking clowns keep conceding.'

'We carry this team.'

'Without our goals they'd be out of a job.'

Now that only one man is required for a restart, it's all changed. You no longer have a fellow striker but two attacking wide men. It's lonely. Those wide men aren't really your mates, not in the same way. Is anyone your mate? God, now the paranoia kicks in. You stand there thinking, I hope they're not talking about me back there …

Still we persist, at the very start of the game, with the pointless clip forward. If, at any other moment in the game, you had the ball at your feet in the centre circle, you would lay it off, always to feet. When the game starts, you instead have licence to punt it out of play. No one complains. It's not like it's about spot-betting any more; no one's interested in jeopardising their career and reputation for a £500 punt on the time of the first throw-in. You clip it forward because there is a natural caution in the first minute. Play the ball back and the next clearance might get charged down, as Shane Long did when scoring the fastest goal in Premier League history. Go long and you might win the header. If you don't, at least the ball is in their half. It's safety disguised as aggression. It's like a fast bowler sending down a bouncer way over the opening batsman's head. He's not taking a wicket, but the batsman's not scoring any runs off it either.

When Sir Clive Woodward had his brief spell somewhere in the back rooms of Southampton, he came out with the arresting claim that we should be scoring from nine out of ten set pieces. If that was ambitious, there is still a great premium placed on coming up with something new and different. Because the manager has to go big picture, he typically hands this responsibility for fine detail to his assistant, who will seize his rare chance in the spotlight by getting very stressed about it. The only time you'll see ever an assistant manager out of his seat during matches is when you're either defending a set piece or about to take them.

So nervous are they that their work or lack of it could undo all the team's hard yards, they become frantic in word and action. Arms wave. Eyeballs pop. Phrases fly out heavy in profanities. 'MARK YOUR FUCKING MAN! NO! NO! YOU'RE DOING IT ALL WRONG!' There will be a certain amount of arse-covering, so the manager understands it's not his fault that the opposition striker has just had a free header on the six-yard line. 'I TOLD HIM! I FUCKING TOLD HIM ABOUT THAT RUN!'

After 150 years of association football there is little room left for the truly groundbreaking, so when you do see something new, it blows your mind. I loved the penalty that Robert Pirès tried to pass sideways to Thierry Henry against Manchester City in 2005, even if it had been borrowed from Johan Cruyff, and even if they did stuff it up. I used to love the little near-post corner routine that Teddy Sheringham would work, which we pulled off once with Stoke at West Ham with Jon Walters in the Shez role. Harry Kane does something on wide free-kicks where he has two players over the ball, one right-footed and the other left-footed, already monkeying with the central defenders' minds, and then he deliberately goes offside as the first man fakes to take it. The defenders then drop in when the second man steps up, so Kane is now onside, and yet the defenders are chasing him, on the wrong side and out of position. I love the free-kick that is deliberately sent under a jumping wall, all disguise and sleight of foot, and I still swoon at the memory of Matt Le Tissier getting the ball played back short to him, rolling it up his foot and then dipping the sweetest of volleys home.

When you do hatch a plan, hammer it in training and see it come off in a match, it's an amazing feeling. You celebrate the goal but you celebrate the subterfuge too. With it often comes a sense of relief, because as a striker there will be a split-second when you know you have lost your man and that the exact right ball is coming in, and you are so excited about the free header that you have to keep it all together and actually make proper contact rather than taking your eye off it because you are already imagining the giddy aftermath.

You can overthink them. Rafa Benítez loved an elaborate routine. There were times where I would be doing some bizarre dummy-run beyond the near post with team-mates splitting behind me in all directions like the Red Arrows at Farnborough Air Show. I'd be thinking, Rafa, I'm six foot seven, Sami Hyypiä is six foot four. Stevie Gerrard can put a dead ball on a six-pence: let's just cross it and I'll head it in.

You can certainly over-train them. If you haven't been picked to play on the weekend, you begin to loathe set pieces, because on Friday your job will be to don a bib and act as the opposition while the first team practise and practise. You become a mannequin, a guinea pig, a stooge in someone else's fun, and you feel insulted. It'll probably be raining. You're having to walk, because the big boys are still learning the moves in slow motion, so you're cold, and you understand there's no real point in trying that hard either, because the sooner they get the routine right and score, the quicker you can all go in.

The accepted etiquette in that situation is that you shouldn't be too busy. Don't bust too big a gut as it looks bad on the first-choice team. But occasionally something is lost in translation, and all hell breaks loose. We had a German defender at Stoke called Philipp Wollscheid, and he refused to do anything but his absolute best, almost as if he were a professional being paid to do it. Our assistant coach Mark Bowen set up a drill where Wollscheid and his fellow stooges had to break a defensive line that the rest of us were holding. That was fine, except that he was taking it far too seriously, barging into me, and then I'm losing my head and giving him a little dig with my elbow. Before I know it, he's kicking out at me and cutting my leg, and I'm grabbing hold of his nose. He was very camp German about it. 'Oh my God! You haff all seen this! Captain!' (This to Ryan Shawcross.) 'Captain! I haff been punched! I cannot believe this – because he is English you let him get away with this!'

All because he was being too busy. All because he was doing the job he had been asked to do as he had been asked to do, rather than as the unspoken rule that he had never heard suggested he should. But Phil was always different. On a team trip to Dubai we went out for a few beers, and ended up in one of the lads' rooms for a few more. Suddenly he's grabbing the phone on the bedside table, looking distressed, shouting at us all.

'Argh! I'm so angry!'

'Phil mate, what's the matter?'

'I am so very angry!'

'You're angry? But why?'

'No, not *an*-gry. *Un*-gry! I'm so, so ungry!'

Turned out all he wanted was a cheese and ham toastie.

On our pre-season training camp in Austria we were given a rare afternoon off. A few of us decided to play golf, a few stroll into town for a coffee. Phil decided to go off on his own. When I saw him later, he again looked distressed.

'I had absolute nightmare! I was stuck in the fun Ekulah!'

I had no idea what he was on about. What was an Ekulah – a local Austrian bar, some sort of rural jail? How could it have been so bad when he himself had described it as fun?

It took several minutes to work out he'd been on the funicular railway. Being a footballer I neither knew there was a railway in the area nor that the word funicular existed. English was Phil's second language yet he was schooling me in an obtuse technical backwater of mine.

We thought he was weird. But he thought we were weirder. Phil used to wear tracksuits so baggy it was as if they belonged to a man twice his weight, yet he wasn't bothered. He would bring the ball out of defence with the gait of a fashionista carrying a handbag in the crook of her arm. He would run in such a strange fashion that mates of mine coming along to watch us would say to me afterwards, what the hell is wrong with your centre-half? Maybe in Wadern, the little town he came from in south-west Germany, they all ran like that. And he was a really good player. Just different, like Rob Green was different. Different in a way that football dressing-rooms, cruel as they are, struggle to handle.

Set pieces. Attacking ones are always more fun for a striker. I have nothing to lose and a possible goal to gain, unless the manager has instructed me to do a near-post Bould-style flick-on, in which case I can't score and will thus be quite grumpy. Defending an opposition set piece as a striker is miserable, not least because you've usually got to run all the way back from at least the halfway line to your own box. The whistle goes, the crowd cheers. You sigh heavily. 'Fuck's sake ...'

As one of the taller gentlemen in that team – okay, that county – my job is usually the same: either picking up their tallest player, or as a free man, attacking the ball to get it away. There will be four men marking, one on the near post for anything short, and me in the middle. I'd much rather be free than marking. If you lose your man and he scores – easily done, whether blocked off by another player if you're man-marking, or given the dummy and slip if it's zonal – there's no escaping the shame. You go into the dressing-room at half-time and it's there in black marker-pen on the whiteboard: VIDIĆ = CROUCH. Angry faces staring at you every way you look. Some just looking disappointed in you, which is of course far worse. You sitting there with a sports drink in your hand and your nose on your chest. 'But I'm a striker ...'

The free role liberates you. If the ball coming in is low, the man at the near post will get rid of it. If it's too high the keeper can come to claim it. If it's in your zone, great, because heading the ball away as a striker who is defending is so much easier than heading a ball in as a striker who is strikering. No need to angle it into a corner, or keep it down. You can pretty much head it anywhere, as long as it's away from your own goal. It's everything that being a striker isn't. As a striker trying to score you can go delicate glance (always tricky) or use the pace on it to power it back the way it has come. Defending it you just smash it up and away, and when you do get a big pie on it, you'll be guaranteed a lusty cheer from the relieved crowd. Your only concern is to make sure your brain is calibrated for the correct end of the pitch. No one wants to see a defending striker jump for an opposition corner and give it a nice little glance into the 'D'.

We live in an era when every minute aspect of the sport is studied and gamed for advantage. We have goalkeepers who can hit a pass on the move like a midfielder of twenty years ago. We drink shots of beetroot juice to reduce muscle soreness. And yet the humble goal-kick – one of the most used of all set pieces – had so little attention paid to it for years, so little variety in its execution. You go long to hit the striker. You go short to hit one of the full-backs who have split. That's pretty much it. Unless you were Swansea under

Roberto Martínez or Brendan Rodgers, when they went through a spell of insisting that the keeper roll it out to his centre-backs regardless of how the match was going or where the opposition strikers might be lurking. Jon Walters, Steven Nzonzi and I were like coiled springs, knowing exactly where the ball was going but pretending to be oblivious. Until the ball was passed, at which point the three of us would be all over them. In one match we got the ball off them so many times it was hard not to laugh – shots off at goal, passes to someone unmarked in the box ... Their poor fans were going bananas. 'Just fucking lump it!'

There are principles and there is stupidity. You don't have to just punt it. They could have dropped it into the striker, over our heads, take the press out of the game. Clipped it onto the chest of their striker and played it nicely along the deck from there. Had they done it even once, we may have retreated a little. Not even Pep Guardiola will persist with a more theoretically attractive option if it isn't working. Instead, year after year Swansea would come up to Stoke and try to play like that. We would win the ball, get our crosses in, retreat and wait for it to happen again. Our fans absolutely loved it. Few things please a Stokie more than a physical steamrollering of someone who fancies themselves as a little more sophisticated and stylish.

If you win a corner, there are three main ways the ball can come in: inswinger, outswinger and clip – straight and true. The last of these, the driven ball, is the hardest to get right. Charlie Adam was perfect at it, as was David Beckham in my England days. As a striker you can see the flight of the ball all the way. The assumption from those not fortunate enough to play elite football is that the inswinger is an easier ball to head into the goal, on the basis that it's heading that way already. In fact, the opposite is true.

The outswinger comes at you with more pace. You can track its trajectory and attack it. The inswinger is always going away from you and towards the defender and goalkeeper. You're chasing it. It's like when you play swingball, and you're trying to hit a ball in the same direction as it's already heading. You get half a racquet on it at best. The outswinger is the ball coming to your backhand side that you meet flush with a forehand. The inswinger is a glance. The outswinger is BANG.

There are certain memes now attached to the taking of a corner. Corner takers try to get a bit of backspin on the ball as they drop it into the quadrant, even though when you actually take it the ball has to be motionless. Players now try to place the ball as far over the line as they can, which maybe gives you a fractional advantage if you're looking to whip it close in to the six-yard box and don't want it to go out of play first, but mainly serves to wind up the opposition fans sitting nearby. 'LINESMAN! LINO!' The taker may raise one arm, or both, or bounce the ball before placing it down, and each will mean a different delivery – one near post, one far post, one come-short-please. They tend to rotate over the course of a season, in case the opposition have done a Marcelo Bielsa and spied on your drills, which only serves to confuse us. 'But you had both arms up.' 'Yeah.' 'I thought that was …' 'Last week.'

I can feel both a great sympathy and significant anger towards the defender on the post. It amuses me how they always hold onto the post, as if the goal is going to move if they let go, or the post is going to pull a shimmy and lose them. I hate that defender when you smash in a perfect header, the goalkeeper is nowhere, and then they pop up to nod it off the line. I feel sorry for them because they're often the shortest defender, the taller ones gainfully employed marking actual humans rather than vertical pieces of wood. Often the ball will sail over their head, and they're left desperately craning their necks and contorting their faces and making a straining noise. All the while really wanting to stretch up and palm it away, but knowing that's an instant red card, jumping up with arms ostentatiously behind them instead, as if they're wearing handcuffs.

One rule trumps all others at attacking corners: the ball in must beat the first man. I still find it amazing how often in the world of professional football that the first man gets hit. The taker tries to get too much pace on it, or lifts his head too early, and the moans and groans from the crowd are ringing in your ears. It's an absolute heartbreaker at the best of times, and the later it gets in a match, the more you're chasing a game, the more it hurts. As a fan you'd rather see the ball go straight out of play behind the goal than fail to beat the first man. Ninety-third minute with the goalkeeper up, failing to beat the first man should be a straight yellow. No player would ever argue.

PENALTIES

Because I am a footballer, because the game has obsessed me since I can remember and filled my brain with nonsense when it could possibly have more usefully been filled with other things, I will often pose philosophical questions to myself. What would it be like to actually be as bad at football as a goalkeeper? Why does Glen Johnson not appear to suffer from hangovers? What made me once think that paying £800 for a jumper was acceptable?

But the question I find myself mulling over on long coach journeys or late into the night in strange hotel rooms is this: if you had to choose one player – from the start of human existence – to score a penalty to save your life, who would you call up?

My shortlist comes together within minutes. Harry Kane, because I never think he's going to miss. His World Cup ones in the summer of 2018 were almost cruel in their perfection. Into the corner every time, with a lovely crispness and pace. No one's saving a penalty like that. Alan Shearer, because he would never mess about. Shearer didn't tuck a penalty away. He buried it. Same with Steven Gerrard. You put that much pace and finesse on it and the goalkeeper needs not only to guess the right way but be moving in that direction before the ball is struck.

I'm not obsessed with power. Frank Lampard would place them. Teddy Sheringham used to open up his body at the last minute and caress the ball home in such relaxed fashion that he could have been in his back garden. Matt Le Tissier could do it any way he chose, which is why he scored forty-seven of the forty-eight he ever took in competition for Southampton. It was almost as if he could do perfect impersonations of all the others: pace, accuracy, corners, down the middle, inside of foot, gone before the keeper could move, waiting until the poor unfortunate had committed himself and started falling over.

In my life or death scenario, I can't have room for the flash merchants. Eden Hazard is wonderfully cool the way he takes his, all gentle trots in and casual little dinks. Great for him, appalling for my nerves. I'd rather fall on my own sword than be put through that. It's the same with Paul Pogba's technique. It might work for him but for me, waiting for the executioner's nod, it would be far too antagonising. Even the way he approaches the ball is hard to watch.

I wouldn't be adverse to the no-nonsense defender approach. You watched David Unsworth lumber up to a penalty like a mighty digger towards a small rock and you felt certainty that he would come out on top. His successor at Everton, Leighton Baines, had a contrasting physique but a similar stone-cold reliability. Full-backs with a sweet touch are a fine bet – Denis Irwin, Lee Dixon, Kieran Trippier. A striker who is a pure poacher rather than a technical player is not. I would never, ever want Filippo Inzaghi taking a penalty to save my life. Brilliant finisher, too flicky and nudgy to keep me alive.

Even goalkeepers can make great penalty-takers. Kevin Pressman smashed one home for Sheffield Wednesday that is still travelling in the same direction at the same immense pace, somewhere just outside the orbit of Venus. Peter Schmeichel used to hit them so hard you feared the ball would explode on contact with his right boot. René Higuita took loads. Chile's José Luis Chilavert found them so easy he would sometimes take free-kicks just outside the box too. He once scored a hat-trick of penalties in a single match for his Argentine club Vélez Sarsfield. Respect.

A top professional player should be able to put a penalty where they like. Despite that, we all have a default, a spot where we naturally prefer to stick it. When you're under the most pressure it becomes almost impossible to fight that urge; something deep inside you makes a calculation based on risk and seriousness of impact and settles for what you know best.

That doesn't mean it always works. My natural shape is to go for the right-hand bottom corner and whip them with pace. I fell back on it when playing for Stoke against Liverpool in the 2016 Capital One Cup semi-final shoot-out, and Simon Mignolet saved it. Abbey's dad Geoff, a lifelong Liverpool fan, was convinced afterwards that I had celebrated, convinced that my time at Anfield was more important to me than my current employers. I hadn't. I was so angry it had been saved that as the ball rebounded back to me I tried to punch it away. Geoff looked away at the wrong time and looked back to see me with a clenched fist waved in the air. I'm still not sure he believes me.

It wasn't my lowest moment involving Liverpool and penalties. In the depths of my awful goalless run with them at the beginning of my time at Anfield, convinced I was never going to score any other way, I snatched the ball off Gerrard when we were awarded a penalty against Portsmouth. Stevie was okay about it. He understood, and let me have it. Rafa Benítez was fuming, but I was convinced. Right up to the moment it was saved. Thankfully Bolo Zenden nodded the rebound in. I say thankfully. I was supposed to run off after him to celebrate. Instead I just wanted to punch him. You've never seen a player more distraught at his own team scoring a goal.

Grabbing the ball off your usual penalty taker can never end well. If you score, it's not like you're a hero. You've only done what was going to be done anyway. If you miss it you appear both incredibly selfish and mindbendingly stupid. You think of Riyad Mahrez sticking his penalty over the bar for Manchester City against Liverpool, having taken it from Gabriel Jesus. You think of Christian Benteke, eight months without a goal for Crystal Palace, elbowing aside the dead-eyed Luka Milivojević to then miss against Bournemouth as Palace slumped to the bottom of the Premier League. These things haunt you.

I've had my good moments too. Take Southampton against Portsmouth in the FA Cup, January 2005: an always spicy South Coast derby turned red-hot by Harry Redknapp's recent defection from Pompey to the Saints. As a former Portsmouth man I was also less than popular with the away end, even less so when I stepped up to a penalty in the ninety-second minute that could win it for Southampton.

I wasn't the designated penalty-taker. Had Jamie Redknapp or Kevin Phillips been fit then I would have been nowhere near it. Even as I walked towards the spot with the ball tucked under my arm I was vaguely aware of Harry waving frantically from the touchline. Through the bedlam of 30,000 amped-up fans either screaming with delight or disgust I could still make out his desperate message. 'CROUCHIE! NOOOOOOO …'

I was young, I was confident and I was in form. I stuck the ball down and banged it home. Two minutes later, when the final whistle sounded, Harry legged it over and gave me the embrace of an ecstatic man. 'Son, you realise that at 1–1 we're looking at a replay back at Fratton Park. We both know what that would be like. Thank fuck you scored ...'

My personal default penalty is to look bottom right and then hit it the other way. After twenty years as a professional footballer, however, that is now too obvious. Every goalkeeper in Britain knows about it. And so it comes down a game of bluff and counter-bluff that should in theory be thrilling but is in fact mainly confusing. Do I look towards one corner of the goal as I step up and then actually put it there? It's a cunning ruse if you're expecting my usual pen but it's also massively obvious where I'm going to put it, if that isn't contradictory. I'm giving the keeper the eyes but actually I'm not – I'm giving him the triple-eyes, because I'm looking in the opposite direction to my standard pen which is in itself the opposite corner to straightforward eyes. Perhaps it's clear now why I missed those pens for Liverpool and Stoke.

There's also the duration of the gaze. You can't just glance to the fake corner; you have to look long enough that the goalie actually spots it. At the same time you can't stare, because then he knows you're faking it. At that point you've overstated your case. You see a lot of players now put the ball down, walk backwards and go No-Eyes, which blows my mind. How can you be sure the goal and its custodian are exactly where your subconscious now thinks they are? It's for this reason that I like to back away and look at the whole goal, not just to recalibrate my sights but to strike fear into the keeper that I could literally stick this one anywhere. If you run in to the ball off a No-Eyes approach, you might just arrive in fractionally the wrong place for your standing foot. Even drifting off course by a few degrees could be enough to see you wrecked on the rocks. I'm scared of arriving half a foot off and swinging wildly with my striking foot while the other one gently nudges the ball three inches off the spot.

The great cliché of successful penalty taking? 'Never change your mind.' Thing is, what if the keeper moves early, in the direction that you were going to shoot? Surely it's better to then change your mind and go the other way. And so I say: leave room for doubt, but don't be swamped by it. The issue comes not from changing your mind but doing neither one thing nor the other: planning to go right, then becoming unsure about going right, thinking late about going left and finally scuffing it feebly down the middle into the keeper's shins instead. It's certainly worth watching the goalkeeper, and if you have the nerve, wait until he commits, as Yakubu used to do. They tell you too never to lift your head, just as they do when you're playing golf, but I'm not convinced that matters either. If you're hitting through the ball nicely, why not have a little look up to catch it in flight? Equally this may equally explain why, despite me living on a golf course, my handicap is still stuck at sixteen.

It's a cruel thing, a penalty miss. I was nine years old, playing for the year above in school in a cup competition, when I messed up for the first time. I still remember it clear as day. I put it wide. And as we trudged off, having lost because of my mistake, all the older kids were looking at me with disgust on their faces, as if to say, what are you even doing playing here?

You do all you can to make sure it doesn't happen but you can never protect yourself entirely. Lampard was sensational from the spot. With England he used to stay behind after every training session to work on them. But he still missed in our World Cup quarter-final defeat to Portugal in 2006. So did Gerrard. It didn't make them bad penalty-takers and it didn't render all their hours of practice worthless. It simply reflected the odds. A goalkeeper can go left, right or stand up. If you take fifty penalties he's going to get lucky at least once. What matters more than having one saved is that you shrug it off and score the next one. Stick with your method. Hold your nerve.

It's why I will never understand the striker who does not want to take a pen. Yes, you will miss at some point, probably painfully. But it's the closest you get to a free goal. I'd have chalked up way more than 108 Premier League goals had I been the designated taker for my various clubs, rather than in the clean-hitting shadow of Gerrard, Charlie Adam and Jermain Defoe.

You can find joy in the miss too. When you flip it round and the opposition blow one against you, it's like being convinced you've left your credit card in the pub only to find it in your coat pocket. Woo-hoo! If they then stick the rebound in it's worse than if they scored in the first place. It's like thinking you've found your credit card and then pulling it out to discover it's an old train ticket. As a fan you're halfway through a wild celebration when suddenly you have to shut up again. You feel like a fool. Meanwhile the goalkeeper is going absolutely bananas at his defence. The subtext is clear: I've bailed you muppets out once already, and you can't even help me out now? So too is the fact that they're secretly quite chuffed when a pen is awarded in the first place. It's their chance to shine, to be a hero. If it goes in it's the fault of the bloke who gave away the foul. They can't lose.

There are critics who believe the best place to put a pen is down the middle. The rationale: goalkeepers never stand still. Trouble is, when they do dive they will leave a trailing foot or leg, which means that you have to lift the ball. And if you lift the ball it brings into play the horror of popping it over the bar. You can't blast it. The ball will arrive on the goal line too quickly, before the keeper has committed one way or the other. Your best bet is to clip it with the instep, aiming for head height. There's a 1 per cent chance he doesn't move, that he stands there and catches it. You think about Andriy Shevchenko nudging it down the middle in the Champions League final shoot-out against Liverpool in Istanbul and Jerzy Dudek putting his left hand up as he falls right to bat it away. But it's the best way of scoring if you have the guts for it. The goalkeeper is vacating that area. It is yours to claim.

The worst penalty is what we might call the Mannequin Save, where it's not in the corner and it's not down the middle, and it's about a foot off the ground, so a moulded plastic shop-dummy pushed to the side could stop it. Yet the mad thing about penalties is that it can be the best penalty in the world if the goalie goes the other way. The only good penalty is the penalty that goes in. Eric Dier's one for England against Colombia in the 2018 World Cup was nowhere near as technically correct as the earlier ones from Kane and Trippier. It didn't matter. It went in. It won England the match. It sent the nation ripe bananas. It was beautiful.

And so back to my original question. I know I should choose Messi or Ronaldo. They are geniuses. I wish I could strike a ball as they do. But I can't. I can't risk a stutter in the run-up, not when my life depends on it. I don't want to go of a heart attack. I want a blaster.

I want Harry Kane. Of course I do. He's missed a couple, but the many he scores are a thing of rock-solid wonder. Against Colombia the defenders scuffed up the penalty spot, which is truly disgusting behaviour, yet you still knew – knew, not hoped – that he would bang it in. Harry would save me. Not least because, when he was a kid in the academy at Spurs, I taught him everything he knows. Some of what he knows. A little of what he'd already worked out.

Harry, my life is in your hands.

INJURIES

You get towards the end of your career in football and you notice yourself becoming grouchier with each passing season. Everything is worse despite the fact that everything is clearly better. Yet you feel as though the old days were better, despite the fact that you got paid less, played on muddier pitches, trained at worse places, had ill-advised hair and played a less attractive style of football.

I'm a little hesitant to say that more players seem to get injured from tackles these days. I don't really want to claim that some players go down too easily, or take too long to recover, or occasionally milk it. I don't want to say that, but I have to, because to be honest I believe it.

At the time I started out as a kid at Spurs, it was considered a bad thing to be out injured. When George Graham was manager, he brought with him the attitude of a former Arsenal manager: this is a flaky club, these players are soft, they need to be toughened up. He brought in a rule that all injured players had to do three sessions of rehab a day. You arrived straight after breakfast and you left when it was dark. All to make being out seem as unattractive as possible, to turn a fun career into a dreary nine to five. If you were fit you trained in the morning, had lunch and went home to play golf or watch

MTV Cribs. If you were injured you stood there at the window of the training-ground gym, like Annie at the Hudson Street Home for Girls, staring out all tearful at your friends going off to play.

At the time, Graham's tactics worked. Footballers are simple creatures with simple motivations. Let us have fun. Let us enjoy ridiculously short hours. Don't make me do what feels like a proper job, please. But the power of the modern manager has waned. No longer can you say to a player on the deck, get up, get out there. Those decisions now lie with the medical team. They are the ones who decree whether a player should come off injured and when they are ready to come back, even when the player themselves may disagree. I've seen Robert Huth wandering around with a great flap of skin sliced open on his forehead, blood pouring down his nose, asking the physio to bandage it up, looking positively pleased with the scenario despite appearing to have been attacked by a shark. Tony Pulis was bang up for it: 'That's my boy. That's the attitude.' And the physio taking one look, shaking his head and still having the last word on whether he should play. Have-a-go heroes are not appreciated as they used to be.

There are players who are bizarrely competitive about their injuries. 'Oh yeah, I had that one, but far worse.' 'Oh, is it only a grade two? Mine was a seven. Yeah. First time they'd ever seen anything beyond a three.' There are players who sense an injury before they are actually injured. 'I've got a feeling that something might go. Better take me off.' I can't get my head around that. It might go, so you won't play? It might not. You could still play. It might do, in which you can't play, but you're not playing now anyway, so what's the difference?

There is one at every club. Their names and reputations are known at all the other clubs. There is one player in the Premier

Football is a serious business at all times.

When I tell people that I once had a night out in Brighton dressed as a chicken, and that I popped in to the local branch of Toni and Guy to get my feathers trimmed, they have sometimes accused me of exaggerating, as if the idea of a 6'7" chicken is somehow weird.

A magnificent welcome in Burnley. A local butcher also gave me my own sausage, which was less painful than it sounds.

This fella tweeted that if he could have my shirt, he would do the whole away trip in Speedos and a snorkle. Here I am giving him his reward.

They say never meet your heroes. They have clearly never met former QPR defender Justin Channing. I couldn't believe he was real. I couldn't believe he was wearing jeans – at this stage I thought all footballers wore full kit seven days a week.

Showing Fabio Capello my right-arm off-spin. You didn't argue with
Fabio, even when it came to a sport he'd never heard of.

Rudi Voller reaches back into his magnificent permed thatch to discover Frank Rijkaard has flobbed in it. An awful moment for any player, and one guaranteed to lead to fisticuffs.

'No, I'm not sure why I'm on this pitch with you either.'

When I found out about Gareth Bale's magic beans, it blew my mind and changed my world. I could out-jump him even if I couldn't quite out-pace him; one 'out' out of two isn't bad.

Jermain and I had a prolific record playing together from U21 days to England, Portsmouth and Spurs, although I'm sure he could have passed a few more times!

I originally asked for the England shellsuit top at Christmas 1990. At the age of thirty-eight, BT Sport finally made my dream come true. The twenty-nine intervening years had done nothing to damp down my excitement; bat-wing was everything I hoped it would be.

Jeff Winter and Mike Dean, two referees born for the stage. There is a
reason why you don't see kids in the park in replica referee's kit.

Play to the whistle, they always say. Here I'm simply appealing for the
whistle so we can all get on and play.

After I scored against Arsenal from a corner, Arsene Wenger described me as a 'basketball player'. In that case, this was a three-pointer.

Two of the finest penalty-takers of all time. Every man has a default place to put a pen. The best just have more defaults.

The phrase 'og' initially confused me. Had legendary Coventry goalkeeper Steve Ogrizovic gone up for a corner and stuck one away?

It astonishes non-footballers how little actual footballers carry with them. Here I am sporting the latest designer luggage from the Parisian fashion house G'Arbage.

Tackling is part of the game … unfortunately.

You put the luminous subs' bib over your choice of wet-top or big coat. It gets stuck on the hood or caught up at the back, and you look like a hunchback or a tortoise. You look like you can't even dress yourself.

Loved this day. Pepe, Robbie and I are certainly not hungover here at all. Two of the greatest characters I've ever played with.

The fab four, or at least the quite good quartet: me, Steve Sidwell, Glenn Johnson and Sean Davis. Very, very close to the dream night out. Not very close to the dream fourball.

Andy Cole scored more Premier League goals than me. Les Ferdinand regularly used to out-jump me when we went for headers at Spurs training. Both were polite enough not to mention these facts when I interviewed them for my new Amazon show.

My last game in football! Nice to be able to spend it with my beautiful kids Sophia, Liberty and Johnny. Sophia was actually trying to get Aubameyang's shirt in this snap.

Possibly my favourite non-footballing moment. Singing live at the O2 with Kasabian. A quiet, sober, low-key affair.

Which one is the real Iniesta? Thanks to my podcast, I am now best friends with both, so I'm not really bothered.

I arrived at Crouchfest fearing no one was going to turn up. Then Tom, Chris and I spotted 2,600 half-cut fans of the podcast. And Liam Gallagher. And Katherine Jenkins.
I love doing the podcast as much as I can't stand Karl.

League who is notorious for both being brilliant when he is fit and also never being fit. He is rumoured to pick and choose his games based on the standard of the opposition. When it looks like a run of easy matches, games where he can make a flashy impact, his injury concerns clear up. When the opposition are bigger, nastier and far superior, he's back on the physio's table.

Football is not a game for dabblers. From the age of twenty onwards, you will almost never go into a match feeling 100 per cent fit. Most of us spend ten years playing at around 70 per cent. There will always be a niggle, always be soreness. You keep going because you can. You don't stop because as soon as you do someone will take your place, and they might not give it back. It's not something we like to advertise or that is probably good for our long-term health, but anti-inflammatory pills are passed out like sweets. The physio will ask on a Friday who wants an Ibuprofen, and on a Saturday before a game, who wants a Voltarol or two. I don't like them. I never have; they make me feel awful. But I'm in a small minority. Most players will knock one down. I know many who have been on them for years.

No one talks about the silent pill-swallowing heroes, because it's seen as standard behaviour. But everyone talks about the malingerers. We had one at Stoke, in the season when we were relegated, who was stretchered off the pitch in apparent agony. We assumed he had a career-threatening compound fracture. It turned out he had a groin strain. I got into the dressing-room at the end of the game to see him having his shorts sliced off, as if he was being cut out of a car wreck or being readied for amputation. He could have stood up, taken his shorts off, jogged on the spot and put them back on again. Instead he lay there with an arm thrown over his face like a man about to be humanely put down.

A few weeks later the same player sustained a small nick on his thigh – the sort of thing that a five-year-old might look at with interest, wash off under the tap and subsequently pick the scab off. Each morning there is always at least one player in the physio's room being treated, some for serious long-term injuries, others being strapped up for training or pounded by the masseurs and chiropractors so they can stumble out for one more session. This player would go in each morning and ask for a sticking plaster. He would then ask the physio to apply it. This went on for a week, the player totally unapologetic, the rest of us somewhere between astonishment and disgust.

I played in the League Cup match between Liverpool and Arsenal where Luis García tore his cruciate. In the same game our Chilean winger Mark González was stretchered off, his leg in a brace, medics giving him gas and air. We lost the match 6–3 and the atmosphere in the dressing-room afterwards was sombre. We'd lost two players to long-term injuries. Poor sods. Hope they can somehow come back to play for us again.

I came in to training on Monday. The first thing I heard was that García was going to be out for a year. The next thing I saw was González doing squats. In the gym. With 100kg on the bar. I thought I'd witnessed a miracle. I walked out and walked back in again. He was still doing squats, if anything at greater pace.

'Mark. What happened?'

'Yeah, I get bang on leg.'

'But I saw you stretchered off. On gas and air.'

'Is good now. I no need treatment Sunday either. How your weekend?'

A decade later, I was still being asked by players at other clubs if that story was true. It had spread throughout the Premier League at such a rate that most assumed some form of exaggeration or Chinese whispers. I was there. I witnessed it with my own eyes. It happened. A stretcher, gas and air, ten minutes added time – and squats on Monday.

Easy though it is to see such scenarios as serious moral failings – and quite often that is the case – sometimes it is about fear as well. We had a player at Portsmouth who had spent the majority of his career in the Championship. He was comfortable at that level. As we moved through the Premier League, deeper into competitions like the FA Cup and UEFA Cup, he began to look scared. The bigger the game, the more intimidated he appeared to be. Often the team for Saturday's game would be announced on the Thursday. If he was in, the charades began as soon as we went out to train. He would sprint over to take a corner and then pull up, clutching his hamstring. He would shake his head, swear about his bad luck. 'Yeah, I think I've pulled something. Better go in, hadn't I?' And then he would overdo it, going round to each player later as we got changed, looking for support. 'I'm feeling it bad, what do you reckon? I don't want to let you boys down. I should probably pull out, shouldn't I? Don't you reckon …?'

I couldn't behave like that. I would be lying to myself. I was devastated enough when I was actually injured, the only fear being that someone somewhere might think I'm one of the skivers. Once I was injured over Christmas. That's an old favourite of the slack – pull something minor before that frantic run of games so you can have the festive period at home with your family. The thought that anyone might have believed I was faking it made me die inside. I wanted to bring the MRI scan in to training to prove it to everyone. Look! There it is! That indistinct white blurry bit on the other white bit by the grey and black areas!

I couldn't make it up because I've seen bad injuries close up and I've seen what they do to players. I was there when Stephen Ireland shattered his left fibula and tibula in training, and it was almost as horrific as the infamous David Busst moment. Phil Bardsley was the closest player to Stevie, and as soon as it happened he grabbed his head and started yelling in horror. None of us could look. Everyone felt sick. We all knew that it could have been any of us. It just happened to be him.

You always analyse such moments in the aftermath, when the whole training-ground complex seems to have fallen silent. Stephen had been injured before. He was coming back and going in for bad tackles, trying to prove himself. The one that did for him was a 60–40 against, stretching out against a team-mate we called Johnny Brazil – Dionatan Teixeira, a South American-born Slovakian who was a terrible player but a lovely lad. There was nothing either could do, but it changed both their careers.

Stephen eventually came back. Not all players do. There was a burgeoning talent I played with who was just breaking into international football when he got injured in what looked like an innocent tackle in training. It was nothing more than the smallest player on the pitch standing on his ankle, but it damaged his ligaments and led, eventually, to the end of his career. When the medical advice came that he should retire, we all felt sympathetic – until he started phoning all the players who had been there that day, trying to get us to go on the record and say it had been an appalling, premeditated challenge.

It was clear that he wanted to sue the person who had injured him. He was lining up witnesses. 'Come on, Crouchie, it was a shocker, wasn't it? You'll say that for me, won't you mate?' But I couldn't say that, because it hadn't been. It wasn't Kevin Muscat on Matty Holmes in 1998, where Matty was lucky not to have had his leg amputated. 'Don't worry, Crouchie, he won't be liable, the club would cough up for it on insurance.' But I wasn't having it, and I couldn't look at the player in question in the same way ever again. He had always been very confident in his abilities, made it quite clear that he didn't need the other players as mates. He certainly didn't have any mates about that campaign.

There are the unlucky ones. Harry Kewell played in every major final Liverpool got to in his time there, but only a partial role in each: coming off in the Champions League final of 2005 with an abductor muscle problem; doing his groin in the FA Cup final of 2006; only a sub in the Champions League final of 2007. He was never the player he had been at Leeds and it could never come back. Then there is Michael Owen, such an extraordinary talent in his early days and almost unplayable at his peak in 2001, when he snatched the FA Cup from Arsenal almost on his own. He was just a small kid from Chester but quicker than any player I'd seen first-hand at that point. But as the injuries kicked in he had to hold something back when running rather than opening up fully, because he knew that if he were to go full gas then something would tear. I had enormous sympathy even if the concepts – explosive pace, delicate hamstrings – were alien to me. My hamstrings were as powerful as Cheestrings. It's hard to pull a muscle that isn't really there.

Word gets around when a player is faking, but word gets around too when injury has taken a player's edge. It might not always be visible to the public but other players can see the signs. You can train on your reputation but you cannot dominate in matches on the same. Not that it always matters. A player at 80 per cent of what he used to be might still be superior to everything else you have in the squad. It's why degenerating talents can keep moving around and keep getting deals. There is always someone hoping that the shadow of the old you is still better than no shade at all.

You find yourself wondering sometimes how good a player might have been. I played with Ledley King in the Spurs youth team so I understand how superior the original model was even to the Rolls-Royce of a defender who played in the Premier League for a decade and went to two World Cups with his country. The two of us were caught messing around in one session as under-18s and got called in to see the coach for a ticking-off. It was quite clear from the coach's lecture what he thought of us both.

'You, Ledley, you need to behave. Stop messing around and you WILL play for England. You, Crouchie … you might. Yeah. But you, Ledley …'

I was the spare part, the mate who was allowed to tag along to keep the star happy, the Jonathan Wilkes to his Robbie Williams. I was fine with that. I could see the same things they could. That I ended up with twice as many England caps as Ledley was a source of sadness to me. Watching Ledley at Spurs, sitting in the gym trying to use the arm-bike to keep fit while the rest of us legged it off for training, used to break a little piece of my heart every time.

Footballers are lucky boys now. Clubs are like the most amazing private hospitals. Everything gets taken care of. You have a toothache, they will bring in a top dentist. You have a callous on your little toe, there will be a chiropodist to gently file it away. If you need a scan, you can get one that afternoon, rather than waiting for a fortnight as most have to. It used to be that each club had one physiotherapist. At a Premier League club there will now be three or four, as well as three masseurs, a club doctor, an osteopath and a chiropractor.

The chiropodist I have found very useful. When I run, my toes curl over for some unknown reason, and I end up putting most of my weight on my nails. It creates a build-up of hard yellow dead skin, which may sound like nothing but – if you are still with me, rather than being sick in a bucket – can become so painful that I can only walk with a limp. A career on the line, all because of one toe. Don't tell me modern footballers don't see the darker side of life. Your feet are your tools. And your head in my case, but still. Let me protect them.

The scans I appreciated but found more difficult. I had a CT scan once that involved almost total immersion in the white plastic tunnel of doom. They gave me headphones to take my mind off the incessant beeping and a mirror so I could partially see out, but the claustrophobia was still too intense. I'm alright if it's just the ankle in the tunnel. You can enjoy quite a pleasant little snooze in that scenario. But anything else and I'd rather run it off.

Only once have I truly let myself down. It came towards the end of my career, when I was given a rare start in the first team, only to find ourselves 2–0 down early on. I gave the ball away, chased after it and – furious with my own performance, angry about the team's – launched into an absolute horror of a tackle. I got a yellow. It should have been a sending-off. But it might as well have been; my hamstring, already sore, suddenly became an excuse. I just wanted to get off the pitch. I went into the dressing-room at half-time and thought: I'm done. I'm no longer the footballer I thought I was.

I texted Abbey at full-time. She told me to sleep on it. She was right; by the morning I felt better about my future, even as a sense of shame lingered. The team had come back from 2–0 down to snatch a point, and all the talk afterwards had been of how much character we had shown. Not me, I thought. I nearly became the player I never wanted to be.

There are players who appear to feel no pain. John Terry played as if his skin were some strange artificial sheath over a metal skeleton. He would wear short sleeves in training even on the most brutally cold day, like a Geordie teenager going out in the Bigg Market. Huth looked genuinely chuffed to have half his forehead missing.

And then there are the players who seem to feel too much. Their bodies are either more sensitive or their minds are somehow a funnel for all the pain at the club, and all the dark agonies of the world. Harry Redknapp used to grow so weary of Gareth Bale going down in training at Spurs that he instructed the physios to leave him there. We played around him as he lay on the pitch. Eventually he would get up, too. With England it was Emile Heskey who was more sensitive to contact than anyone around him. At the time he was starting ahead of me and I was on the bench, which became doubly galling. Not only was he getting picked, but when he played, he turned me into a yo-yo. He would go down. Fabio Capello would signal for me to warm up. I'd do twenty seconds and Emile would climb to his feet. Five minutes later he'd be down again, and I would be off for another twenty seconds. By the end even the physios would be getting arsey with him, sighing as they stood up, grumbling as they picked up their medical bags. I just wanted to shout at the pitch, shout at Capello. 'HE'S FINE! HAVE YOU LEARNED NOTHING?'

Treatments have moved on from the magic sponge. There is what I refer to as the Horseshoe, a piece of metal that is held like a knuckle-duster and scraped down your calves and thighs to release tight fascial tissue. There is the Game Ready, a red rectangular box filled with ice that attaches to a black compression sleeve that you fasten around your injured limb. They're so popular now that players will buy their own if the club refuse to supply one. You see lads with one Game Ready on one leg and one of the other, looking like they're off to the moon.

You see other players sitting on tennis balls or going up and down on foam rollers. Pretty much everyone wears compression tights after a game. It doesn't matter how shaky some of the scientific evidence behind some of these gadgets might be. If it might work, if you know others who swear it does, you will give it a go. I still remember seeing Robbie Fowler in those thin brown nose-strips and pestering my mum until she bought me some. I wore them down the park and ran about with a look of amazement on my face, which may have been as much to do with how tight I'd stuck it on as anything else. 'Boys! Look how fast I am! I'm faster with this on, aren't I?'

My personal favourite now is something called the Hypervolt, a sort of massage gun that I apply to my back and glutes to loosen everything up before a game. My team-mates will always take the mickey when they see me using it, and quite rightly so: it looks like I'm pummelling myself with an instrument purchased in a Soho back-street. But it was all I needed to get me ready for a game, whereas others had the most elaborate regimes. Huth would do what looked like a full gym work-out – grunting press-ups, swinging kettle-bells, sweating heavily, balancing on things that made it difficult to balance. Meanwhile I would be chatting to a few mates while dildoing myself.

Different strokes. I've also developed asthma in the last few years, something the club doctor told me could come on at any time. The dildo does nothing for that, although maybe I'm using it at the wrong end. I have to use a brown inhaler like everyone else. At least I'm not Mario Balotelli, who claimed he was allergic to grass. And training. And early nights.

Our paranoias about injury, our desire to stay a step ahead of everyone else, means that players become attached to particular physios and their idiosyncratic treatments. Jonathan Woodgate brought his old Leeds man into the England set-up, and the physio subsequently got a big-money move to the New York Knicks NBA team. Ledley brought Nathan, his rehab man at Spurs, into Capello's England camp, which went down badly with Fabio.

Capello had his own men and his own strange ways. One of his masseurs used to follow every treatment by blasting you across the back of the legs with a hairdryer. We were never told what it was supposed to do, which made for some uncomfortable moments as you lay there naked on the massage table, your arse-hair parting beneath the blasts of hot air like a wheat field in a storm. I was also instructed to practise a breathing technique which involved standing in my room with one arm out to my side and the other holding on to the wall, which was something I only usually did after coming in from a big night on the sauce. I tried it, it did nothing. Still, my arse-hair had never looked better.

You'll be familiar with some of the embarrassing ways footballers have got themselves injured. Dave Beasant, the former Wimbledon, Newcastle and Chelsea goalkeeper, dropping a bottle of salad cream on his foot. Kevin Kyle, one-time Sunderland and Scotland striker, holding his eight-month-old son on his lap while trying to heat up a bottle of milk, spilling boiling water all over his family jewels and having to phone in sick with burned testicles. Sam Henderson, a goalkeeper with Queen of the South, damaging his shoulder after being hit by a runaway cow on his dad's farm.

I have my own to add to the list. While a young man at QPR I used a spare weekend to visit some mates over at Bath University. On the way home from school a few years earlier we had developed a game that involved diving into bushes. You could go front-side or back first, the technique a matter of personal preference. The best hedges were dense enough to hold your weight and offer sufficient spring to launch you at least partially back out. There were some absolute crackers along Ealing Common. With the right speed and angle of approach you could pull a full somersault off the best.

In Bath, bellies full of cheap student drinks, heads full of schooldays nostalgia, we went for it again. I will say this about the West Country: it has some absolutely first-class hedges. Ealing was good, but Bath was a whole new level, a real Mecca for the bush-jumping enthusiast. Bang back into form, at the absolute peak of my game confidence-wise, I spotted a beauty coming up, accelerated away and launched myself into a trademark parabola – only to spot, at the very last moment, a large metal spike sticking up through the middle.

Thank God my reactions were still sharp. Twisting in the air, I somehow managed to brush it with my leg rather than catching it amidships, where it surely would have killed me. As it was, I still sustained a brutal gash up my thigh. As I lay there on the pavement in agony, blood coming through my jeans, I thought: is this how it all ends? Is this how I go out of professional football, when I've barely even begun?

When I got back to London I had to lie to everyone. I told manager Gerry Francis I had tripped and fallen on a coffee table. I was certain he didn't believe me, and I was so relieved by my relatively swift recovery that I vowed to change. In an emotional phone conversation with my mate in Bath, I formally announced my bush-jumping retirement. Of course I missed it: you don't commit to a new sport like bush-jumping, take it to fresh heights of daring and skill, and not have your regrets.

Mine was that we had just opened a fresh front in the sport, based more around the gritty urban scene than leafy provincial towns. We would jump on the train from Ealing up to Soho, wait until kicking-out time when all the bars and restaurants were lobbing out their rubbish, and then focus on the biggest pile of grey bin-bags we could find. It was a halcyon period. Find the right back alley and you could get stacks of rubbish bags sixteen or eighteen deep. One night all of us were on fire – speed, aggression, the most innovative of angles. We thought the night could get no better – and then one of my mates let out a yell, and started waving something in the air. 'TWENTY QUID! I'VE FOUND TWENTY QUID!'

He was still shouting that when a taxi came round the corner, failed to spot him and drove right into him. As in slow motion he flipped up in the air, rotating over the bonnet and crashing down on his back in the road. We stood frozen, aghast. The driver stepped out, hands on his head: 'Son, are you okay? Son?' Nothing for what seemed like an age. And then our mate raised first his head and then one extended arm, a huge grin spreading across his dazed face.

'I got twenty quid. I'm brilliant!'

NERVES

You hate nerves as a footballer and you love them too. You grow accustomed to them and you never really learn how to lose them. They come in the big games and the small games. When they go, you know deep inside that maybe your time with football is coming to an end.

When I played for England we were often told to have a little sleep in the empty hours before games, particularly when it was an evening kick-off. The hotel would be quiet, the bed large and comfy. You'd lie there after your doze, all warm and cosy under the thick duvet, no one to bother you, understanding that in three hours' time you would be running out into a cauldron of 80,000 screaming fans, half of the country watching on television. And then the thought popped up in your head: I could just stay in this bed. I could just stay here and not have to face those nerves, not have those knots in my stomach, not have the sick feeling fizzing round my guts. What if I don't answer my phone, or the knock on my door? What if I just don't go out? Later, having played the game, you ride a wave of adrenaline so strong you can't sleep again until close to dawn. You forget all about the nerves, until the next match comes around, and they begin again, and you remember once more that they never end.

There was a night, up in Manchester, with England playing at Old Trafford while Wembley was being redeveloped, when I almost gave in to them. We were on the team coach from the Lowry hotel, driving slowly through the traffic around Salford Quays, when I glanced out of the window at a pub by the side of the road. At a table by the door was a bloke about my age, sipping a pint, messing about on his phone. In that precise moment, I would have done anything to swap places with him – to be sitting there with a beer, not a care in the world, ready to enjoy watching England on the telly and then go home without millions of people discussing every aspect of what you'd done. I'm pretty certain everyone in the pub would have given anything to have taken my place, on the England coach on the way to play for their country, getting very generously rewarded for it too. It was a ridiculous, stupid thing. But for about thirty seconds, it seemed like the most attractive idea in the world.

I got it again during the World Cup finals in Germany in the summer of 2006. Playing in the World Cup is the pinnacle of any Englishman's career, something I'd dreamed about as a kid and had hoped for desperately for the previous few years as I'd tried to establish myself in the Premier League. In the dressing-room before our opening group game, I looked at the players getting changed around me – David Beckham, Michael Owen, Steven Gerrard, John Terry. The enormity of it all hitting me all of a sudden: oh my God, Peter, you're at a World Cup! You're actually about to play!

It was as if I were watching the whole scene on TV, as if I were back home seeing it all relayed to my front room. And with that came the butterflies. There is a whole country watching this, I thought. There will be everyone I know and care about watching me, and millions and millions more I have never met who will be passing judgement on everything I do. I sat there, swallowed and thought, why didn't I just become a bin-man? And yet the moment I walked out of the tunnel it all turned to excitement.

If it was bad for me, it was worse for my family. They were powerless to do anything about it; at least I could lose myself in the game. My mum and dad felt more uncomfortable the longer the game went on. They cared so much, and they just wanted to protect me from the worst consequences. My dad would find himself going to specific cafés for his pre-match lunch in the hope that it would somehow bring the luck of the week before, walking the dog at certain auspicious times, pulling on the same lucky pants.

Before that World Cup my mum sat me down and made me promise that, should we find ourselves in a penalty shoot-out, I would not take one. It was a tricky situation for me. I could see where she was coming from, but I could also picture the look on Sven's face in the team huddle out on the pitch as I told him his striker couldn't step up because his mum hadn't given permission. As it turned out I got lucky, although it was also as unfortunate as it could be. Because Jamie Carragher had been banging in penalties every time we practised them in training, he was given the fifth one when we played Portugal in the quarter-finals. I had come on as a sub after Wayne Rooney was sent off, and was lined up for number six. Carra cracked. Ricardo went the right way and palmed it onto the bar. I had kept my promise to my mum but at the expense of England going out of the World Cup. In that scenario the only real winners were Portugal.

You can feel it on the pitch when the nervousness has spread to the fans. The atmosphere sours. You don't hear individual shouts but you can sense the vibes. There is a different sound for 'we-need-a-goal' nerves, a distinct one for 'this 0–0 is killing me', another for 'we're 1–0 up and hanging on'. You can also see it in the eyes and the actions of a manager. When he changes his mind on something, you know he's struggling. A manager has to be decisive, even if that decision is wrong. It's like being an army officer leading mutinying troops. You might be wrong, but you have to convince all the wannabe rebels that you're right. Even if you don't know the answer, pretend you do, or else the players will be all over you.

At Southampton Paul Sturrock used to say something, listen to an assistant and then change his mind. It might have made sense but it also weakened him in our eyes. We didn't want weakness. We wanted a leader. It's like Frank Abagnale in *Catch Me If You Can*, attempting to perform an surgical operation with no previous experience. 'Do you concur?'

Nerves should be crippling and for some players they are. You survive because you know that if you can get through them, if you can overcome the abject terror and fear of failure, then the release that follows will be the best feeling you ever have. There will be a blast of endorphin that you could never replicate any other way, a buzz so intense that you almost feel sorry for someone who never gets to experience it.

I played professional football for a long time. Even at thirty-eight, sitting on the bench, I would feel the full force of the old panic and pleasure when the manager signalled at me to get ready. I'd be thinking, 'Do I actually want to go on?' at exactly the same time as thinking, 'For God's sake, man, get me on, yeah?' I'd be standing on the touchline, stripped down to my kit, see my squad number come up on the electronic board held aloft by the assistant referee and go almost weak at the knee with nerves. It happened in league matches with Burnley when we were safe. It happened with Stoke when we were down in the Championship. All of it worse as a substitute, with more time to think about everything, with more noise from the fans seeping into your brain, with no physical release to distract you from the sick feeling building and building in your stomach like a toxic soup.

And the weirdest thing of all? Every single footballer knows exactly what I'm talking about, and yet none of us really discuss it. It's the elephant being sick in the corner of the room. It's the one taboo subject in an environment where you will happily chew over the freakiest and darkest things known to mankind.

Maybe it's a strange kind of machismo. Maybe it's because everyone has to find a way to cope and so just gets on with it. But you can see it all around you, in the way that normally chatty team-mates fall silent, or the funny ones go serious, or the cocky ones start going pale and dropping things. In 2019, I took part in a BBC documentary about mental health with the Duke of Cambridge. Gareth Southgate told a story about one of his early games with England, when David Seaman sat down next to him afterwards and said, 'Oh, I was so nervous before the game.' Gareth had been shocked. 'I was thinking, Dave Seaman gets nervous? Now that can't be. And suddenly the whole dressing-room changed for me, because I suddenly started to look at how everyone was carrying on before the game, getting their own mind right ...'

Gareth can talk about these things. Most players go the other way. The worse they feel, the less likely they are to share it with anybody. I attempted to cope with humour and messing about, trying to make it clear that I wasn't really bothered at all by trying to look like a man bothered by nothing. Others stick on their headphones and don't talk to anyone. Some – those who would usually rather eat a book rather than read one – suddenly immerse themselves in the duller parts of the match-day programme. 'Give me a moment lads, I'm catching up with what the groundsman's been up to in his latest column.'

Even though I believe it's good to talk, I also believe it would make me more nervous if I did so. By talking about my nerves I would be focusing on them more. By listening to other people's worries, I know I would be helping them but I'd also be introducing fresh fears into my own head. 'Are you worried about the physical power of the right-sided centre-half, Crouchie?' Not until you flagged it up I wasn't. 'Yeah, there's a record-breaking television audience expected for this one, mate.' Brilliant. Cheers. That's really helped.

It's not like my system is flawless. Pretending not to be nervous only works if your pretending is convincing. I got quite good at reading out choice selections from the programme, an act most team-mates seemed to swallow. It genuinely looked from the outside like I was taking it all lightly, when actually the reason that it looked like I was taking it lightly was because I was taking it very seriously indeed. Everyone has a coping mechanism. This was mine. On my face, a big grin. On my lips, a quirky stat from an opposition pen-pic. Inside, a voice dying to cry out: 'I've been this way all my life! School games! District trials! On loan at Dulwich Hamlet! The Championship, the Champions League, the World Cup!'

The Middlesex schools athletics finals, Perivale track, west London. I'm fifteen years old, down to run the heats of the hundred metres. We are being called to our blocks in rows of eight, and I am still three lines back when the nerves take over. I can't do this, I think. I don't want to be here. I do, but I don't. I wanted to be picked. I now want to be anywhere else than a part of suburban London that even most people in suburban London have never heard of. I want to run so I can win. I don't want to run because I can't win, because I can't run. I can't run because I am so nervous my legs won't move. Woah.

Suddenly my heat was being called. My line had reached the start. All the cool kids from my school were on the grass around the track, watching on. Every cool kid from west London was there. All the nice girls. All my mates. Everyone.

I got down in my blocks, heart bashing against my ribcage. The gun went. I got up again, just, like a section of pipe being winched into place by a crane. I started trying to run, and it was as if my limbs were all working independently of each other – right leg and right arm going forward at the same time, left arm going across my body, feet as heavy as blocks of stone. I cramped in my left calf at twenty metres. I cramped in my right calf at thirty. By forty metres I was last and feeling as if I were breaking up in flight, bits of me separating off and spinning away in all directions. At fifty metres I lost all control. One moment I was upright, albeit at a weird angle. The next I was face down on the dark red track.

There was silence from the hundreds of kids watching. Then laughter, spreading from one little group to the next, and then the next, until all of them – the coolest kids in town, the ones from my school, my own mates – were all roaring and screaming and rolling about in the stands. I got up. My life could get no worse. And then I looked down the track and realised that I still had forty-nine metres still to run, and that rock bottom was still quite a long way further on. I started a humiliated jog down the remainder of what was now an empty track, dead last by ten seconds in a race won in twelve, trudging back round from the finish line to our school's place on the grass, every kid looking at me, every kid pointing, every kid laughing.

More than two decades on my mates still wind me up about it. That fall was because of nerves, and I vowed that day that they would never stop me doing what I wanted. At least with football I know what I'm doing. I know the nerves will side-swipe me but I understand that once I get going I will be in my safe place and at my comfort level. With golf I'm lost and alone. I love the sport: I took it up much later than most footballers, and I enjoy every second I play, even if I'm still not ready to play a round with Jamie Redknapp.

Yet the prospect of playing in front of any sort of gallery brings me to my knees. I'm often asked to play in pro-ams, very much as an underwhelming am to be paired with a disappointed pro, but I can't do it. The Alfred Dunhill Links Championship at St Andrews, Pep Guardiola's one in Catalunya. I could be playing spectacular courses with spectacular partners: Hristo Stoichkov and Ronald de Boer at one, Samuel L. Jackson and Michael Douglas at the other. I can't because of what might happen. I can't because there is nothing to get me past the nerves. A crossbar challenge in front of 80,000 people is intimidating but achievable. An eight-foot downhill putt in front of Bill Murray is not.

A little while ago my dad persuaded me that I was ready to play the East Course at Wentworth. I wasn't, but even in your late thirties, you defer to your old man. Even as we walked to the first tee I was awash with doubt and remorse. Dad, I'm not good enough. Son, neither am I, keep your voice down. I loosened my shoulders and took out my driver. I saw my dad turn round and look a little startled. Behind us was standing Bernard Gallacher, eight times a player in the Ryder Cup, three times the European captain.

I was ready to stick the driver back in my bag and clear off. I've got a swing like a man trying to wriggle out of handcuffs. Even at seventy, Bernard hits the ball like a man breaking rocks. My dad, like all dads, sensed my distress and tried to do something about it.

'Mr Gallacher!' he shouted (my dad had never met him before). 'Why not the West Course this morning? Isn't the East a little dull for a player like you?'

Bernard shrugged. 'Ach, I just fancied a little tickle. You lads crack on.'

My dad saw the look on my face and strode over. 'Listen,' he hissed in my ear. 'Who cares where your tee-shot goes? Forget about Gallacher. We'll never see him again.'

It worked. I stepped up to the ball, took a breath and clattered an absolute beauty down the middle of the fairway. I glanced back at our celebrated gallery in time to see a little nod of approval. Yes, Bernard. It's what I do.

My dad glared at me. 'See?' he whispered, sticking his ball down and waggling his driver. 'I told you. Nothing to worry about.'

He pulled back his club and let rip. The ball shot sideways at incredible pace, just past my ankles, directly at a large detached house off to the side of the tee. The last we saw of it was as it burrowed under a white picket fence and disappeared deep into a millionaire's garden.

Neither of us looked back. Straight to the buggy, slamming it into gear, off down the cart path without so much as a wave at Bernard. There was no question of looking for the ball. It would have taken a team of archaeologists to unearth it. Dad just dropped a new one by mine and took the penalty. It was almost dignified.

When I see the effect of nerves on others now, I try to help them as best I can. Sometimes that means giving them space to roll out the weird superstitions that make them feel slightly better. At Burnley you learned that whatever worked for Tom Heaton worked for the team. Sometimes that means giving them space so they could vomit in the toilet rather than on your shoes. The memory of Shaun Derry throwing his guts up is like a time machine taking me back to Fratton Park in 2001.

You see it worst in the young kids who have just come into the team. On the outside you put on an understanding smile and attempt to talk them through it. On the inside you're thinking, thank God I'm not you. The message you give is the same one that I used to get as a lad at Spurs, and then QPR: 'You're in this dressing-room for a reason – because you're good enough. The manager has seen what you can do and he trusts you. Whatever you've done to get here, just do that. Don't change it just because you're in a superior team. What you do is enough.'

I've been lucky in so many ways. I'm naturally upbeat. I try to find enjoyment in everything I do. It's the introverted ones who struggle, who over-think it, who lose themselves in what ifs and oh no's. I know great players who were brought low by thinking too much. I had mates from home who had the ability to make a career of football but who had the mentality of a troubled singer-songwriter and lost themselves in self-analysis.

The majority of footballers aren't great thinkers. We take the mickey about the rare ones of our breed who dare to read books or attempt to learn another language. But thinking rarely helps. Thinking gets in the way of instinct. Choosing to be judged by millions of strangers each week makes no sense as a wellbeing choice. It's madness. If you thought about it too much you'd end up at the obvious answer: don't do it. So instead we behave as if we're the title characters in a sad children's cartoon. *The Boy Who Thought Too Little.*

It's not even about negative thoughts. Just thoughts are bad enough sometimes. To take a penalty in a World Cup finals you need to clear your mind of all but the simple mechanics of striking a ball. There is no room for consequence and there is no room for imagination.

It's a skill as much as being able to strike the ball itself. Some players learn it; most come ready-made. Here I'm lucky again; I can only ever concentrate on one thing at one time, even if as a father of four I would like to be capable of coping with more. As soon as I started getting ready for a match, anything else that may have been going on in my life or the wider world was elbowed out of the way. There was never a point in twenty years of professional football where I was playing and thought about anything else but professional football, and in some ways that is the most beautiful thing. When I faced huge problems off the pitch I began training or playing, and all those worries just disappeared. Those times on the pitch were completely free.

It's why I've never understood when a player's dip in form is blamed on 'off-field issues'. You play to escape. It's why taking a break from football to solve those issues makes even less sense to me. I can't think of anything worse than sitting at home obsessing about it all. Even if the things that are bothering you are all over the newspapers, football provides its own special refuge. You go into training and the other lads will make a big joke about it, and suddenly you think, actually, this is all a joke. It's not life or death. You arrive at the club feeling like your whole world is falling in. You kick a football and, like a happy young puppy, you just want to chase after it. It's insulting and beautiful at the same time.

I remember one period in 2006 when it felt like I had the weight of the world on my shoulders. And yet training with Liverpool that week was the most enormous fun. We played Birmingham away at the weekend and I scored twice before the first half was even up. To look at me jumping about with Steven Gerrard and Luis García you wouldn't think I had a care in the world – celebrating in front of the fans, grinning as I walked back to the halfway line, beaming even as I was subbed off on fifty-six minutes with a hat-trick up for grabs.

Playing at Anfield could be hard on the nerves. I was so anxious before my debut, in the Champions League against FBK Kaunas, that I tensed up Perivale-style and pulled my hamstring the first time I tried to put on the after-burners. But there were so many times when Anfield lifted me close to joy – ninety minutes of running, jumping and avoiding tackles, all of it in a cauldron of noise, staggering into the showers afterwards physically spent and soaked in sweat but feeling so alive. My head was so clear, my body tingling, buzzing so much that it would be several hours and many beers until I could even think about going to bed.

There are psychologists now at every club to help you through. Sadly not many players want to use them, because of the unspoken fear of somehow appearing weak to others. It doesn't matter that in cycling much of the success of the Great Britain track team at the Beijing and London Olympics could be put down to the work that former clinical psychiatrist Steve Peters did with Sir Chris Hoy, Victoria Pendleton and others. A football club is still a tribal environment. It can be unforgiving and it can be ruthless. I could never ask a psychologist for help in coping. You fear that if you show weakness then someone else will take advantage. That needs to change, but it will take time.

In place of dialogue, there are slogans. Everywhere. In the dressing-rooms, in the gym, in the canteen. All of them are cheesy. Most are meaningless. Here are some classic examples.

INDIVIDUALLY WE ARE NOTHING. TOGETHER WE ARE EVERYTHING. That's going to boost your confidence, being told that you are worthless without the presence of Bruno Martins Indi. Together we are everything? What, a crack team of decorators? A boy band? The cosmos? We're just footballers. We're probably mid-table. We're trying our hardest. That may have to be enough.

TRAINING IS EVERYTHING. Hang on, I thought we were everything? Also, matches are everything, not the drills we do while wearing gloves and luminous bibs on a Tuesday morning. There are no fans' songs about dominating the five-a-sides. No one bangs on about how good Oasis were in rehearsals.

CULTURE COMES FIRST. Only in a yoghurt factory. People will tell you that New Zealand's success in rugby is because they have star players humble enough to clean the dressing-rooms after matches. Yes, because the fact they are all big, fast and have unbelievable handling skills from having played the game since the age of three pales into insignificance with the ability to pick up their dirty pants and lob them in a laundry skip.

THE SCORE TAKES CARE OF ITSELF. Take it from a striker: it doesn't. Don't insult me and my goals. I worked my arse off to get in position for that three-yard tap-in. You should have seen what the centre-half was trying to do to my Achilles on the edge of the box. Show some respect.

Sometimes there are big photos of you too, by your spot in the dressing-room, of you scoring goals if you're a striker, or you standing on a striker's toes if you're a defender. They are always specific to you and designed to highlight your contribution to the team. In the fag-end days of my time at Burnley I will always grateful that no one stuck up a picture of me sitting on a bench for eighty-three minutes, wearing a thick warm-up coat. I've always preferred science-fiction to gritty realism.

Sport often bleeds into business. All those slogans have been borrowed or repurposed by seminars or in offices across the country. You take your inspiration where you can, although I've never been entirely convinced that there is too much similarity between running a large HR department and spending your mornings trying to hit a team-mate on the arse with a spare ball. But I do like the image of Nigel in accounts returning to his desk one day to find a giant photo on the cubicle wall of him at his finest: polishing off the final column of a complicated Excel spreadsheet, index finger poised over the return key. This is the best you, Nigel. Be Inspired. Be Inspiring.

TROPHIES

In an upstairs cupboard in my house is a large plastic box. In that box is my lifetime in football: almost every trophy I ever won, from five-a-side tournaments as an eight-year-old to an FA Cup winners' medal, from little wooden shields to empty bottles of champagne. There are deflated footballs with the faded signatures of old team-mates, silver salvers with neat inscriptions. There's also strange-shaped pieces of carved glass, cups with big handles, bits of cheap black plastic with team names from my past and wins that almost no one else can now remember.

Each of them takes me back. I've played in Champions League finals and at World Cups but I used to love the summer five-a-sides as a kid as much as any of them. The weather was always baking, the grass usually brown and parched. You would have to wait an age for your next game, and when it did come round it would be over in blur of shouts and blocked shots and trying not to fall into the 'D' and give away a penalty. In between matches you would shovel down a burger and an ice-cream and then stand around in the small tent where the organisers were sat, trying to work out what that result might mean for who you would face in the next round. All the time there'd be sweat dribbling down your back, your face red, knees and elbows grazed from landing on the hard bare earth.

You can say that none of it mattered, but it did to me. I'll never forget the feeling in my stomach as we parked up outside Craven Cottage for the Middlesex County Cup final, my West Middlesex Colts team up against Enfield Rangers. I was ten years old and allowed to use the actual dressing-rooms. I walked out of the tunnel looking for my dad and his mates in the main stand. I even banged in one of the goals as we won 3–2.

The little individual trophies you got at the end-of-season awards would usually all appear to be from the same trophy factory somewhere in the Far East. They'd consist of a square black plastic base, a gold-leafed player caught in the act of striking a ball with the top of his foot, leaning back slightly, head down, other arm perfectly balanced with outstretched foot. No matter that the only man to ever kick a football like that was Bobby Charlton during the 1966 World Cup: it was the totem for all us, whether striker or midfielder, Player of the Season or Top Goal-Scorer; maybe even the trophy that was a prize and an insult all rolled into one, Most Improved Player.

Sometimes the gold figure might be involved in a frozen tussle with an opposition player. Sometimes it might be a creative central midfielder with his foot nonchalantly on the ball, another man sliding in for an old-school challenge that was almost definitely going to take man as well as ball and should really end in a yellow card. Never did there seem to be a trophy showcasing purely the defender's arts – a towering header, a casual interception and classy piece of distribution. It almost made me feel sorry for defenders good enough to win Player of the Season. But then again I was a striker, and defenders were my enemy, so they could suck it up.

When I signed my first professional contract I thought: wow, I wonder what the real trophies look like in this proper adult world. And then I saw a few, and they were a bit rubbish. The medals might come in a felt-lined box but some of them look like chocolate coins. The designs were either underwhelming or, in the case of newer competitions, unpleasantly gaudy. The five-a-side ones might only have been won by teams from suburban west London, but they were often more creative.

As a kid the trophies came most seasons. West Middlesex Colts were feared throughout west Middlesex. As a professional I won almost nothing for years. Nothing at QPR. Nothing at Portsmouth. Not really a success at Aston Villa, the first actual bit of silverware coming on loan at Norwich when they won the Championship title to get promoted to the Premier League. Even then I didn't really feel part of it. I had only been there for the last three months of the season: part of the temporary cavalry with Darren Huckerby and Kevin Harper. I was still given a medal but I wasn't certain I'd earned it. There was still a week of the Premier League season to go when Norwich were confirmed as champions, so I was back at Villa even before the open-top bus parade. Great to see you again, Mr O'Leary.

But here's the strange thing I began to understand about trophies as a professional sportsman. They don't matter. Not the physical things, anyway. What you care about is the achievement itself, the memory of that special day. The lump of metal, the little square box? Far less frequently in your thoughts. There is a reason why they are all in that box in the cupboard rather than up on the walls or in a cabinet.

Take the runners-up medal I got from the Champions League final of 2007. I saw it on the night in Athens, and I haven't looked at it since. You should be proud of something like that. You've got through the qualifying round, the group stage, the two-legged nightmares of the knock-out rounds. You've beaten some of the finest sides in Europe, and ended up with a silver medal, which in the Olympics is considered a pretty special thing. But in football it is something far, far worse, a reminder less of how far you have come than the fact that you failed to go all the way. It's why the expression on the faces of the runners-up as they collect their medals are akin to men having a fresh turd placed on their palm. The medal itself is the same size as the winners' one. It's not unattractive in itself. It has some heft when you pick it up. But you still don't want it, which is why quite a few players leave it at the ground or lob it into the crowd. Who wants a permanent reminder of the time they messed up on the biggest day of their footballing careers?

Walk into the house of most footballers and you won't see any silverware. At mine, in place of the bling, are the photos. They'll only go up in my office, so they are nudges for me rather than show-offs in front of visitors ('What, this old thing? Hadn't even realised it was up – that's me scoring for England at a World Cup. Take your time, enjoy the fine detail …'). There are photos of the scissor-kick for Liverpool against Galatasaray; lifting the FA Cup with Robbie Fowler, one of my childhood heroes; doing the Robot in front of Sven and Prince William; the volley for Stoke against Manchester City; the Kasabian gig at the O2 when Serge shoved a mic in my hand and I ended up singing my heart out to the entire arena. All of them seemingly impossible moments for a kid from Ealing who grew up booting a ball against the tennis court fence in Pitshanger Park – little stories from the past with the happiest of endings.

Sometimes when you travel the world and arrive at a set-piece sight you can find yourself a little underwhelmed, just because you've seen so many photos of it, so many films, that the reality is slightly disappointing. The pyramids at Giza look smaller than you imagined. The Sydney Opera House looks less impressive from the perimeter wall than it does from a helicopter shot above the Harbour Bridge. The best trophies in football don't have that problem. The FA Cup is an absolute beauty. It has grace, it has style. I always think of it as the brother of the Wimbledon men's singles trophy: two beautifully dressed old gentlemen, their suits as crisp and ageless as they were in their youth. The history of them matters. I like the fact that the Wimbledon trophy has the inscription, 'The All England Lawn Tennis Club Single Handed Championship of the World', as if there was an alternative tournament for players who hit forehands with both left and right hands. I love the thought of all the other players down the past century who have also held the FA Cup aloft, those famous fingerprints that were there before mine. I like that there is a slightly smaller replica that looks exactly the same, made by the same jewellery shop in Bradford at the same time but used instead by the North Wales Coast FA for their annual trophy.

I had so much fun with the FA Cup. It was like going on a date with someone I had fancied since school. I drank champagne out of it. I wore the lid as a hat. I cradled the base. It's heavier than you think, which adds to its appeal for me. It shows that it has class and substance. The day after we beat West Ham at the Millennium Stadium in Cardiff, Robbie Fowler and I were waving it from an upstairs balcony of a Liverpool bar to all the fans down below, in the way that Liverpool captain Phil Thompson had taken the European Cup to his local pub, the Falcon in Kirkby, in the back of his Ford Capri after beating Real Madrid in Paris in the final of 1981. I thought my life had peaked.

The Champions League trophy is the FA Cup's big brother. Taller, wider, bigger handles, but still the same casual beauty. The UEFA Super Cup, played for between the winners of the Champions League and the Europa League, is an often-forgotten attractive one, all easy curves and shining silver. I'm also a firm defender of the Community Shield, both as a trophy and a contest. I scored the winner for Liverpool against Chelsea in 2006, three months after our FA Cup win in the same stadium, and it felt almost as good – same packed stands, same celebrating fans. I appreciate for most people it's forever attached to the phrase 'traditional curtain-raiser', but it was part of my childhood, signalling the fun about to begin, and it's lovely to lift – unusual shape, good heft.

A good trophy should be instantly recognisable. Hence the appeal of the League Cup, with its three handles, as distinctive as its current sponsor is forgettable. It's a decent quiz question: how many can you correctly name from Milk Marketing Board, Littlewoods, Rumbelows, Coca-Cola, Worthington's, Carling, Capital One and Carabao? The Premier League trophy is perfect in that it is everything the competition represents: flashy, cost a few quid, not particularly tasteful. It's got lions, it's got a gold crown. No one knew where to stop. It's the trophy equivalent of a new-build mansion.

A good trophy should have handles. It's why the UEFA Cup doesn't work for me. It's too ice hockey. The exception to this is the old Football League Division One champions one, as held aloft by Tony Adams when Arsenal beat Liverpool at Anfield with Michael Thomas's late goal in 1989. It was a silver ball on a silver spike but it was as elegant as it was short-lived.

The current World Cup trophy is the other great handle-free controversy. Baddiel and Skinner were right to point out on *Fantasy Football League* that it looked like a man's hand holding a grapefruit and dipped in custard, but it works against all the odds. There are so many flaws – the fact that it's almost certainly hollow, because someone worked out once that a solid gold version would weigh as much as an adult man, and thus be impossible to hoist triumphantly into the skies; that the original version of it was nicked in Rio de Janeiro in 1983 and probably melted down; that the base was made too small to be engraved with the names of many winners, and so will need biffing off in a decade or so. I'd also like there to be more than one element to it, because a trophy needs to be shared around – a lid for one man, a plinth for another. You can't drink out of the World Cup, and I could never have been the skipper to lift it, because we couldn't have done that thing where all your team-mates put a hand on it as you hold it up. The photo on the front of the papers would have been me, the World Cup and a load of stretching fingertips. The alternatives – team-mates stroking my face, me lifting it while sitting down – would be even less iconic.

It still works. The warmth of the gold, the contrasting green of the base, which is maybe more of a nod to Brazil than is fair on the rest of the world. The balance of the thing, the fact it can be held with one hand but equally looks magic when borne aloft by two. Nothing looks like the World Cup, which I'm sure is one of the reasons they were happy to let the old Jules Rimet trophy go to Brazil back in 1970. The 'won it three times' clause had been stipulated by Jules back in 1930, but the argument doesn't work for me. Manchester United weren't given the Premier League trophy in perpetuity in 1996. Roger Federer doesn't get to keep the All England Lawn Tennis Club Single Handed Championship of the World. I think FIFA were secretly a bit gutted that Pickles the dog found it in that hedge back in 1966 when everyone thought it stolen and gone for good. They were ready to move on, and Pelé, Rivelino and the rest gave them the perfect excuse. You know when it's time for an upgrade.

Everyone's happy in a trophy presentation photo. Everyone except the bloke doing the presenting. They're the most awkward-looking person in the stadium: part of it but in no way really part of it, someone who has looked forward to their big moment and then realised as it unfolds that no one could care less about them, that they are purely functional and that function is merely to pass something to someone else more popular. With champagne going everywhere, he's right in the mixer and can't wait to get out. I still feel sympathy for Sheffield Wednesday's players, who won the League Cup at Wembley in 1991 and had it presented to them by Rumbelows' employee of the year, a woman named Tracy. You wait half a century for a major honour, beat the Manchester United team of Sir Alex Ferguson at the home of football and get to shake hands with someone who has flogged a slightly higher than average number of microwaves.

I've always fancied a play-off winners' medal. Not because of the tin itself, or the gaudy trophy, but because of the day itself. As a player and fan, going up by winning the play-off final at Wembley is surely better than going up as champions. It's Wembley, it's a sensational day out, it's doubling your wages in one game. They're always good games. So much hangs on them. There is so much to lose, which is why the gate receipts from the Championship play-off final all go the loser. The club that's just gone up to the Premier League won't even notice it. Have a few crumbs off our table, lads, we don't flipping need them now.

I will never get one of those awards but I've had some personal beauties that mean a great deal to me. Stoke gave me a lovely trophy to mark my 100th Premier League goal. The player of the season ones I got early in my career at QPR and Portsmouth are still precious and appreciated. I would have loved the Premier League goal of the season award in 2011–12, and thought I had it in the bag after crashing home that volley against Manchester City, only for Papiss Cissé to pip me at the death for his goal for Newcastle against Chelsea. I'm still fuming all these years later. I'm convinced his was fluky.

The match ball you collect after scoring a hat-trick is always special. I have one from Liverpool against Arsenal, England against Jamaica. I got one for Stoke in the League Cup and gave the ball to a little lad in the crowd. There is a pleasing tradition where all your team-mates sign it for you, typically with moving personal messages like 'Couldn't have done it without my crosses' and 'Should have had four, that miss was a disgrace'. No one ever likes to point out that the ball you're given may not actually be the one you scored your hat-trick with, merely the last one lobbed onto the pitch by a ball-boy. But you go with it, in the same way that at 2am after a big summer barbecue in the back garden you end up playing headers and volleys with a half-deflated ball that represents one of your happiest days and by the end contains signatures which are smudged at best and erased more often than not.

On those same boozy nights you can also make the most chastening of discoveries. Running out of beverages, you remember those bottles of man-of-the-match champagne you have stashed away. You dig out a couple of the ones from the Liverpool days, pop the cork, slosh it into the waiting champagne flutes to cheers from your assembled guests, make a toast to all assembled and then knock it back … only to find out it's actually Carlsberg. I enjoy a lager. I just don't enjoy it when I think it's champagne. Tepid Carlsberg in a flute at two in the morning is probably not the best drink in the world.

None of those trophies is the most popular one in our house. The one that brings the most joy to guests wasn't even won by me: it's the glitterball given to Abbey after she won *Strictly Come Dancing* with Aljaž Škorjanec in 2013. My daughter keeps it in her bedroom, while Abbey carries her own reminder with her everywhere she goes: a chip on her tooth, after she pretended to bite it, in the style of Olympic gold medallists nibbling their medals. The trophy bites back.

AGENTS

You hear a lot about agents. About how much money they make. About the deals they do. About how they persuade a player to sign for them in the first place: hundreds of thousands of pounds, free cars, houses for the extended family.

My own sweetener was a box of free Adidas gear. I was fourteen, so it blew my mind. There was a pair of the latest Predator boots, some lounge gear, shorts, trainers and a few tops. I remember staring in joyous disbelief at the agent. 'You mean I don't have to pay for boots?' He gave a nonchalant shrug. 'Yeah, got you some moulds, some studs ...'

I was right at the start of it all for the agency I'm still with, quarter of a century later. Ledley King was the first, Ashley Cole one of the next few. We were all teenagers and something of a long-term punt. It was Ledley who recommended me: Crouchie is a proper player, he told them. You should take him. He also gave them advance warning. 'When he walks in, don't laugh. You'll want to, because he's six foot seven and weighs about nine stone, and you'll never have seen a football player who looks less like a football player.' They listened but not that carefully enough. Apparently when I arrived at their offices the main man was fuming. 'Fuck's sake. This is actually a wind-up. Nice one, Ledley ...'

At the time I was on a YTS contract at Spurs, getting paid the grand sum of £45 a week. When I signed full-time professional terms I did the negotiating myself, and got it up to £275 a week for the first year, rising to £300 in the second if I did well. I thought of myself as a prototype Alan Sugar, which was a mistake when the chairman actually was Alan Sugar. There was only one man walking away from that deal having got value for money.

When my agent found out he was furious. 'How long is this deal? Are you sure it's not for five years? You could be banging them in for the first team and still be stuck on that. Leave this stuff to me.'

Unfortunately at that point I was yet to understand how ruthless the game was. It still is. If someone can take advantage of you, they will. I went to see Gerry Francis at QPR, told I had no future at Spurs, excited that my local club might be interested in taking me on. Gerry was an experienced manager. He understood what agents do and that his life was a constant running battle with them. So the first thing he said to me was, 'Son, I'll give you a chance, but you need to know that I never deal with agents. If you try to get one involved, the move is off.'

I panicked. I thought, right, better not tell my man. If it could kill it, it's not worth the risk. I told my dad. He agreed. So we went to Loftus Road and did it all ourselves. They offered us £800 a week. I couldn't quite believe it. Almost triple my previous deal! Not for a moment did I remember that the existing wage was a sorry sort of benchmark that anyone with both an agent and sense would have pied off rather than sign. I just thought I'd made it. I was still living at home in Ealing: that would be £800 in my pocket every single week. I thought I was flying. I told my mates, who had all left school and were slogging around in the dullest of jobs for that much every three weeks. They thought I was flying too. Dad, we've played a blinder here.

And then my agent saw a photo on the QPR website of me holding up the home shirt. The call was brusque. 'What the hell do you think you're doing?'

'Yeah, but Gerry doesn't deal with agents.'

'Deal with agents? I spoke to him last week!'

I had no idea that there were senior players at the club on £8,000 a week. I did by the time I was voted player of the season as some of them were spending Saturday afternoons sitting on the bench, but by then the leggy horse had bolted. I had no idea that managers and agents consider it part of the circus, that they get on but spend most of their time trying to get one over on each other. Gerry had called my agent up in fits of laughter. 'I've done you!' My agent called me up as I looked at my £800 in a rather different way. 'If this happens on your next deal, it's over ...'

I'd learned my lesson. When I moved to Portsmouth at the end of that season, a £60,000 signing turned into a £1.2 million transfer and my agent handled the deal. Over the years, I think I've made it up to him – moving to Aston Villa, Southampton, Liverpool, Portsmouth again, Spurs and Stoke, all in the decade that followed. Each multi-million pound move came with with a cut for him, that slice of £800 long since eclipsed.

The cut. My professional career stretched to almost twenty years, but I still couldn't tell you the standard cut an agent might take from his player's move. Part of the reason for this is that there is no standard cut. There's no standard anything with lots of agents. There is a cloud of secrecy over the money they earn from a transfer, even from the person who is being transferred.

You shouldn't lose a chunk of your weekly salary. When I was on my £45 as a kid at Spurs, my agents weren't demanding £7 of it. They didn't need peanuts when the whole peanut-farm would be coming along later. As a grown player, the cut is supposed to be a percentage of the value of your deal, but the exact percentage might forever remain a secret between the agent and his accountant. Back in the day, a player would be told that the agent would get their slice from the buying club. 'Don't worry about it, it's not your money.' The player would think, great, not realising that it was a rather obvious conjuring trick. It was still your money, and you were still paying: you just weren't seeing it before you paid it. You were better getting the actual amount, asking what the agent's chunk was going to be, and then paying it. At least then you knew.

Transfers can happen without agents. They don't partly because of the money that can be made and partly because everyone involved – players, buying club, selling club – usually find it makes things easier, even if can also make it more expensive.

The buying club invariably works out in advance whether a player is keen to go. An ear will be put to the ground. By the time that you the player get to the buyer's training ground, the agent will have given you the ballpark figures for what you're going to be earning and for how long. A great deal more will go into the contract, but you usually know most of the rest – what the stadium's like, how good the support in the stands is, the facilities at training. You want to speak to the manager, to work out what his plans are for you, to see if he understands your game as you do, to discover which other players might be coming or going. Meanwhile your agent is speaking to the chief executive. He calls you and tells you the exact figure for what they're offering. If you tell him you're not happy he'll go back in. If you tell him you're happy he'll still go back in. That's agents.

There'll be some to-ing and fro-ing and a fair amount of thrashing about. Meanwhile, the player will be sitting in reception or a spare office, twiddling their thumbs and looking at their phone to see who else is moving where for how much. You'll get bored and hungry and someone will be sent to administer to your needs. When I signed for Stoke, the deal was still to be signed as midnight approached. Tony Pulis made a couple of the girls at the stadium stay behind and rustle us up a curry. There was me, Pulis and Cameron Jerome eating curry off plates on our laps, while our respective futures were argued about in a room three doors down.

I was always glad to have my dad for my dad. Despite the QPR shenanigans, he understood what might be going on behind closed doors. He had a lifetime of experience in the advertising business and while he didn't know all the answers in football he knew what questions to ask. What's that for? Where's that bit going? Who gets that bit? Left on my own I would have struggled far more.

But even with my dad, I still needed an agent, because I couldn't say the tough stuff on my own. I hate confrontation. I don't like arguing with people. Agents enjoy being the bad guy. Gary Neville? He could have negotiated with Kim Jong-un, and enjoyed every second. When we were with England, he loved going into meetings with the FA, just to say the opposite to what they'd said. You might remember his appearance on *Rio's World Cup Wind-Ups* before the 2006 tournament in Germany. He was stopped by two actors dressed as traffic policemen and offered a choice between six points on his licence or match tickets for one officer to make the whole thing go away. I would have crumbled in seconds: if you've seen the episode where Rio set me up with some fake Russian gangsters you'll know my style. Gary, by contrast, argued with them. He refused to take the easy way out. He relished the opportunity for a ding-dong, even with the long arm of the law. And that's why he could never understand why players didn't do transfer deals themselves. To him it was fun. To him it was a relaxing break from the football.

If you don't have that natural spikiness, you need someone with you. Sir Alex Ferguson understood the mentality of young players. He knew that a lad of twenty-two would find it difficult to contradict a man with his track record of winning trophies and promoting precocious talent. And so he would secure the best deal for the club, rather than necessarily what the same player may have been able to get elsewhere.

Sometimes players will know that an agent isn't being entirely honest with them. They'll see through the smoke and mirrors and work out that they aren't being shown how all the sums are being worked out. They reconcile it with the thought that they are getting more than they could on their own. You might ask the agent, 'What are you actually getting out of this?' and never get a straight answer. You might know that this is a straightforward deal that could be settled by a single phone call. The club wants you. You want to go there. But the size of your slice of the pie will be bigger this way, even if someone else is filling their face too.

And it's not just transfers. One of the most useful aspects of the agency I'm with is the team that comes with them: accountants, mortgage advisors, a commercial manager for boot deals and adverts, a financial advisor. When you're twenty-one and suddenly on thousands of quid a week you don't realise that you need an accountant, but you do. You have no clue how to buy a house. You've spent your entire life thus far in the football bubble. Footballers do not talk about variable interest rate loans. Believe me.

Players need that help and sometimes think they need a whole lot more on top. Some use agents like adult nannies. You want a new car: you phone your agent and they sort it out. Your car gets a flat tyre: you call your agent. Can't be arsed organising your own child's birthday party? You lob the responsibility on them and spend the afternoon playing golf instead. Tables at restaurants, tickets for gigs: a percentage will be added to each deal, but what do you care when you have one phone number that can deal with everything?

It's why good agents get passed around. A gentleman with white mutton-chop whiskers named Harry Swales made Kevin Keegan English football's first millionaire, was then recommended to Bryan Robson, and was then in turn passed on to Ryan Giggs and Paul Scholes. Personal recommendation works when you're a young footballer with strangers coming at you from everywhere.

There is a downside. If someone else does your life for you, what happens when that person is no longer there? You still don't know how to do your tax return, or buy a house, except now you're forty and lost rather than young enough to learn. As soon as football is done with you, a lot of agents are finished with you too. You might have a contract with an agent, but there's no stipulation that they have to call anyone for you. They might be contractually obliged to get you the best deal possible, but if there are no deals being chased, best means nothing. The moment most players stop kicking a football they are no longer making their agent any money. And money is why it starts, finishes and ends.

Sometimes you're best off with a big agency. They do one deal and they use another player as a makeweight. They get one pro on a big TV show and they have the number and trust of the executive next time they want to boost the profile of another part of their stable. There's also a lot to be said for what we might call the Jerry Maguire model: one man working himself into the ground for you and you only. You feel special, you feel reassured that they won't be eating if you're not eating. They are the pilot fish to your whale, or at least the plover bird to your crocodile. It works for Ed Sheeran and his manager Stuart Camp. Total dedication, total dependency.

Agents are seldom quiet men. They have charisma, or an edge, or both. Mine began as a cricketer, became a cricket intermediary, went into football with us young guns and was once spotted by me riding a motorised trike lit by UV lights around Marble Arch, wearing a fur coat and smoking a cigar. Before I met Sky Andrew, the man who did Sol Campbell's infamous free transfer from Spurs to arch-rivals Arsenal, I assumed he must be an awful man. I had been raised at Spurs. How could anyone who countenanced the sale of another homegrown talent to the Gunners possibly be anything but a rogue? And then I met him, and I really liked him. He was funny, he was interesting. I found out he'd represented Great Britain at table tennis in the 1988 Seoul Olympics. He'd won three Commonwealth gold medals two years on. He may have made a couple of million from Sol's move, but Sol wanted to go, and Arsenal were getting a defender worth £20 million on a free transfer. It all made sense. Unless you were a Spurs fan.

It was the same with Pini Zahavi. You hear so much about him – about his power, that he's a super-agent. But you meet him and he comes across as a lovely little man. I had mentioned to Rio that I fancied going to Israel on holiday with Abbey. He told me that Pini would look after us. And he did, even though I had no contract or other links with him. Hotels, trips out, transport. It was like having an extraordinarily well-connected travel agent.

They're different, the big dogs. I think of Jorge Mendes, who represents Cristiano Ronaldo and David de Gea, José Mourinho, Diego Costa and James Rodríguez. He began as a DJ and nightclub owner, and got his first deal with a player he met in a bar, which tells you quite a lot about agents. He brought Mourinho to Chelsea, Pini brought Chelsea to Mourinho.

At Wolves he has dominated their transfer dealings, bringing in six of his own players plus the manager in two years. You look at Wolves in 2019 and it's hard to argue with where they are, and it's hard not to see it happening at several other clubs. For an overseas owner, naïve about football and how transfers work, it's far easier to hand all responsibility to one agency. They will tell you they can provide the players you need. You give them the money. Sometimes it works, sometimes it does not. As a player you only understand how great the reach of the big dogs is when the team-mate sitting next to you casually asks how so-and-so is. It's like discovering the existence of some vast secret society. What, you're one of us too?

Quite a few agents know very little about football. It matters less to them than you might think and sometimes less to their players too. You don't want their advice on tactics: you want their ability to convince someone else that their tactics will only work if they sign you and pay you handsomely. I knew one agent who was a season ticket holder at QPR just so he could enjoy the catering facilities of the club's CClub private members' area. He used to arrive two hours before kick-off, have the full dinner, then leave before kick-off. No one batted an eyelid.

Quite a few players don't trust their agents. The real revelation is that this is probably a good thing. It is sensible to realise that they are doing a useful job for you but don't necessarily care about you. You trust an agent when you see that you can trust them. As long as you're careful, an agent is a good thing to have. That doesn't mean that you need three agents when you're seventeen years old and yet to play two games for the first team, as I have seen recently. It doesn't mean you should let your agent talk to the manager if you're not happy about the way you're being used or not being used at all. I saw a couple of lads at Stoke who were fuming about being left on the bench. I asked them when they were seeing the gaffer. They told me their agents were flying in from Spain and Italy to do it for them, which meant you now had an unnecessary game of Chinese whispers rather than a simple direct conversation between two grown adults.

Managers hate players coming to see them. They say that their door is always open, but they seldom mean it. But they hate agents coming to see them even more. They're in all the time at training grounds now, easy to spot as the only ones in full suits, the only ones who drive both expensive cars and step out of them with leather briefcases. They will be looking out for their clients but looking out for others too. Agents like to fish and they like to cast some bait. One of the lads will sidle over and say, my agent wants to speak to you, do you mind if I pass on your number? And the next day the call will come, always beginning the same way: 'I don't want to step on anyone's toes ...' they'll say, before proceeding to step all over them.

It used to be like warfare: agents going after other agents' players, slipping little sleeper deals in, driving in a wedge, offering what the other agent never could, knowing they couldn't either but by the time the player realised that, the goalposts would have moved again. And then, like the cartels of Colombia, it was as if a truce had been called, as if they realised enough blood had been shed, or more likely that there was even more money to be made.

I don't know whether Pini or Jorge or Kia Joorabchian summoned the others to a secret meeting in a car wash, safe from prying ears, but a new way of working came into practice. You will still get the call about stepping on toes but it will now be followed by a 'I've already spoken to your man, and he's fine with it.' It's just business. Two will go halves on a deal that otherwise wouldn't have happened. The player may not be privy to it. They're the pawn being bought and sold, the commodity to be traded. Their life is a good one so they don't complain.

And they don't complain because the money has never been so big. More players getting paid more by more clubs. You know it's too much, but you know the clubs are getting more, and you know the clubs are getting more because the media companies paying for television rights are making more money out of it too. Unless they're Setanta or ITV Digital, but that's another story.

THE BENCH

They say that if you want to know how something works, ask an expert. In which case, as the man who has made more appearances off the bench than any other player in Premier League history, I feel much of my career has been waiting for this chapter to arrive.

There's a strange synchronicity to many careers. You begin as an unproven young player being given the occasional chance to impress off the bench. You end it as an overly proven old player given the occasional chance to remind people that you're still actually alive.

In between, even when the bench has become a place to walk slowly to having been taken off five minutes from the end to save your precious legs for the next match, soaking up the adoration of the grateful supporters as you do so, you still reset to the beginning every time you move up a level. You start games in the Championship, you score goals. You get a move to the Premier League and you're on the bench again. You score goals, you get called up to England. Back on the bench, at least until you've proved yourself again.

It's an odd thing, being a sub. You train all week with the team, prepare with total attention to detail. You work on the team's set pieces, you study the planned tactics. And then someone tells you

you're not playing, and it all goes to waste. It's like a musician rehearsing all week, travelling to the venue, doing the soundcheck and then the gig being cancelled. Except the musician probably hasn't eaten a massive and unattractive breakfast of plain pasta and chicken that he now has no way of burning off except by jogging along a thin strip of grass near the touchline every twenty minutes or so.

It makes you angry. As one of football's older gentlemen I could understand that I didn't start every week any more. I had opposition fans shouting, 'OI CROUCH – YOU NOT RETIRED YET?' at me as I sat there, just in case the manager needed something to back up his decision. I knew I could still do a job if given the chance, and even at thirty-eight I felt as capable of moving slowly around a restricted area of the pitch as I did at twenty-three. But as a younger man, full of self-righteousness and raw passion, I was furious every time I wasn't picked to start.

You question the manager. You question yourself. It's like being dumped by a girl you secretly really fancy, or at least ignored on a big night out by a girl you thought you were already dating. You're in your best shirt. You've remembered to wear smart shoes. You've had a proper wash, and you're wearing an inappropriate amount of cologne – and yet the only time she speaks to you is to tell you she's going to dance with a bloke who you'd always worried was a slightly better-looking, more charismatic and successful version of you anyway. And there's very little you can do about it. She might shun you every week. And you have to sit there on the edge of the dancefloor, watching your rival busting his moves and everyone loving it and no one even remembering those amazing shapes you were making yourself just a few short weeks ago.

Being on the bench takes a certain mentality. There are players who are so furious with the manager that they don't want to go on.

If the team are losing, they consider it unarguable proof that they should have started in the first place. If they do get on they'll jog around rather than run, just to make sure the manager knows quite how unhappy they are. 'How dare he? Doesn't he know who I am?'

That makes no sense to me. It's you that looks like the idiot. Imagine if I'd sulked my way through the Champions League final of 2007. What would have been the precious memories to pass on to the grandkids? 'Yeah, I came on in the greatest club game there is, playing for a side that's won it six times against one of the two clubs that's won it more, but I couldn't believe that a Dutch bloke with strange wet-look blond hair started instead of me, so I moped in the centre circle until it was over.'

I've always wanted to win the doubters over. Dump me and I'll change my wardrobe and get a new haircut rather than lie on the sofa all day getting drunk and swearing at daytime TV. Leave me out and I'll want to score a goal or at least create one to show you what you're missing. The trouble with that approach is that you can be too keen to impress. You're so all-action and aggressive when you come on that you end up clattering around like a lunatic. I did it for Stoke, coming on against Southampton: released from the traps with eyes blazing, one yellow card almost before I've touched the ball, another one before I've had the chance to do anything constructive. I wanted to get stuck in. Instead I went slightly mad.

I came on at Stamford Bridge once, the stadium where I used to spend Saturday afternoons as a ball boy, playing the team my dad has loved all his life. Desperate to show everyone that I should have been on from the start, I chose to do so by inflicting on Cesc Fàbregas the worst tackle I've ever made. It was horrific. I had to text him afterwards to apologise. The Stoke lads were all looking at me in the dressing-room afterwards as if they no longer knew who I was. 'What the hell was that about?' I couldn't explain. I hadn't wanted to do it. I liked Cesc. We'd appeared together in a critically acclaimed World Cup commercial for popular tube-packed potato snacks Pringles. Experiences like the summer 2010 Pringoals campaign bond you, yet the anger and desire had grabbed hold of me and taken me to a place I never wanted to go. Frightening.

It could be confusing on the bench. I always wanted the team to do well even when I wasn't playing, but deep down, I didn't really want the strikers to score. Why would I? They were doing my job. They were on the end of crosses that were meant for me. If they kept scoring I'd be finished. I'd never get off that bench.

I've experienced it both ways. Sometimes the manager is keeping faith in you and naming you in his starting eleven and you're not scoring, and you know that certain players will be going to him behind your back to tell him he's got it wrong and he needs to select them instead. I've had it at club level. I've seen it with England. You try not to take it personally. Professional football is a horribly cut-throat profession. You're either on the way up or you're on the way down. All those players you've leapfrogged over the years? You've taken their livelihood for your own gain. You have been ruthless and so will they, because it has happened at every level you have played at. You go to district trials as a kid: they take one striker. From the entire youth squad of a Premier League team, only one kid gets a pro contract. You've got to be that guy, and then you have to be the kid who gets in the reserve team, and you have to win that battle, and you have to be the one who gets a chance with the first team.

The higher you go, the more selfish you have to become. Rio Ferdinand once told me that Ruud van Nistelrooy would be fuming if Manchester United won 3–0 and he hadn't scored, but had he scored a hat-trick in a 4–3 defeat, he would be absolutely buzzing. I've played with strikers who would shoot from anywhere rather than pass to you and risk being benched in your favour. When Jermain Defoe scored five in one match for Spurs against Wigan in 2009, he could have slipped me in with four of them. I don't begrudge it. It's a selfish business. Anything to get picked. Anything to avoid the bench.

There are players who don't want to perform when they come off the bench, not to punish the manager but so as not to make him think it was the right decision. If you play well as a sub, you might be thinking it's a solid case for you to start the following game. But the manager may be thinking it's proof that you're the best game-changing sub he has, and decide instead to make it a permanent role. I've often been seen as that last resort, a sort of desperate Plan B. Even when I was scoring in every match for England I was still thought of as the back-up, something that was ticking things over while they worked out a better idea. I scored eleven goals in one calendar year for England. It hadn't been done since 1929 and it hasn't been done since. Despite that I was never really Plan A.

On the upside it helped prolong my career. I was a decent Plan B. My appearances as a substitute in the Premier League constituted about 9 per cent of my total playing time but almost 15 per cent of my goals. Defoe has scored more Premier League goals as a sub than anyone else, and he was still playing into his late thirties too. But there is a stigma that comes with it. Apart from Jermain and me, two other players high on the list of most sub appearances are Shola Ameobi and Carlton Cole. Both big lads, both target men. Because when you do get sent on as a striker, you're usually losing.

You're chasing the game. You're there to make things happen, and so the team panics and resorts to lumping it long.

Maybe I shouldn't complain. No one throws on a centre-back when they're losing. You're the cavalry. You're a superhero. It would just be nice if they could keep the panic in check. Keep playing good football. Get the ball forward in wide areas and fling some decent crosses in. Play it in to feet. I'm a substitute, not an incompetent.

It's the first training session on a Monday when a lot of that anger can come out. The players who actually contributed on the Saturday will do a light session to ease out their legs. Everyone else has to do a proper full run-out, a run-out dominated by furious rebuffed man-boys. The slightest thing can set it off: a late tackle, a poor pass. Suddenly you have men slapping each other when they really want to be slapping the manager. The manager understands this and often chooses to stay in his office, pretending to work on his post-game analysis. Everyone knows the real reason: he wants no part of the fall out from ten angry men, and everyone takes it out on the unfortunate coaches instead. Football being football, it's all out of everyone's system by Tuesday, and by Wednesday all the players are best mates again and looking forward to the weekend.

Competition not to be on the bench, competition when you're on it. Only three of the seven substitutes can come on. There are often two strikers. So you're warming up in the corner, next to the other sub forward, and the assistant manager points in your direction. Suddenly you're panicking: does he mean me, or him?

The charades begin. Thirty thousand people in the stands all around you are singing and shouting. No one is able to hear a thing, so you start mouthing silently from corner flag to bench.

'Do you mean me?'

'Yeah you.' (Points again.)

'Sorry gaffer, you're pointing at both of us.'

Coach going red in face: 'No! You!'

Still mouthing silently. 'Dave, your pointing over distance is impossibly imprecise. Could you clarify?'

The coach kicks a water bottle in frustration, then points to the sky. Right, that's me. He points to my waist level. Right. That'll be the other one.

If it's you – great, but not that great, because you're still only a sub. If it's not you, the anger explodes again. 'What? Why the hell not me?' It's like the girl you thought you were dating but who had blanked you comes over with a smile on her face and a pint and then gives the pint plus a peck on the cheek to the bloke standing next to you. It's double humiliation. You're not just Plan B. You're the Plan B to the Plan B.

Your rival knows. The crowd knows. You have to make the sort of face seen at awards ceremonies when the cameras are on you and your rival gets the big gong instead – a fixed smile that says I'm so happy for them even when inside you're somewhere between punching them and crying. And so begins football's own Walk of Shame: back to the dug-out, keeping your big coat on, the man next to you unzipping his for action. Your head down, everyone laughing at you, and even you don't know what you are, because you're not the forward on the pitch, and you're not the one coming off the bench, so really what is the point to you at all?

There are times when you hope it isn't you. Finding your team 4–0 down against Manchester City with half an hour left and them playing keep-ball, or Liverpool cutting loose. A thankless task, knowing there is no chance at all of you scoring four goals to bring it back, their centre-backs showboating, even their goalkeeper's flicking it over your head and making you look a fool. Worse still is when you get two minutes at the very end, with the team already nailed on for defeat. You find yourself muttering under your breath as you pull off your tracksuit bottoms. 'Don't even flipping bother. This is degrading ...'

Referees are supposed to add thirty seconds to the match for every substitution, as well as the same for every goal and each card handed out. As a player coming off or coming on for a team that's in front, you drag the whole thing out for slightly longer and you feel like you've won a small victory. If you're still on the pitch you completely fail to take any of the above in when complaining to the referee about the amount of added time at the end of the ninety minutes. You just tell him it's too much if you're winning and too little if you're behind. Most of the time it just appears to be random. It may well be an in-joke among the officials, something to give them a little tickle in a job that sees you relentlessly slagged off by everyone else in the stadium.

The fourth official prepare to holds up the board. It's 0–0 and there have been two subs. Six minutes flashes up. The referee tries not to laugh too openly. The linesman is having to pinch his own thigh to stop himself cracking up. A word into his mic. 'Kevin, you wind-up merchant. Classic ...'

Not all benches are equal. What used to literally be a bench is now like the sort of set-up you get in executive cars: heated seats, deep padding, a recliner, adjustable headrest. The old White Hart Lane had everything but a massage function. At Stoke it's possibly the best furniture in the city. If you've been to the bet365 Stadium for a winter midweek game you'll understand that the heated elements are also close to a medical necessity. At Elland Road the bench is really low: you can barely see across the pitch. At Old

Trafford you're so far back you're in with the fans. The poshest now are at the Emirates or the Etihad. The worst I've experienced recently were at Ashton Gate. It lashed it down with rain all afternoon, and the bench was directly in the deluge. It brought on a personal crisis. I'm approaching forty years old and I'm sitting on the bench against Bristol City in the pouring rain. What am I doing with my life?

For all the money in football, no one has yet developed clothing for substitutes that is appropriate to all the conditions one experiences. You have a choice between a wet top – what in civilian life is known as an anorak – and a big padded jacket. One keeps you dry but makes you cold. The other keeps you warm but gets you wet. Why not provide a jacket that does the best of both? The club-issue wet top is rarely efficient even at its basic task. The Galvin Green stuff I wear on the golf course is far superior. So much money being spent in football but none of it on beading fabrics. The shame of it. 'FOR THE LOVE OF GOD, WILL NO ONE BRING ME GORE-TEX?'

You get cold on the bench, so you stick on bobble hat and gloves. You do your warm up and you're baking hot, so you take them off as you sit down and instantly get cold again. You put the luminous subs' bib over your choice of wet-top or big coat. It gets stuck on the hood or caught up at the back, and you look like a hunchback or a tortoise, and now the fans are not only thinking you're past it because you're on the bench but that you can no longer dress yourself.

You don't expect to come on in the first half so you don't bother putting your shinpads in. Then a player on the pitch gets injured after half an hour and suddenly you can't find your shinpads. You don't want to be warming up in your shirt so initially you don't put it on, and then the call comes and you realise with a lurch that you've left it in the dressing-room, and you have to send the kit-man running in to get it.

When the panic sets in and the manager is raging, you will see substitutes lose the ability to perform basic motor skills like taking off a coat or tying a lace. At Portsmouth the signal would come back from Harry Redknapp to some of our overseas players, and they would quite casually stand up, stretch, sit down again and start pulling their tracksuit bottoms off. Pads in, taping ankles, tie-ups for socks. Harry would be turning round again, going purple with rage – 'FUCKING GET READY!' – and the subs would be unzipping their two layers of big coats to find they've forgotten their shirts. The kitman would be shrugging his shoulders, and now they're on their hands and knees looking under the seats. The referee sees the signal from the touchline that a sub is coming on for an injured player and blows his whistle, except the sub has now disappeared from view, so the game goes on with you down to ten, and Harry is now ready to explode. You're watching through your fingers thinking, he might actually kill someone here. There was always a meeting called by the assistant coach the following Monday: 'Lads, if you're a sub, you have to be ready to come on at ALL times ...'

You hydrate as a sub as if you're playing, because you might be. But because you're not, you don't sweat any of it out, which means that as soon as the half-time whistle goes, you'll see all the subs go sprinting down the tunnel for the changing-room toilets. You'll have another pee before the end of half-time and then be desperate again around the eighty-minute mark, which is exactly when you're meant to be coming on.

So many negatives, and yet coming off the bench can be the most wonderful feeling. Some of my best times in football have come when I've begun a day devastated not to be picked and ended it as the man who's scored the dramatic late winner. That ten-minute cameo when you arrive in a flurry of limbs and change a game that was going the other way. You're the one everyone is talking about, you're the one in all the headlines. It lets you point out to all your team-mates that they were a heinous collective failure until you arrived to save their backsides.

There was a period under Mark Hughes at Stoke when I kept doing it, and the amount of love I got in the dressing-room afterwards was an absolute delight. I felt like Superman. At the very start of my career, as a stringy nineteen-year-old at QPR, I came on with us 2–0 down at Gillingham, smacked in a volley for 2–1 and then set up the equaliser for Chris Kiwomya. My first Robot for England was as a sub against Hungary. Even at Aston Villa, where I didn't really do myself justice, I came on late to score the winner against Middlesbrough that got us into the UEFA Cup.

There is an accepted protocol to being a substitute. You can't sit there slagging off the player in your position, no matter how much you might like to. You can't pretend to have all the answers and you can't forget that you're not a supporter in the stands. It's not acceptable to shout, 'What the hell is he doing?' or 'Easy ball, you idiot!'

You can choose who you sit next to, which is nice. No need to sit in formation or ascending squad number. If a player alongside you says something funny, remember that someone somewhere will be filming you, and soiling yourself with laughter when your side is getting thumped is not a good look.

Do not look too desperate in front of the manager. I've seen players deliberately do their warm up in his direct eye-line – sprinting flat out, stopping in front of the bench, sticking in ostentatious tuck-jumps. Have some self-respect. You're still a sub. When you do warm up, do so towards the corner flag at the end where your supporters are. The middle of the pitch is the posh seats. The ends behind the goals are the noisy sweary ones. Go too far and you'll be abused. Don't go far enough and you'll annoy the chairman.

You'll have seen subs loosen up thousands of times. What you might not realise is quite what each stretch means.

One knee on turf, other knee up. Usually seen early on in a game. An entirely token effort. You're only out there because the coach has told you. Purpose: to look like you're warming up when you're actually watching the game. Pro tip: every now and then throw an arm in the air so it looks like you're doing something.

Standing with legs wide apart, looking forward. You're looking forward because you want to watch the match. You're not running because you know there's no chance of you coming on for ages.

Standing with feet shoulder-width apart, rotating torso round to either side. You're bored of the match and want to see what's happening in the crowd.

We're footballers, yet we will not touch a ball with our feet as we prepare to come on. No professional golfer would ever walk to the first tee without having hit a bucket of balls on the range first, but subs don't have the space or opportunity. Multiple stray balls would end up on the pitch, and suddenly you'd be trying to sneak on in your big coat and subs' bib hunchback like an overgrown kid climbing over the neighbours' fence. Excuse me, could I have my ball back?

We now see some clubs wheeling out exercise bikes onto the touchline for players to warm up on. It makes no sense to me, unless they want me to do a bike race first. You use your body in a totally different way on a bike, or in my case, not at all. I've done pre-season training with Tony Pulis when he made us ride up near-vertical mountains. I would have been quicker putting the bike on my back and running as fast as I could. I climb off a bike like a man getting out of a car after a four-hour journey. My backside hurts, my hamstrings are tight and my quads are on fire. If you want to bring out random pieces of gym equipment, an elliptical trainer would be an improvement. A treadmill would be better. At least then you're running. Does Geraint Thomas prepare for a mountain stage of the Tour de France by kicking a football around? Quite.

It is an art, watching a game as a substitute. You have to analyse what is going on, but specifically to your position. I might have had no idea at all whether we were playing three in defence or a back four, but I'd have worked out which of the opposition centre-backs I was going to pull on to, who was crossing it where, what corners we were using, where the little pockets of space in the box might be. When the time comes to go on, you hope your manager understands that your brain is fried with adrenaline and keeps his instructions simple. But he's also caught up in the game, and he can't both watch it and talk to you. You try to get little dregs of information out of him, but then something dramatic happens on the pitch and he's on his feet – 'FUCKING HELL SMUDGE!' – and you have to apologetically ask him to repeat the critical tactical re-jig bit he's now forgotten.

Only when the whistle goes for the change do you actually have his full attention. Then his arm is around you and you're all his. 'Right son, what I want from you is . . .' You hope it's one thought, maybe two max, rather than the approach taken by the lovely Graham Taylor with Nigel Clough in the aforementioned England documentary *An Impossible Job*: a complicated, contradictory briefing which leaves you pretending to know your role when in actual fact you are utterly clueless. Personally I'm always fine with my own bit but I'm so wrapped up in the excitement of it all that I forget what I'm meant to be telling the rest of the team. I'll run on thinking, oh God, what was it, and then the winger will look at me and the sight of his face will trigger it – oh yeah, it was you! You're going wide!

Over twenty years as a professional player, I've experienced both sides of what we might call The Hook. There is the coming on, and then there is the coming off. For every man that leaves the bench, one must take his place, and you can almost always feel it coming.

Seventy-ish minutes have gone. You give the ball away. The crowd groans. You glance over at the touchline and see the manager sending his two sub strikers out to loosen up. You're pretty much done for at this point. It's just a matter of when. You run around frantically, trying to make something happen, but your desperation only makes it worse. You see one of the subs taking his tracksuit top off. Right. You've got a minute absolute max to do something amazing. You start shooting from everywhere, praying for a juicy back-post cross to come in, all the time thinking, I just want to sit that sub back down on the bench. Stick your jacket back on, son, I'm not done yet.

Occasionally, very occasionally, it will happen. You smash one in. The cross you've been waiting for all game finally arrives all perfect and wrapped in a bow. Now you've ripped up all those plans. You're not coming off now. You've stuck two fingers up at the manager and his flawed ideas. What, you were going to take this bloke off, the one who's just won us the game? More often you're trudging off, trying to remember to high-five the man replacing you rather than dig him in the ribs. Strikers might be the most likely to come on but we're also the ones most often taken off. Goalkeepers: never. If a centre-back is subbed off when he's not injured, it's a story.

Taking any player off in the first half is both ruthless of the manager and a bit of a show. If you're subbing a player at forty minutes, why not wait until half-time and spare him the humiliation? You pray that you'll never suffer the ultimate ignominy: being subbed on and then performing so abjectly that you get subbed off again. José Mourinho did it to Nemanja Matić at Chelsea and then again to Juan Mata at Manchester United. Pure degradation.

If your goalkeeper has been sent off, an outfield player has to make way for the reserve keeper. The fall guy is usually a striker or winger. The indignation is intense. Hang on, why me? I'm not the one who messed up! Through his decision the manager is basically spelling out that you are a luxury player, the most dispensable he has, the one man he's not going to miss. In your head you tell yourself instead that it's because you're the most creative. You're actually too good for the slog to come. 'This is backs to the wall now, they only need cannon-fodder.'

Being taken off can be a great reward. If you've played well, the manager will be standing on the touchline to greet you with an affectionate cuff round the back of the head and a light slap on the arse. 'Well done, son, you have a rest, we need you for next week.' You can milk it from the crowd as you leave the pitch – a slow walk, an obvious reluctance to leave the arena that you had graced so beautifully. Raising your hands above your head to clap the fans who are singing your name. A rueful smile. 'Ah, I was only getting started ...'

When the final whistle goes you return to the pitch, ostensibly to congratulate your team-mates, in reality to milk it a bit more. Big coat on but unzipped, so they can see the sweat on your shirt, no tracksuit bottoms to they can see the mud and toil on your legs, socks rolled down to emphasise how relentlessly you worked. A grand show, a masterful humblebrag, all disguised as a simple desire to shake Pascal Chimbonda's hand.

That's if you've done well. If you've had a shocker you're off that pitch like a rabbit chased by a dog. No one there to meet you on the touchline, the manager pointedly looking elsewhere. Fellow players on the bench are only giving you a high-five out of sympathy, and everyone knows it. It's patronising but no one else has even acknowledged you, so you take it gratefully and pull the hood up on your big coat and try to take solace in the protein shake the fitness coach has handed you – even if you know that one of the reasons he's given it to you is that the club gets £1,000 from the drink manufacturer every time it gets shown on television, and the fitness man is probably on his own commission too.

Substitutions are tough for us, but they can also be brutal on the manager. Coaches can live and die by their decisions. Get it right and you change a game and a career. Look at Sir Alex Ferguson bringing on Ole Gunnar Solskjær and Teddy Sheringham for Andy Cole and Jesper Blomqvist in the 1999 Champions League final. United were 1–0 down to Bayern Munich and lucky it wasn't more: then a stolen goal from each and United have made history. Graham Taylor, by contrast, took off Gary Lineker in his last game for England, brought on Alan Smith rather than Alan Shearer and the team crashed out of the 1992 European Championship.

Too often the timing appears to be based on habit rather than logic. Managers make a change at seventy minutes but rarely at fifty-five. If it's not working, why not crack on? At least Mourinho was ballsy, subbing off his subs. It's an admission that you got it wrong, but it's better to accept that rather than let it cause more damage.

Don't make pointless substitutions. What is the use in bringing someone on at eighty-nine minutes when you're 2–0 up? What was the point of those international friendly matches when each side would make eight changes, and the bench would be littered with one-cap wonders? Jon Flanagan. Michael Ricketts. Francis Jeffers. These were games ruined by substitutions, careers mockingly defined by what should have been crowning glories.

Look, it's not easy. You get your sub ready, give him his tactics, and then the other team make a change that renders yours outmoded. You're winning, so you take off a striker and stick on a defensive midfielder, and they equalise. Now you need to score a goal with insufficient strikers and too many crabs going sideways in midfield. Do you put your striker back on?

It's 0–0 so you lob on a third striker. He scores. Now you want to defend that lead, except you're all forwards. You're wide open through the middle. You've done exactly what you wanted to do and it's only made it worse. Sometimes you throw on an extra man up front and it perversely makes it harder to score, since the opposition will now drop deeper or the new striker will make the same runs as you and mess yours up. Often the best form of attack is to keep the same shape and balance but to move the ball more quickly.

I seemed to be about panic. When I came off the bench the other team would often make a reactive change too – stick a big defender on, go to three at the back, send their tall striker back at set pieces to mark up. Panic and confusion are good things to see in your opponents' eyes. I was an agent of destruction bringing terror and fear in his wake, even when in my head I was a dashing combination of Paul Gascoigne and Gianluca Vialli.

The greatest subs make you proud to be one of them. Solskjær: seventeen Premier League goals off the bench, including four in one insane sub appearance against Nottingham Forest in February 1999, as well as the Champions League final one a few months later and another famous peach against Liverpool in the FA Cup. Defoe: twenty-four Premier League goals as a sub; Olivier Giroud twenty goals by summer 2019.

These men understood the tiny nuances, the little gaps left open to you. They know that even when you have so little time you can't go too hard too early. There are times when you're so keen to make an impact that you make five flat-out sprints in the first six minutes and spend the next ten breathing out of your arse. The half-chance comes and you're not there to pop it home because you're in the centre-circle feeling sick.

Not for the super-subs. Geoff Hurst, England's great hero at the 1966 World Cup, was only in the side as a replacement late in that tournament because first-choice Jimmy Greaves cut open his leg. Mario Götze played seven minutes of Germany's World Cup quarter-final in 2014 and then didn't feature at all as they walloped Brazil 7–1 in the semis. For eighty-eight minutes of the final against Argentina he sat on the bench. Then Joachim Löw pulled off Miroslav Klose, record goal-scorer at World Cups, and gave Götze his chance. 'Show the world you are better than Messi and can decide the World Cup,' he's supposed to have told him. Seven minutes from the end of extra time, Götze volleyed André Schürrle's cross home to steal away the biggest prize in football. All of it as a substitute. Beautiful. If perhaps still not quite as good as Messi.

CHAIRMEN

There may well be football club chairmen in this world who are quiet men or women with very little backstory of note. Characters with no obvious eccentricities, shy individuals as happy pottering around in their garden or curled up on the sofa with a good book as sitting in the single best seat in a football ground. They could conceivably exist. It's just that in twenty-five years in football I've never met one. Every single chairman of every single club has been different to the average human being in some way. There is always an edge, always an angle. There is always a story.

And there is always an ego. I was a youngster at Spurs when the memo came round to everyone at the club: if you see Alan Sugar and his wife at any point in any part of the stadium or training ground, you are to address them as Sir Alan and Lady Sugar. It conjured up in my mind the image of the combative star of *The Apprentice* cantering around the White Hart Lane pitch on a grey charger, armour gleaming in the sun, helmet visor pushed up, jabbing a lance at groundsmen and ball-boys and shouting, 'You're fired!' while Lady Sugar trotted after him on a palomino mare. No matter that he had received his knighthood for services to the home computer and electronics industry. Like Ben Kingsley and Nick

Faldo he took his honour both with great pride and as a permanent prefix.

Other people might think of chairmen and picture would-be Manchester United owner Michael Knighton juggling the ball in front of the Stretford End, or Ken Bates buying Chelsea for £1 and selling his shareholding to Roman Abramovich for £17 million, or Peter Ridsdale leaving Leeds United £103 million in debt, Cardiff £66 million in debt and being acting chairman when Plymouth fell into administration.

I also think of Simon Jordan, Crystal Palace chairman during the 2000s. Simon always had a lot to say. I was still a young player at Portsmouth when he was in his pomp, a time too where there was a decent rivalry between his club and mine. I had never met him personally before a curious incident took place while I was on holiday in Marbella. I was with two friends, strolling down a hill towards the beach. A Mercedes convertible roared past us with the roof down and slammed on the brakes. Then it reversed at pace, to reveal an even more tanned than usual Jordan behind the wheel, sunglasses up on his head.

'CROUCHIE!'

Straight in, no hellos, no introduction.

'Crouchie! Who's your agent?'

I told him. He nodded.

'Tell him I'll be in touch, yeah?'

No goodbye, sunglasses down, accelerating off down the road.

My agent never did hear from him. I'm not sure Simon left the game really liking footballers. As someone who had made his money with the Pocket Phone Shop, he may have resented the amount they expected to be paid. As things spiralled out of control at Selhurst Park his players got the blame. Perhaps he was not particularly fond of managers either: he got through five in his first three years at the club. When you call your autobiography *Be Careful What You Wish For*, you perhaps move on with a few regrets.

I moved from Sir Alan at Spurs to Mr Wright at QPR. Circumstances weren't great. Chris Wright had been successful in the music industry, signing Blondie, Spandau Ballet and the Specials' 2 Tone label. At QPR he had been less successful, signing Paul Furlong and Steve Morrow. The only special thing was the debt: £570,000 being lost a month.

Administration was the inevitable result. There were supporter demonstrations and attempts to claw back some of those enormous losses in hopelessly petty ways like making everyone at the club pay for their food at the staff canteen. It wasn't too bad for the players, but for the staff, a proportion of whom wanted to bring sandwiches from home, it was too much. With the club sinking towards the third tier, new chairman Nick Blackburn came to see me. 'You've done well,' he told me. 'We've got to sell you to keep the club from going under.' And so a skinny kid from Ealing who had arrived at the start of the season for £60,000 was offered at the end of it to Preston, Burnley and Portsmouth for £1.2 million. Portsmouth won the auction; Nick got my affection for telling me I was welcome back any time for inadvertently helping a club we both loved.

What QPR didn't realise was that, with the subsequent arrivals of Bernie Ecclestone, Flavio Briatore and Tony Fernandes, life was only going to get messier. What I was about to discover was that the chairmen in my life were about to get louder.

Milan Mandarić knew a little about misbehaving footballers. While in charge of the San Jose Earthquakes in the late 1970s he had become good friends with George Best, which made the carpeting I received from him just after I had signed all the more galling. Due to an unfortunate angle on the security camera in a marina bar and a beer-based prank from Shaun Derry, it appeared that I was hammered midway through an otherwise quiet Sunday afternoon. I wasn't, but I was able to take a little revenge over the next few months as I sat on the balcony of my flat.

I had bought a place down on the marina. I was on the third floor. Milan had the penthouse on the top floor of the development across the way. I had a pair of binoculars out on the balcony, ostensibly to look at the yachts coming and going, but in reality to watch their owners messing about. Occasionally I'd lift the bins a few degrees and check out what our chairman was up to. I could see right into his flat and precisely what was going on. It was probably for the best that he never worked this out.

Mandarić was the sort of chairman who desperately wants to be involved with every aspect of the club. He had massive plans for Portsmouth, and he would eventually see many of them come to fruition under Harry Redknapp, but in these early days all of us were struggling. We were training at HMS *Collingwood*, a windswept naval base where the sailors clearly despised us. We had to wash our own training kit. When we failed to win a single match in a month, Mandarić came down to the dressing-room and told us he was therefore not going to pay us. Except because he was a naturalised American who had lived in the States for thirty years, he didn't quite put it that way. 'I hate coming down to the locker-room, but you guys aren't performing, and I'm not happy,' he said. 'You've not done your job, so I'm not paying you for it.'

I was twenty-one and juvenile. After the locker-room reference I was in my own world of childish mirth. The older players, though, were incandescent. We had contracts. They had families to support.

When I left QPR I had been on £800 a week. My new flat had cost me £217,000 and I thought I had made it. While everyone else was shouting about what a disgrace Mandarić was, I was thinking, I've still got loads left from last month. And also thought he had a valid point.

Milan was aiming higher. Despite the fact that Portsmouth were on a run of thirteen consecutive seasons in the second tier, that they had only been higher for a solitary season in the previous forty years, that the average attendance at Fratton Park was around 11,000, Milan managed to sign Robert Prosinečki, recently of Real Madrid and Barcelona, a man who at the previous World Cup had scored the goal that won Croatia the third-place play-off. Prosinečki had genius in his boots and a red Marlboro hanging off his lip as soon as those boots were unlaced. He had no interest in running but wasn't asked to. He had no interest in speaking English so Mandarić signed a nice lad from Slovenia called Mladen Rudonja (nickname: Turbo Rudi) to act as his unofficial interpreter.

Prosinečki probably shouldn't have played at times. Marlboro Reds are not famed for their cardiovascular benefits. But manager Graham Rix had clearly been told by the chairman, and had to swallow that one, just as he had had to swallow the locker-room invasion that undermined him even more. And so the fading maverick was allowed to both cut teams apart and do nothing defensively for his own. In a game against Barnsley he scored a hat-trick of sublime quality to put us 4–2 ahead with time running out. We drew 4–4. Mandarić watched on from the stands and began to plot Rix's demise.

When I returned to Portsmouth six years later, by then an established England international, the club had changed just as much. Mandarić had sold up to Sacha Gaydamak, a man who appeared star-struck by big-name players, whose father Arcadi had at the time been convicted by a French court of illegal arms trading to Angola, and who was later charged with money laundering.

As a player you assume an owner will not spend money he does not have. And so you looked at the crowds of 15,000 and a team that included Lassana Diarra, Sulley Muntari, Nico Kranjčar, Jermain Defoe, Sylvain Distin and Sol Campbell and thought, you really are very successful at quite a young age, aren't you?

You never got to meet him. Gaydamak was quite distant, unintentionally aloof, much like a budget Abramovich. You'd glimpse him occasionally through the open dressing-room door, gliding past with two huge bodyguards, never looking in, never speaking to any of his expensively assembled team.

We genuinely thought he was building something special. The club finished eighth in the Premier League. We got into Europe and were beating Milan at Fratton Park until a Ronaldinho free-kick and Pippo Inzaghi goal in the ninety-third minute nicked them a draw. We were walking over teams. Talking among ourselves, we reckoned we were a couple of signings away from getting into the Champions League.

Harry spotted the cracks first. When he departed I was initially puzzled. 'Why is he leaving? We're flying!' He'd worked out what others would soon realise: Gaydamak's funds had dried up, been frozen or just disappeared.

It got no better for Portsmouth. A Dubai-based businessman named Sulaiman Al Fahim bought the club off Gaydamak for a quid, and things were so grim no one even thought this cheap. It wasn't even the low point for Fahim, who nine years on would be sentenced to five years in a United Arab Emirates jail for stealing £5 million from his wife. Forty-three days into his regime, and with none of the players paid, the club was sold again, this time to a Saudi Arabian called Ali al-Faraj, who had never been to Fratton Park. The unconventional chairmen kept coming – Balram Chainrai; a Russian named Vladimir Antonov who was then arrested for asset-stripping. Only when the supporters bought the club, with relegation from the entire football league a real possibility, did the recovery finally begin. Maybe Mandarić had been a delight after all. A great institution in turmoil. It shouldn't have happened to a club like that.

No matter where they come from, no matter how long they last, there is a universal look for chairmen. A wool overcoat in the English winter, in dark grey or black, never a puffa jacket or anything from the club shop. A sober scarf, a self-conscious and badly muted celebration when their team score, like someone who has never truly celebrated a goal as a child; someone next to them who looks massively bored, who when the camera cuts to them mid-match is messing about on their smartphone.

The seat they sit on will literally be the most comfortable one in the entire ground. That's the sort of privilege your investment secures you. The area around Abramovich's box at Stamford Bridge has overhead heaters, because south-west London is obviously parky when you've spent much of your childhood in the far north of Russia. Having seen his yacht docking when I was on holiday in Sardinia, such designs almost seem spartan: the boat had two swimming pools, two helicopter pads and a submarine on the back. I assumed it was reversing into port because the front of it was sticking out so much in front of the super-yachts either side. It wasn't. It had been moored for hours. It was just three times longer than all the others. It was almost twice as long at the Stamford Bridge pitch. Maybe the submarine was to get from the stern to the bow without tiring your legs out from the walk.

It was the frogmen swimming around the hull, keeping it safe from nosey Sardinian fish, that made me realise that Roman must have viewed the purchase of Oliver Giroud like I would a pint of lager – a momentary decision with minimal financial impact to bring a couple of minutes of brief pleasure. When John Terry and Frank Lampard were at Chelsea he let them use one of his other five yachts for a free holiday. The staffing was apparently nuts – forty of them looking after four guests. If you dropped a drink on the floor a crack team of cleaners swept in like pinafored SAS and instantly made the incident invisible for you.

A chairman will generally have a personal suite at the ground. They will usually have a boardroom, and they will always have their own reserved parking space. It was when Erik Pieters stuck his car in Peter Coates's designated spot at the bet365 Stadium that I realised a certain malaise had set in at Stoke. Had it happened at Spurs, Sir Alan Sugar would have ripped the players head off. Coates is a very nice man, and instead sent the security guard up to ask Erik to move it. But you could tell he wasn't happy, and you could sense that the attitude which said it was better to sling your car in the owner's space rather than in the players' area thirty metres away was not going to translate well on the pitch. It wasn't the only reason we got relegated from the Premier League in 2018 but it told its own small tale.

Peter Coates was the last chairman it should have happened to. He was Stoke City through and through – one of fourteen kids in his family, his old man a miner, a regular at the old Victoria Ground from an early age, an amateur player with the club sixty years ago. He used to come into the training ground on a Friday, say a quick and pleasant hello to his players and then have lunch with the manager. He never came down to the dressing-room and never tried to throw his weight around. When I left Stoke for Burnley he sent me a lovely personal letter, thanking me for my eight years, telling me I'd been a great ambassador, inviting me to come back any time I liked. It was a simple but wonderful gesture from a fantastic club.

Coates lived and breathed it. He invested in a new stadium and in an excellent training facility at Clayton Wood. None of that was done with an intention to sell on for profit. Now it's his daughter Denise who runs the ship, who took his original chain of betting shops and turned it into the bet365 online behemoth. She's obviously the most able of businesswomen – in 2018 she paid herself a £220 million salary with another £45 million on top in dividend payments, more than twice as much as the entire first team squad earned. She pretty much owns the town of Sandbach. Ryan Shawcross has seen the grounds of her £90 million house there, and he says that the lake actually is a lake – not a vast ornamental water feature, but something you can happily race sailing boats on.

No matter what their character and personal tastes, the chairman seldom influences you when you're choosing which club to sign for. You never work with them on a day-to-day basis. They're the top of the tree, while you're mere foliage. When I joined Spurs in 2009 I wasn't thinking about Daniel Levy's financial acumen. When I had rejoined Portsmouth I wasn't doing due diligence on Sacha Gaydamak. I looked at the manager, the other players coming into the club and the value of my contract. You are concerned only with the playing side. You're not storming into the chairman's office to ask him about his loan structure. 'Sacha, man, what interest rate are you paying on this? In God's name, why have you leveraged your buyout on the future season-ticket sales of a club with an average attendance of well below 20,000?'

David Moores was the Liverpudlian equivalent of the Coates family. He had been chairman for sixteen years, his family involved in the club for more than half a century. Littlewoods, the Moores family company, employed thousands in the city, its headquarters a local landmark. I always found him a genuinely nice man, someone trying their best for the club. He had turned down offers from Sheik Mohammad and Dubai International Capital before selling out to George Gillett Jr and Tom Hicks.

He had looked into Gillett and taken Hicks on Gillett's word. No one predicted how spectacularly it would go wrong, how the two new owners would fall out, how the club would have its worst start in fifty-seven years and start losing fine managers and appointing questionable ones. There was a banner on the Kop by the end, 'Built by Shanks, broke by Yanks', and you could feel it going wrong even at our level. One of their sons was sent over from the US to keep an eye on things. You'd see him at the training ground in his chinos and deck shoes, talking loudly in an American accent about subjects that seemed outside his comfort zone, and then you'd see him out that night in the Newz Bar in town, trying to persuade female supporters to inspect his personal investment portfolio.

It could never end well. Hicks and Gillett had no affiliation to the club at all. They hadn't come because they loved football, but because they loved money. When it fell apart, they were unable to handle it, which is often the way. Chairmen love the adoration that can come with running a football club. Mandarić used to beam away in the directors' box when the Portsmouth fans were singing his name, getting to his feet to give a patrician wave, with south coast personality and club director Fred Dinenage usually alongside him. Most have been successful in business. They're used to winning. But football is a volatile game, much harder to control than a typical company's fortunes. If they don't get that success straight away, they can struggle to cope. When the fans turn on them, they stop coming. The manager can't escape. He has to go. So he gets the abuse by proxy, the players too. Most chairmen lap up the adoration and run a mile from the blame.

I know a fair few Aston Villa fans who had no great love for Doug Ellis. Some of the criticisms were fair: after he ended his first spell as chairman, Villa won the league title and the European Cup; five years after he returned, they were relegated. You don't end up with the nickname 'Deadly' by being backward in your HR dealings. Thirteen managers were sacked on his watch and he sold the club to American billionaire Randy Lerner, who then burned through managers at an even faster rate, and got the club relegated again. By the end, in his dotage, you feared some others at the club were taking advantage of Ellis. But Ellis wasn't rinsing the club. He put money in, and he only occasionally came into the dressing-room. When he did, he would never publically slaughter the players. He just loved to talk about football.

He was certainly eccentric, not just for his habit of wearing carpet slippers to games, or bowling about in a Rolls-Royce with the personalised plate AV1. I remember being in the boardroom at Villa Park, twenty-one years old, having just signed for my first Premier League club, and standing with manager Graham Taylor, the chief executive and the club secretary. 'Ah,' they said, 'you've got to meet Doug.' They brought him in. He waved dismissively at the rest of them. 'Everyone out.' Just him and me, me wondering what he was going to say – welcome me to the club, tell me about the great Villa strikers I had to live up to, or maybe go old-school and offer me a brandy and cigar?

'You know I invented the overhead kick?' he asked.

It's quite hard to know how to react when a seventy-eight-year-old football chairman who has never played the game professionally makes that his opening conversational gambit.

'Yes,' Doug continued. 'We were playing, the ball bounced up, and I just did this thing. Everyone said to me, what was that you did? And I said to them – that was the overhead kick ...'

It was the only thing we talked about. When he led me back out of the boardroom a few minutes later, the manager, chief executive and secretary all said the same thing to me – 'Did he tell you about the overhead kick?'

Graham Taylor was a very nice man. He had my sympathy with Doug. It is a cross that many managers have to bear: deferring to a boss who knows far less about the game than they do. I found it very hard to imagine Rupert Lowe kicking a football. I'm pretty certain Abramovich could never do a Knighton on the pitch. But in what other industry does the top man have no experience of the company's primary product? Maybe that's like expecting the current boss of John West to know how to handle a fishing trawler. Yet chairmen are the ones who choose the manager. The success or failure of the club begins with them. It's almost impossible for a manager to contradict them without raising their hackles and quite possibly getting the boot. Can even Pep Guardiola go to Khaldoon Al Mubarak in Abu Dhabi and tell him he and Sheikh Mansour have got something wrong?

You can have your run-ins with a chairman and still respect them. Levy has impressed me at Spurs. He does all the deals himself, has signed their brightest talents – Harry Kane, Dele Alli, Harry Winks – on long-term deals. Kane might be on £150,000 a week but Real Madrid have players on £350,000 a week. He buys young because of the resale value. He plucked Pochettino from Southampton when the manager's English was still poor and he had only eighteen months' experience of British football. The club have a world-class training facility and the best new stadium in the game. If I were an owner of a football club I'd have Levy as my chairman every day of week.

Rupert Lowe always seemed more like a rugby club chairman than a football one. When he took over as chairman he had only seen his first game of the association code six months earlier. I personally found it hard to even call him Rupert. I'd literally never called anyone Rupert. I didn't grow up with a Rupert. There wasn't a single Rupert in my school. The difference in cultures between him and Harry Redknapp was amazing to witness. It was like a 1960s sitcom about the owner of the mill and his foreman.

Fortunately I never had to call him by his first name. Just as every manager is always known as 'Gaffer' or 'Boss', every chairman is always addressed by a player as 'Mr Chairman'. If you meet the owner and he's not the chairman you still call him Mr Chairman. You'd never say Mr Owner. It just doesn't work. Also, they'd never stand for it. It's the twenty-first century, but we're still expected to know our place: many, many rungs below them.

FORMATIONS

There is a constant debate within football around formations. Not only which one works best, or which is coming next, but if systems should dictate the players you sign or the players you have dictate the system, and whether the coach in the stands with his playbacks, playbooks and Prozone stats knows better than the lads actually trying to make the theory work in the real world out there on the pitch.

To which we should probably insert the views of Tony Pulis, one of the most astute managers I've worked with and a man whose dream day was three hours of shape drills with the defence and midfield while his strikers were sent to a different pitch to do whatever they wanted. There was a point at Stoke where, having consistently finished in the top half of the league, having made it into Europe and started to attract the sort of players that had not traditionally been interested in spending a portion of their lives in the wider Stoke-on-Trent area, some within the squad felt we were ready to loosen the stylistic straitjacket and play a little more.

A meeting was called with the manager. Reasoned points were made. 'Gaffer, we're ready to go to the next level.' 'Boss, we can be more fluid. We're a proper Premier League football team now.'

Pulis looked back at us, gave his cap a tug and sighed heavily. 'Don't get carried away, lads. You're just average players in a great system. We carry on as we are.'

The subtext was clear. My formation comes first. I've made this team. And while this may be a strange thing to say about a man who habitually wears tracksuits, trainers and a club-branded baseball cap, Pulis understood that formations are like fashion. You find a look that works as well as possible for the lumpy shape nature has given you and you stick with it. A short man with the leg girth of Will Carling should not attempt to wear skinny jeans. A man of six foot seven should not wear a short-cropped swimming short, even if he is a professional footballer. A Stoke team based on set pieces, aggression, long throws and a good defensive shape should not attempt to play out like Barcelona.

But fashions come and go, on the pitch and off it. The trick is to not only realise what suits you but what might be coming from the catwalk into the high street in the weeks to come. For so long, British football was all about the 4–4–2. It made sense to us. It worked. You looked at the number on a player's shirt and you knew where they would be standing on the pitch.

I was aware as a kid that continental football was different. I loved watching *Football Italia*, and I could see *catenaccio* in action most Sunday afternoons. The first World Cup that had me smitten was Italia 90, when England switched to five at the back with Paul Parker and Stuart Pearce as wing-backs and were suddenly turbo-charged where before they had been stuck in second gear. But I hadn't seen anything radical in the flesh until I went to Stamford Bridge with my dad one week and found Glenn Hoddle playing himself as a sweeper.

It blew my mind. At a time where most goal-kicks were routinely booted as far down the pitch as possible, Hoddle was taking them off the keeper. He had a wall of big defenders ahead of him, and with that protection was using the time and space not to push little passes out to his full-backs or deep-lying midfielders, as you might do now, but instead to spray the most glorious passes around the field.

In truth it was a formation entirely based around making Glenn Hoddle look good, but I still loved it. Even as a kid I was so obsessed with football and how it worked that I used to watch it more intensely than anyone around me. My dad would ask me how the formations were changing and who was free where. I was purely about monitoring the flow, the tactics. He would defer to however I called it. For ninety minutes every fortnight, I was the boss.

When Hoddle moved upstairs to manage he brought Ruud Gullit in to play the same role. It seemed the perfect balance between system and personnel. The sweeper-quarterback worked. Gullit could pass like a god. Yet it failed, because Ruud was too instinctively forward-thinking to be a defender. He kept wanting to rampage forward, which you could understand given his rampaging-forward success throughout his career, but was no good when you had Erland Johnsen and Frank Sinclair constantly looking over their shoulders. The formation did not work without the right player.

The innovations keep coming. I had never seen nor understood the box midfield until Joe Allen explained to me how it worked for him and his team-mates with Wales. They had wonderful free spirits in Gareth Bale and Aaron Ramsey who would be wasted in a conventional three or four. They had Allen and Joe Ledley who would run and track for you all day long. Two attacking mavericks, two holding midfielders. The box was the shape that allowed Chris Coleman to maximise the talents at his disposal.

If a formation works, it drips through into other sides. When Terry Venables used the Christmas-tree formation with England before Euro 96 it led to a number of top Premier League clubs using the same shape with some of the same personnel. Three at the back won Chelsea the league title under Antonio Conte in 2017 and was suddenly spotted at Stoke. Spain used a false nine, turned their forward line into a series of constantly shifting small wingers/attacking midfielders: Liverpool and Manchester City dominated the 2018–19 Premier League with an updated version of the same.

As a footballer, because you are selfish, your favourite formation is the one that leads to the greatest success for you personally. The false nine upset me because I'm a genuine nine. The false nine might be radical but it does not involve me, so I can't pretend to feel anything but seething resentment when I see it working so successfully.

Because I was a selfish footballer I would blame the formation if I didn't score. My dad, genetically predisposed to also watch football specifically from my perspective, would back me up. Together we would drive away from a game in which I had struggled to make an impact, bitching furiously about the shambolic waste of getting the best from three other younger attacking talents instead. I really required a nice old-fashioned 4–4–2, which was increasingly a problem in the later years of my career when managers were as loath to set up in such a dated way as they would be to stand on the touchline in flares and a crocheted tank-top. I needed crosses. A runner up front alongside me with two wide men getting crosses in worked a treat. My strike partner could get in behind or feed off my chest-downs and headers. I could receive the ball to feet, get it wide and then canter gamely into the box for the return. When I had Rafael van der Vaart in the hole alongside me at Spurs, with

Gareth Bale and Aaron Lennon charging up and down the flanks, the full-backs bombing on – it was CrouchBall at its purest, and I loved every second. It was the formation that did for Inter Milan and then AC Milan at White Hart Lane. It worked.

The alternative – me on my own up top, three midfielders, wingers playing on the wrong side so that they instinctively wanted to cut inside to shoot rather than clip a cross over first time – did not. I was too far away from the midfield and with the primary source of crosses cut off. Those were lonely days for me, and if you were the sort of football fan who assumed that a striker should keep striking as long as he is starting, you would have assumed that my form had gone, that my mojo was on the wane. It wasn't. I was the same player. I was just in a system that neutered my better abilities.

During my golden spell with England, the year when I scored eleven goals and felt I could have had more, the formation was geared up for me. I had the beautiful combination of David Beckham and Gary Neville down the right, Gary whipping crosses in on the run, Becks either driving balls onto my chest or bending them in with that glorious right foot. I knew that Joe Cole on the left would shape to go down the wing, pull a trick and curl it in first time with his right, which meant I could still time my run and still get in ahead of the centre-back. It was the same with Liverpool as we charged to the FA Cup and Champions League finals in successive years – Stevie Gerrard running off me everywhere, Harry Kewell and Steve Finnan with the pacey crosses off either side, lots of support all around me.

Like I say, selfish. But when it works for the man scoring the goals it usually works for the team too. And when it's not working for the team, the manager's highest principles and avowed methodology never last long. You can work all pre-season on one formation. You drill it in training and roll it out in warm-up matches.

The coach spells it out repeatedly: this is our pattern of play. Keep working at it and the results will come. This is the way we now are. You begin the season, lose your first three games and the whole lot gets jettisoned. No one cares about grand ideas when you're in the relegation zone. None of your fans get on the radio phone-in shows and declare how happy they are with a home defeat because you were easy on the eye as you capitulated. I saw it writ large in my final season at Stoke: Nathan Jones came in as manager, having had great success at Luton with a midfield diamond, and told us all that the diamond was the only way he ever played. We lost, lost and lost again, and the diamond was gone. Nathan will implement it in time, but you need to win games to get that time.

When you ask whether the formation comes first or the players, just look at the team's position in the table. You might wish to play with a holding midfielder, but if you don't have a good one, you can't. Unless you have the sort of multi-faceted player who can operate in the hole behind the main striker, you will have to consider playing two or three up top. You can be stubborn, as Maurizio Sarri was in playing N'Golo Kanté, the world's premier defensive midfielder, in a position other than that of defensive midfielder, but you cannot bend reality. At Stoke we were able to play Jon Walters in the hole because he had the fitness to make it work, to push up alongside me when we had the ball and to drop into midfield when we didn't. But only Jon in our squad could do that. If he was injured, the formation had to change as well as the line-up.

It can be hard to fight the fashion police. Arrigo Sacchi's sensational Milan team of the late 1980s and early 1990s lined up in 4–4–2. A lot of flair teams down the years have done. Play that way now, in a far funkier era, and it's seen as an asterisk against your name. 'He's a good manager but ...' It can be harder still to remember that fashions come and fashions go. When I did my coaching badges I looked at research that indicted that 90 per cent of teams at major tournaments – World Cups, European Championships – play the same way. The formation might look slightly different but it resolves itself into the same patterns. Even when you think you are radical, you are often just reshaping what has come before.

I felt at times with Liverpool that Rafa Benítez – a man who could have a tactics-off with Pulis and emerge bloodied yet victorious – could occasionally become too obsessed with formations. Harry Redknapp believed it was players first. Five-a-sides in training, one little sentence as you ran out onto the pitch for a big match – 'Go out there and be brilliant.' It gave you such confidence. There was a system there, but if Luka Modrić wanted to go all mazy and beat two men, someone would fill in behind him. At Liverpool we had Gerrard and Xabi Alonso in midfield, a rock-solid defence of Sami Hyypiä, Jamie Carragher and Pepe Reina, yet we'd set up for Wolves at home with two holding midfielders. We would spend the week working on what Wolves were good at rather than thinking, we're Liverpool, let's go out and beat them. We would draw some games we had to win.

There is a huge amount to admire about Rafa. Yet I wondered sometimes if he thought of footballers as static pieces on a chalkboard. We are three-dimensional characters who will not always do what you expect, and those skills need to be nurtured. If you lock great players into rigid formations, you shackle them. You watch the Manchester City teams of Pep Guardiola and at several points in a game you will lose all track of what formation they're meant to be playing. They're so fluid that anyone in midfield or attack can slot into any of the other positions and be completely at home. There is the formation at kick-off and there are the limited times before the final whistle when you could genuinely say they were holding that shape.

It's not a happy accident. They all know precisely what Guardiola wants from them and where to be to make that happen. You only have to see his agitation on the touchline when he feels one of his players is not carrying out the masterplan. But neither can you deny how effective Rafa's methods were. In European competitions in particular he got the absolute maximum out of his team. A two-legged Champions League tie is about as tactical an occasion as football can throw at you: how you balance attack and defence home and away with the away goals rule; new players to combat; coping with an atmosphere in the opposition stadium that is far removed from the Premier League norms. Rafa invariably got it right. People at the club will admit privately that the team which won back the European Cup in 2005 was punching considerably above its weight, but who cared in the aftermath of Istanbul?

Rafa would drill you and drill you. Each player in the team would be told where to pass the ball in a variety of different scenarios. Get it here, knock it there, get it back, go wide. All of it was mapped out. He would even make us practise what do to if the plan broke down. But it could be difficult to take in because training became monotonous. Some of the enjoyment was lost along the way.

At a game away at Watford, Rafa pushed me out wide left. I'm nobody's idea of a winger. I understand the requirements but lack the constituent skills. I could not work out why I was there. I was in a grump from the first whistle. And yet I scored two goals and we won 3–0. The manager had seen that the right-back and right-sided centre-half were both smaller than average. He got Gerrard and Finnan to hit me on the diagonal and play off my headers and knock-downs. I hated it and walked off thinking I'd had a stinker, thinking that maybe if we'd just set up the conventional way we could have won 5–0. Selfish and ungrateful. A footballer.

Managers enjoy the intellectual stimulation that a funky formation brings. They have two great weapons to use: tactics and man-management. If a player defies their chosen formation, if they don't buy into their system, the player will lose. They will be dropped or sold. If the manager gets it right, particularly with the unconventional, it's almost their finest hour. I remember how Rafa took off Gerrard in the Merseyside derby of October 2007 and brought on Lucas Leiva for his debut. Our best player for a callow defensive midfielder. In added time Lucas had a shot that Phil Neville handled on the line. We buried the pen to win it 2–1. Rafa just nodded sagely.

There will always be one player who either does not understand the system or chooses not to. When Xherdan Shaqiri was at Stoke he probably should have been given a completely free role. It would have made the most of his talents and saved the rest of us a lot of grief. Instead he was asked to play on the right hand side of midfield, which brings more singular expectations at Stoke than it does at Inter Milan and Bayern Munich. You have to help out the full-back behind you. You have to cover as well as sparkle. If you let Eden Hazard have a free run at your defence there will be team-mates who want a stern word with you. Shaqiri could be brilliant. He'd set off, dribble past two men, end up on the left wing – and stay on the left wing. Then we would be totally out of shape. Joe Allen would dash over to help the full-back, inadvertently leaving us short in midfield. At least drop in to left midfield, you'd think, so we could all shuffle across. Instead it would take Shaqiri an age to reanimate. We would eventually lump the ball clear and he would be caught offside on the left touchline, as a right winger.

There is a fine line between being mercurial and just doing what you want. Fans love to see a player beat a man, but if it keeps leaving you exposed, if it is more likely to lead to you conceding a goal than scoring one, it's the wrong option. People will point out, rightly, that Shaqiri scored eight goals and had seven assists during the 2017–18 season in a team that was relegated from the Premier League. But for eighty-five minutes each weekend he would be making everyone else's job slightly harder. Resentment grew in the squad, resentment grew with management. Neither system nor player could mesh.

Because formations matter, because every nuance of the game is now being worked for an advantage, managers take the training from the pitches to the classroom. Each Friday you will be shown video clips of the weekend's opposition – their general shape and preferred patterns of play, the specifics of the opponent you will be up against. This winger favours this trick first, this midfielder's default pass under pressure is to this team-mate.

Most of the time it's mildly stimulating, even if footballers hate sitting still indoors. It's the same angles and moments you might watch at home, just clipped up and highlighted. When Fabio Capello was in charge of England, his favourite instead was a helicopter view taken from a camera he had installed on the top of the stand above Wembley. The idea was that you could see the entire team shifting around, see absolutely everything that was going on. The reality was that you could barely make out anything. You would sit there in silence, watching a ninety-minute game slightly edited to bring it down to an hour, and frequently lose track of the where the ball was. You'd miss goals. You'd forget it was England, because it could have been anyone. You'd suddenly see one team moving slowly back into their half en masse and think, oh, I think I've just scored.

It was possibly the most boring way ever invented to watch football. Capello wouldn't even say anything as we watched – not pausing it to make a point, or standing up to gesture where he wanted a particular player to be. All of us were on classroom chairs, usually after a busy morning running about and a good lunch, desperately trying not to nod off. Capello had managed to take something every single one of us loved – watching football, watching ourselves – and turn it into something we dreaded. Oh look, you'd think idly while shutting one eye to give it a rest. That's me warming up on the touchline. Looking like a leggy ant.

It could have been so good. Players might be selfish but they are fascinated by anything that can make them look better. You show a team playing 4–4–2 that they are up against a team with three in midfield and they will understand that they need to drop an extra man in to avoid being overrun when they don't have the ball, because midfield is where the game is won and lost. Strikers at other Premier League clubs were looking jealously at their counterparts at Liverpool when Andy Robertson and Trent Alexander-Arnold were both contributing assists in double figures during the 2018–19 season. I look at the struggles Fernando Llorente had at Spurs that season and feel a great wave of sympathy, because he was a fine target man being played in a system that makes him look like a poor man's Harry Kane. Christian Eriksen and Dele Alli are sensational to play with but they are not about getting wide and swinging crosses in.

Players will come up with their own shapes. Sometimes they'll deliberately ignore the careful instructions they have been given, because they don't see how they could work. It's like a benign mutiny – you're deckhands taking over the ship, but you're saving it from the rocks. At other times you sense it's wrong but there's nothing you can do about it. At Stoke, Gary Rowett wanted us to sit off opposition teams when we were at home so we could break on them. The concept was fine but the setting was not. Stoke supporters were used to the Pulis way. They wanted us up in the away team's faces, chasing them, clambering all over them. Being out-skilled they could accept. Appearing to be out-fought they could not. The same formation with similar players may have worked a treat at another club. At the bet365 Stadium it never could.

Players see little patterns and ruses that even dedicated fans do not always spot. All formations fundamentally come down to one key aim: drawing the other team out of position so you can exploit the space that's left. That is it. It's why teams try to play out now from goalkeeper to full-backs; if you go long from a goal-kick every time, the opposition will always been in their optimum shape. If you can get them to press you high and yet get through them, they cannot then get back into shape as quickly and effectively as they would like.

It's why Pep Guardiola sang the praises of Jonny Evans, a defender who some might otherwise have considered too unassuming to attract his attention. Guardiola could see that Evans not only brings the ball out of defence well but tries to attract a couple of opposition players before offloading it. He creates space. He lures you in. It's why Naby Keïta's goal after fifteen seconds for Liverpool against Huddersfield in April 2018 looked like a mistake from midfielder Jon Gorenc Stanković but was in fact a beautifully laid trap. The strikers cut off the ball to the centre-backs, who had split wide for the pass. The goalkeeper wanted to play out. Stanković was left alluringly free – until the moment Jonas Lössl passed to him, whereupon Keïta emerged from the shadow of another Huddersfield player at pace to arrive on Stanković as the ball did. A touch, a return pass from Mo Salah, a finish – all planned by Jürgen Klopp, all about luring Huddersfield onto the snare.

It's not just a Klopp *gegenpress* thing. As a striker at Burnley I was told that on goal kicks I should close down one full-back and one of our midfielders would do the same to the centre-back who was most comfortable on the ball. When the ball was then passed out to the other centre-half, wide on one side, we would pen him in – me shutting off the return pass to the keeper, the other striker closing in on the man with the ball. Our whole team was now on one side of the pitch, and while that looks weird from the stands – Lads! There's a winger over here completely unmarked! – it doesn't matter and you don't care, because the only ball out is a sixty-yard diagonal pass. Not many under-pressure panicking centre-halves can make one of those – and even if they do, it'll be three seconds in the air and another couple of seconds to bring under control, by which time you can shuttle over to close that space down too. There are so many goal kicks in a match that it's become a big part of the game. Let's say you're playing Leicester in 2018–19. Harry Maguire and Jonny Evans love the ball at their feet, so you close down those first two and leave the weakest full-back open, inviting the pass into him by angling your body away. He gets the ball, the winger gets all over his backside, he goes long and hopefully you win it back.

Every formation has a downside. With an equal number of players on each side, any attempt to overload one area, side or player will inevitably create stresses elsewhere. If you play with three centre-backs and the opposition have one man up top, one of the three is either redundant or has to be comfortable stepping into midfield and playing. Both the left- and the right-sided players need to be comfortable on the ball, because they will have to split to take the ball off the keeper, almost as if they are full-backs in a 4–4–2. We tried it at Stoke, and only Kurt Zouma, who had grown accustomed to its peculiar demands at Chelsea, could make it work. We could not. Either way your wing-backs have to be amazing, capable of bombing up and down all day long. If you play one up top, you need great support breaking on from midfield, otherwise you are isolated and incapacitated.

Looking forward, I can only see tactics getting more fluid, and it becoming harder to work out formations in real time. Bernardo Silva, Kevin De Bruyne, David Silva, Raheem Sterling, Leroy Sané – they're not midfielders or wingers or strikers, they're just forward-thinking players. Sergio Agüero is the only non-defender at Manchester City who you could describe as a traditional striker. Sané and Sterling might have a preferred wing, Sané a little more than Raheem, but they're all comfortable in all positions. And that's a mark of the very best sides. You look at them and you're not sure who is where.

It works so well because you can't follow a player who doesn't have a position. Back in the day, the left-back would size up the right winger and think, he's my man. David Silva doesn't line up anywhere. Is he the responsibility of the holding midfielder, the right-back or the centre-half? He's none of them and all of them. He's a nightmare, just as the false nine terrifies traditional defenders. They will simultaneously be thinking, 'I'm not doing anything,' and 'Oh dear God there are runners coming at me from everywhere.'

If I were eighteen again now, rather than in 1999, I could not play as I did twenty years ago. Maybe I would no longer be able to fit in with the Liverpool and Spurs systems as I once did so well. I like to think I could adapt to pure passing teams, but the gradual extinction of crosses make me wonder. I look at the height of today's strikers – Sterling five foot seven, Agüero five eight, Sadio Mané and Mo Salah both five nine. That's my legs. My name would have to become an instruction.

And I look at the English national team, for so long one of the last bastions of 4–4–2, and I see only excitement. A coach who qualified with one formation, switched to another just before his first major tournament and then changed it up again despite making the World Cup semi-finals. Gareth Southgate has got young players happy to play free and floaty, players with the technical ability to slot into any shape they might choose. We could win a biggie. We really could. If only we get the formation right.

OWN GOALS

There are moments in football that unite us all. Linesmen falling over. Sprinklers going off before a match and soaking the unsuspecting TV presenter. The club mascot attempting to join a minute's silence, a giant hammer or combi-boiler trying to bow whatever they have that is closest to a head and look gutted.

But nothing pleases us more than the own goal. So joyous if it's not yours, so incomprehensible if it is. A stricken fall-guy, a supporting cast of the angry, baffled and delighted: it's tragedy and it's farce combined, a series of unfortunate events that could only be improved by the addition of the Benny Hill music or some cartoon klaxons/saucepans being dropped.

There are those own goals that cannot be helped – the inadvertent deflection of a shot otherwise going wide, the ones where a defender slides in desperately to prevent a striker getting a tap-in and instead diverts the ball in from a few yards out. These are very much the bottom of the barrel. They're accidents rather than pratfalls, brave attempts that just happened to be a few inches out. As a forward the last-ditch defender one just makes you angry. You think, why didn't you just leave it? I could have nudged it home from sixteen inches. It's the same outcome – goal for us – except it would be transformed into an entirely positive experience for all concerned. I'm happy. I've scored a goal. You're happy, because you haven't.

It's not simply the moment the ball enters the net that is so rewarding. It's the little dramas that play out all around: the little panicky dance a goalkeeper does when he's come out to take a ball bouncing through, only for his defender to assume he is still safely in his penalty area and head it past him; the expression on the defender's face when he makes the ideal contact with his head and then looks up to see the goalkeeper going past him and the ball bouncing gently into the net. The blame-game that follows – it's your fault; no it's your fault; I gave you a shout; what, in Portuguese?

Perhaps the peak of this scenario is the actual collision: the goalie clattering into defender, the defender poleaxed, only the ball untouched as it continues its path across the line unmolested by anyone. As an outfield player my sympathies are instinctively with the defender. I've been in positions on corners where the keeper has given it the big 'KEEPER'S!' shout, just as I'm about the head the ball clear, and I've gone through with the header on the basis that it's better to bang it away now and argue later rather than pulling out and risking calamity. I've also experienced that intense five seconds of private grief when you do stretch out and watch in horror as the ball flies backwards and in. It's the loneliest feeling you'll ever have on a football pitch: surrounded by team-mates and opposition players, no one wanting to look at you, no one coming over for what seems like an age before the goalie trudges across and gives you a sympathetic if meaty slap on the arse. If you've made a different sort of mistake – letting a runner go, sending a pass into touch rather than to feet – you'll get an immediate bollocking from your fellow players. If you score an own goal you won't hear a squeak.

I like the way that goalkeepers struggle to dive to save an own goal, so completely stunned are they to be fielding a shot coming from one of their own. They might wave a token arm, but more often they fall backwards slowly, or stand entirely motionless. It frames the frozen moment all the better. I like the hands-on-hips disgust, the hands-on-face horror, the arms spread out in silent appeal: what in God's name was that? I also like the unconfined joy among the fans of the club who are the beneficiaries. They're screaming but also laughing, pointing in disbelief at the culprit while also grabbing each other by the arm – did you see *that*?

Even seeing the abbreviation 'og' coming up as the scores scroll across the TV gives me a little kick of pleasure. As soon as you spot it your brain starts whirring. What could have happened? A great adventure opens up in front of you, a series of wonderful scenarios. You hope desperately for a belter, one for the canon of all-time classics. If you see the goalkeeper's name next to the 'og', it's even better, because now a mere touch or deflection on the ball is no longer enough. Has he thrown it in? Has he done an unintentional back-header from a shot cannoning off the crossbar or post? Has he attempted a desperate clearance and somehow managed to kick the ball backwards?

As a kid watching my dad play football, I would pile into the clubhouse at full-time, request a blackcurrant and water from the bar and watch the scores come in on *Grandstand*. The phrase 'og' initially confused me. Had legendary Coventry goalkeeper Steve Ogrizovic gone up for corner and stuck one away? It was all the more perplexing because I knew he had actually scored once, a long goal-kick against Sheffield Wednesday that bounced over the head of his opposite number Martin Hodge and into the net. With time

I understood, and with time I learned to celebrate the sight with a shout of triumph. 'Og! Dad, there's been an oggy!'

The own goal, prized as it is, is something of a rare species at training grounds. I can only think that the same desperation that is present in match-day scenarios is not there in practice. It also works the same way as it does for strikers; serial own-goal scorers can really get on a run sometimes. Richard Dunne scored ten in the Premier League, which even across the number of seasons he played is a magnificent run of form. Jamie Carragher managed seven, including two in the same game against Manchester United, the sort of hot-streak to make a number ten jealous. It's still not as good as Aston Villa's Chris Nicholl, who in 1976 scored every single goal in a 2–2 draw with Leicester – two for Villa, two for the Foxes. To his eternal credit he did it the right way round, too – first an 'og' to fall behind, then an equaliser at the right end, a second 'og' to seemingly ruin everyone's day and then a second sweet equaliser. That's what you call spirit. That's what you call oggy guts.

Own goals have decided big games. Poor old Des Walker with that bullet header in the 1991 FA Cup final, Gary Mabbutt scoring for both Spurs and Coventry in the final of 1987. Tommy Hutchison scored the only two goals when Spurs came from behind to draw with Manchester City in the 1981 FA Cup final. All those dreams Hutchison and Mabbutt must have had of scoring at Wembley. Then actually scoring at Wembley and thinking they would be the hero. Then scoring again to ruin their own day and everyone else's.

Mabbutt's own goal in 1987 was unlucky, a straightforward looper off an outstretched leg. Hutchison's in 1987 hit him on the shoulder as he tried to clear a Glenn Hoddle free-kick. Even Des's own goal was only six yards out. But to be a true classic, you need much more.

JAMIE POLLOCK, MAN CITY V QPR, 1998

Everything about Jamie Pollock made sense. He had the right haircut for someone called Pollock. He had the right build, he played in the appropriately no-nonsense style. And yet for one glorious moment he transformed himself into a maverick genius, a player of sweet touch, of rich imagination.

It's midway through the first half. The score is poised at 1–1. Pollock is in absolutely no danger when he runs onto the ball. He's got team-mate Mike Sheron ahead of him, although why he then flicks it over him like Pelé in the 1958 World Cup no one will ever know. Even having taken Sheron out of the game he has his goalkeeper Martyn Margetson ready to accept either a header or simply the ball, left alone after its initial clip. Yet Pollock is only halfway through his masterpiece. He now tenses all the muscle and sinew in his neck and lats and, with a perfect combination of power and placement, dinks the header over his keeper and into the net.

It's magnificent. It's so casual, so nonchalant. It reminds me of Matt Le Tissier's goal for Southampton against Newcastle – languid, lazy, totally in control. The technique is so cool and dreamy he could be Chris Waddle. Le Tiss, Waddle and Pollock: together in the same sentence for the first and only time, all thanks to the own goal.

What makes it so special, beyond even those artistic peaks, is that had he tried it at the other end it could never have come off. He wouldn't have tried. Jamie Pollock scored five goals in sixty appearances for City. None of them could be compared to Pelé. In the same situation by the opposition penalty area he would have panicked. Had the flick worked he would have blazed a volley into the stands, except the flick wouldn't have entered his mind. He would have battered a shot away.

The context is similarly perfect. Pollock had apparently spent the day before the game watching own-goal compilations on DVD. His wife had warned him off it, but – enjoying every second – he had pressed on. Had those gaffes somehow worked their way into his subconscious? I don't know. But in true City fashion, the impact of the goal was huge. City desperately needed a win to prevent themselves dropping into the third tier of English football for the first time. Pollock's masterpiece condemned them to a draw. It's why for me it's almost the perfect own goal. It's multi-faceted, a work of art and a car crash all at the same time.

FRANK SINCLAIR, MIDDLESBROUGH V LEICESTER, 2002

This is just a wonderful finish. Thirty-five yards out, Ian Walker in the Leicester goal, a first-time curling clip into the corner of the net. What adds another layer of gloss is that it was the only goal of the game. And that Leicester had long been a bogey-team for Boro. In short, it's a miracle goal.

DJIMI TRAORÉ, BURNLEY V LIVERPOOL, 2005

I played with Djimi at both Liverpool and Portsmouth. He was a good lad. On his day, he was solid. If that sounds like faint praise, he also scored a couple of beauties at the right end – one a curler for Liverpool against Steaua Bucharest, the other a thirty-yard volley for Seattle Sounders that smashes off the underside of the bar and in. He was part of the Liverpool squad that triumphed in the 2005 Champions League in Istanbul. He owns, and earned, a Champions League winner's medal.

None of that matters. You say Djimi Traoré to anyone interested in football and they will immediately see this miserable magnum opus and hear the Jackson Five-based chant that sprang from it. Like all great own goals it came from no sort of threat: a weak pullback from Richard Chaplow, no strikers near to him, just a sudden inability to control his feet. It's like the dark side of a Cruyff turn, except it was two Cruyff turns, both foxing himself. He can't make sense of it, Jerzy Dudek can't make sense of it. Burnley fans don't know whether to laugh or invade the Turf Moor pitch.

It killed him as a player. It was all anyone wanted to talk about with him at Portsmouth, although opportunities to do so were limited, because he used to commute each day from Paris – forty-five minutes to the airport over there, an hour through security, an hour in the air, half an hour from Southampton airport to our temporary training ground. He was never late, but his reputation was already shot to pieces.

Don't blame it on the Bišćan. Don't blame it on the Hamann. Don't blame it on the Finnan. Blame it on Traoré.

FRANCK QUEUDRUE, BASTIA V LENS, 2001

Franck Queudrue was not a pretty player. There was a point in his Middlesbrough career where the club were close to qualifying for the UEFA Cup through the Fair Play league. Franck's three red cards and five yellows saw to that.

There are some left-backs who you might expect wonder goals from. Roberto Carlos. Philipp Lahm. Paolo Maldini. Franck was not one, which makes his forty-yard dipping volley in Ligue 1 all the more exceptional. I also like the fact that he blames one of his Lens team-mates afterwards. Because it's always someone else's fault when you batter one in from an impossible distance.

CHRIS BRASS, DARLINGTON V BURY, 2006

Brass had a fine career as a lower-league defender: 134 appearances for Burnley, 152 for York City. It's his one season at Bury that represents his peak, however, thanks to an own goal so pure, yet so hard to dream up, that it deserves its place at the very top table.

The ball is floated into the Bury box. Brass has it covered. He runs onto it, facing his own goal, clearly realises the danger of putting it past his own keeper, and instead opts for the over-the-head volley. He catches it sweetly – power, pace, timing. Right onto his own nose and back past the motionless goalie like an absolute bullet.

You do something like that and you think your day can get no worse. You then ask the physio why your nose continues to hurt so much, and he informs you that you've almost broken it. With your own shot.

LEE DIXON, ARSENAL V COVENTRY, 1991

It's a famous one, this, and rightly so. Dixon has all the time in the world. David Seaman is one of the best goalkeepers in the world. The Arsenal defence is famously stingy. And yet Dixon, with the peachiest of timing, dinks it up and over the astonished Seaman from thirty yards. Much like Pollock, had he tried it at the other end he could never have pulled it off. By trying not to do it, he made it possible. Get your head around that.

ADRIEN GULFO, PULLY FOOTBALL V FC RENENS, 2017

You won't have heard of Adrien Gulfo. You won't have heard of his team, Pully Football, and you're unlikely to be familiar with the lower reaches of the football pyramid in Switzerland. Yet this may be the greatest own goal of all time: a heavenly set-up, a finish from the gods.

The cross comes in low. Gulfo, rather than getting rid, turns his body and, with the outside of his right foot, flicks it high in the air. No striker challenges him for the ball as it begins to fall, which may be why he launches himself into the air for an overhead kick. It is all so perfect, so balletic, right up to the point when the ball sizzles off at right-angles, straight over the head of his helpless goalkeeper.

It's like Gary Cahill's scissor-kick for Villa against Birmingham, mixed with Luc Nilis's volley for Villa a few years before, but with a hint of Marco van Basten in Euro 88 and a general sprinkling of Cristiano Ronaldo. If it doesn't bring a smile to your face, you're either dead inside or the Pully chairman. The commentary online sums it up a treat. *'C'est pas possible! C'est pas possible!'*

I can savour these pearls because I have been there myself. A year on from scoring the winner at Man City as Spurs pipped them to the final Champions League place, I scored at the same end in the same fixture, this time for the wrong team. City got into Europe, we did not. I was stretching to clear a cross, the ball hit my heel and it was in, a weird karmic reversal. Everyone was very nice about it, but the walk back to the centre-circle to take the kick-off that I had caused was a long one.

I couldn't complain. My first goal for Liverpool, all those eighteen games in, was probably a double own goal – first a deflection, then the Wigan goalkeeper Mike Pollitt palming it over his own head into the net. It still got given to me. And at least I wasn't Jon Walters, scorer of two own goals in one match for Stoke against Chelsea. He was determined to do something about it, took a penalty and smacked it against the bar. He actually did well to get on the end of both goals. They're a lesson in tracking back, not to mention finishing. It was the most cursed form of hat-trick possible, ending a seventeen-match unbeaten run at home, capping a 4–0 defeat, with the Chelsea fans serenading him at the end with 'Super, super Jon …' All we could say to him was that he could fall no further. Even had he buried the pen he still would have been a goal down.

When there are deflections, when there is doubt, the own-goal decision rests with something called the Dubious Goals Panel. Dubious is about right, because no one really knows who they are and what they actually do. The panel is supposed to include former players and officials, but their identities are kept secret: the first rule of Dubious Goals Panel clearly being that there is no Dubious Goals Panel.

They don't bother with whether a goal should have been scored, or who should be given the assist. We don't even know what evidence they consider, because they've never called the players involved to actually ask them. I like to think of them as a secret society, holding massive power over players they will never meet. A group of faceless men, taking away goals that mean so much to desperate strikers.

Written into the rules should be a cash bonus for any striker who taps in a goal-bound shot that last came off a defender. It's not like stealing a goal from a team-mate. It's the opposite. It's an act of selfless kindness. It's a humane execution. In the same way, in the case of a deflected own goal, the supplier of the pass or cross should lead the celebrations. They have created the mistake, they should profit from the adoration that follows.

It can be awkward knowing what to do if the stadium thinks you have scored and yet you secretly know it's come off the bloke marking you. The tannoy announcer has awarded it to you. The crowd are going ballistic. You have team-mates climbing all over you. And yet something is holding you back – the knowledge that some TV analyst, somewhere in a distant studio, is at that exact moment watching back the goal in super slo-mo and uncovering your heinous deceit. You're left with the bashful celebration: a modest nod, perhaps a handshake. Certainly no set-piece moves, no full-length dive or backflip. You can sometimes make something true in life by pretending convincingly that it is. Not in the Premier League. Not with Carragher watching on, trying to get others to overtake his second place in the all-time Premier League oggy charts.

What we should never see – and what the new-look Dubious Goals Court should come down on like a ton of bricks – is when the scorer of an own-goal is tauntingly congratulated by the other team. That man is already in it deep. Do not shove his face in it. Have some common decency. Had a City player clapped in my face or patted me on the back after my own goal for Spurs I would have punched them in the face, and I am not a violent man.

Own goals, funny? Yes, as long as they're not mine.

TACKLING

I was not a natural tackler as a kid. I wanted to score goals, not stop them. I was keen to master overhead kicks rather than stand on someone else's toes as they tried it themselves. The joy of football for me was swerving past a defender and cracking one in the top corner, not industriously cleaning up at the back before laying the ball off for someone else to have fun.

I had to have tackling instilled into me, mainly by my dad. Do not bottle it. Get stuck in. Never show fear. My dad would rather I missed a tap-in from three yards than jumped out of a tackle. As a lifelong Chelsea fan who grew up in the era of Ron 'Chopper' Harris, he may well have disowned me had I done so. And so I took to heart the old adage so many of us are taught as a child: if you pull out of a tackle, it will only hurt you more.

You get told a lot of things as a kid that turn out to be false. If you don't go to sleep on Christmas Eve, then Santa won't come. If you watch too much television you'll get square eyes. As a child, I never saw anyone at school with square eyes. I had never seen any photographs of children elsewhere in the world with square eyes. There was, in short, no documentary evidence that anyone's eyes had become square because they had spent too much time in front of the telly. That's before we get to the issue of why they should go square, of all possible geometric shapes. Almost nothing in nature is square. Even the old TVs were 4:3 aspect ratio; they were rectangular, not actually square.

Yet we believed it, just as we believed that if the wind changed direction while you were pulling a face, your face would stay that way forever. 'Graham, what the hell has happened to you? Was it the wind, Graham? I can't hear what you're trying to say, Graham, not with your mouth all twisted like that – are you saying it was a consistent westerly, so you thought you were fine, and then it threw the old reverse on you? Graham? Is that you now? Graham?'

I still believe the adage about pulling out of tackles, even though the logic doesn't back it up. Why would it hurt more if your foot wasn't anywhere near the tackle? How could withdrawing from a collision be worse for you than being fully involved? But none of it matters. The adage is too embedded in me to be forgotten, and I am not alone. As a nation, the British love tackling. We love players who throw themselves around and we cheer a last-ditch tackle almost as if it's a goal. A full-on 50–50, where both players arrive at exactly the same time with the ball flying straight up in the air, is as stirring a sight as our game can produce.

As a result, we reserve a special kind of disgust for the player who shies away. We interpret it as a character failing, a public demonstration that the individual believes they are more important than the team, that they are not prepared to hurt a little for the long-term collective good. I've seen it even at the highest level. I've played with a defender – a man whose primary task is to tackle – who was jumping out of tackles that cost us goals, jumping out of tackles in a season we were relegated. I had a fellow forward who, when I flicked the ball on from a pre-planned move off a throw-in, was still standing in the empty part of the pitch rather than where he was meant to be. Next throw, same issue. I asked him what the hell he was doing: he pointed at the opposition centre-half and said, I can't go near him, he's crazy. I told him this was an irrelevance, although not quite as politely. He shrugged. I don't want to get hurt. I couldn't think of him the same way after that.

On a pre-season tour with the same team a different tackle-jumper would consistently refuse to eat dinner with the team. He would take only a light soup and then immediately retire to his room. I was billeted in the next-door room and, intrigued, crept out onto the balcony one night to see if I could look through the sliding doors and find out what he was up to. Remarkably, having ordered room service, he was sitting at a table set for two, wearing the complimentary towelling robe, talking at his phone, which he had placed upright across the table. The phone was showing his wife on FaceTime, sitting at her own table at home, eating exactly the same food at exactly the same time. It was a FaceTime dinner date, and it had been happening every single night. In all my years of football, I'd never seen anything like it.

Does that admittedly unusual marital focus at the expense of a communal team dinner really create an attitude that leads to bottling tackles? There is clearly nothing wrong with demonstrating your love for your family. Many people will consider his actions charming. Am I less of a person for not following his example? Possibly. But I couldn't help but think that the man who chooses to dine with a pixelated image of his distant wife rather than his defensive partner was lacking a small but critical amount of commitment. You are a professional footballer. You are paid to tackle. You are paid to be dedicated.

I'm a considerate team-mate. I returned quietly to my own balcony, careful not to disturb him. But only after first taking a photo that I immediately posted on the squad's WhatsApp group. There is a price to pay at every level.

While it doesn't legitimise his approach, this tackle-jumper is not alone. There is a tackle-shy wrong 'un in every team, from kids' football to Sunday League and through the age-groups, and you can be sure that every one of their team-mates knows it. There will be chuntering. There will be shakes of the head and slaggings off behind their back. The only possible way these tackle-avoiders can be granted any dispensation is if they are so extraordinary going forward that their total lack of defensive responsibility no longer matters. We can call this the Prosinečki Protocol, in honour of the great lazy Croatian who decorated the Portsmouth team I played in almost two decades ago. Robert P was one of the most naturally gifted footballers I've ever seen, as well as being one of the game's most consistent smokers. He didn't have enough English to understand the phrase 'Track back, they're all over us' but was fluent when it came to 'Back off lads, this is my free-kick'. We let it go because in the time it took to complain he would have beaten three men, one of them four times, and smashed home a top-corner piledriver from the edge of the box. It's the same if Leo Messi ever jumped out of a tackle. Because he'd probably scored four in the game already, you'd let him off.

The issues come with the bang-average but occasionally mercurial number ten who gets you half a dozen goals a season, a couple of them in the Carabao Cup. The rest of you are on a constant fume. We're all doing shifts for you, what are you doing for us? Sure, you've thrown in a pretty turn and a nice switch of play, but what else are you bringing? You're not chasing back and you're not tackling. Where are the goals, the assists, the headaches for the opposition rather than for us?

In my time at Stoke I remember earwigging as our manager Mark Hughes buttonholed Pep Guardiola after Manchester City had given us a walloping. How do you keep everyone working so hard when they're all superstars? Pep replied that it was easy. When the two players who run the most are David Silva and Kevin De Bruyne, the best two players you have, what excuse do the others have? There are no luxury players at City. All of them run and score and set up chances and tackle and press and never ever stop. It's the same with the front three at Liverpool and the forward players at Spurs. Twenty years ago strikers could just strike. Now Sadio Mané, Mo Salah and Roberto Firmino never stop. Harry Kane, Christian Eriksen and Son Heung-min are relentless.

You cannot be a man down these days, not in the Premier League. Elsewhere in Europe there are still playmakers who play and water-carriers who do their legwork. You can be a Giuseppe Giannini or a Nicola Berti, a Pirlo or a Gattuso, Zidane or Deschamps. The coaches and supporters are fine with that. No one can remember a single Pirlo tackle, and they don't have to. Rio Ferdinand told me that when he came up against the maestro in the Champions League, Pirlo played as if he were wearing glass slippers. He was never anywhere near anything so base as a challenge. Not that it was a problem for the Italian; he dictated the game from a position on the pitch where you couldn't get near him.

The better the opposition, the more tackling back you're expected to do as a striker. If they're not so good you can play further up the pitch, otherwise you're expected to be behind the ball, closing players down and putting in challenges. The problem is that your skill set is elsewhere. Try all you like and you still look like an occasional bowler lobbing down an over of gentle experimental off-breaks to a batsman on 150 not out. I was once deputed to track back at Old Trafford and put Paul Scholes under pressure. It was humiliating. I tried to get tight to him and he turned me as easily as a man leaning on a lamppost. When I stood off him a touch he started spraying perfect sixty-yard passes to all corners.

People used to say that Scholes himself couldn't tackle. It was the excuse given for him totting up ninety-seven yellow cards and four red in the Premier League. The only player to have been booked more times than Scholes in the Champions League is Sergio Ramos, and we know all about him. Not Scholes's fault, you would hear. He just finds it hard to time his challenges. Strange, then, that he was able to strike a moving ball so well that Guardiola described him as the best midfielder of his generation, that Xavi claimed he was the greatest in his position for twenty years. Weird that he could hit the sweetest of volleys direct from an outswinging corner into exactly the small square of the goal he wanted, yet couldn't stop the same wand of a foot treading on an opposition player's Achilles. Strange until you played against him, when you realised he meant every single challenge. Scholes was indeed a genius player. Some might say he also had a dark side.

There is a horrible fascination when you are a footballer about the assassins of the tackle who lurk in the shallows of the game. Kevin Muscat was genuinely unhinged. Vinnie Jones's infamous *Soccer's Hard Men* video might have been the subject of a ban at his own club Wimbledon and landed him with a record fine, but no one could say he wasn't an expert in his chosen field. We all remember the photo of him grabbing Paul Gascoigne's crowning glories but a more typical example can be found in the opening minutes of the 1988 FA Cup final, when he went through Liverpool's Steve

McMahon like a threshing-machine. Because Steve McMahon is Steve McMahon, he gets up as if he's just been tickled rather than filleted. I wouldn't have moved for days, if nothing else to make sure Vinny didn't come back for dessert.

It was the way it used to be. Your first dirty tackle was a free one. It was as if the laws governing bookings and red cards were suspended for the first five minutes of a game. Stick in a reducer early on now and you'll be booked immediately, and then have to spend eighty-nine minutes trying not to get another yellow card when the opposition are doing their best to get you one. The worst tackles these days are seen at training grounds, where you're aware that you should be playing with a match intensity to prepare you for what is to come at the weekend, but you're also conscious that these are your team-mates, and so you forget how to tackle and get half-injured as a result, and then start swinging punches at each other because you're now angry and upset. John Hartson and Eyal Berkovic got on very well before one clattered the other at West Ham training. Berkovic's assists were responsible for the majority of Hartson's chances. One mistimed challenge later and the midfielder is punching his striker in the leg and the striker is booting the midfielder's head like it's one of his crosses.

To my shame, my tackling became worse as my career went on. It might have been the frustration of being stuck on the bench, of me wondering if I was as good as I had been, or because of the fear that I was maybe losing the pace I did have and was now arriving too late to everything. There were ones I wasn't proud of. The most disappointing always come from your own errors, when you chest the ball down and lose control, or overrun it, and a desire to make amends combines with an anger at your own ineptitude to create a horror-show of a lunge. I just hope it balances up the karma of having been kicked all over the place myself as a youngster. As a kid you were always booted if you were the best player. If you tried something cheeky with an older player – nutmeg him, put him on his backside – he would dish out an immediate lesson with his studs. Glen Johnson told me that the young lads at West Ham still talked about how Stuart Pearce had routinely smashed them all in his time there, just to let them know the pecking order. In my early days at QPR, Leon Knight arrived on loan from Chelsea, made the mistake of looking down his nose at the Championship and got booted halfway back across west London by the grizzled old pros Karl Ready and Steve Morrow.

There are players who can make tackling look graceful. N'Golo Kanté takes the ball off you almost apologetically, and is then twenty feet away moving at pace in the opposite direction before you've had a chance to curse him. After four years in the Premier League he was still only picking up a booking once every eight games or so. He's never been sent off in England. He averages considerably less than two fouls per match. That would be decent for a lightweight striker, let alone the pre-eminent defensive midfielder of his era.

Then there are the true defensive heroes, who are so good that they make tackling redundant. Emperor of the Non-Tackle was Ledley King, who I grew up with at Spurs and watched develop into the most under-appreciated centre-half in Britain. He was so elegant at such a young age. He honed his skills in the football cage in the middle of the estates in Bow, east London, where he grew up. It was an unforgiving place to play football – there were kids of all sizes swarming all over you, barely any respite given, and no adults around to call the fouls. I tried it a few times when I stayed over at his. It was terrifying and brilliant at the same time, and it made him so comfortable on the ball. As an adult playing for Spurs he would bring out his speciality three or four times a game: ushering an opposition striker down the wing, easing him out and then turning back with the ball like a magician pulling a playing card out of a stooge's ear, bringing the ball back up the pitch and then spraying his pass to a moving team-mate's feet. It was a beautiful thing to watch. Even at the end of his career I wasn't entirely sure whether he was right or left-footed. He would pass mainly off his right but do all his skills and tricks with his left. He was a Rolls-Royce among stock cars.

Then there is Alex Wordsworth, possibly the worst footballer I've ever seen – if you could describe him as a footballer, which you couldn't. When I was growing up, he would come down to the park in Ealing, the rest of us in full replica kits, him in jeans and a jumper, and be incapable of trapping a ball or more than two keepy-ups in a row. He was useless – until it came to jockeying. He had the ability to stay in front of you whatever you did. Should you manage to get past him, he then had a hook tackle so deadly that it should have been made illegal: one moment you were bringing your foot back to shoot, the next you were face down on the ground, looking at the trouser-legs of his stonewashed denim.

I'd have to describe him as the most naturally gifted defender I ever played against. Sorry, Ledley.

AWAY DAYS

We're not complicated individuals, footballers. We wear the same brands of overpriced clothing, drive the same unnecessarily fast cars, live in the same leafy enclaves. We like things done for us and we like the big decisions taken care of by someone else.

Nowhere is this more obvious than trips to away matches. Not for us the careful use of Google Maps and live traffic updates, of finding charming local lodgings via Airbnb, of planning ahead to secure the best fares and quirky restaurants. You leave for an away match not only sometimes unable to point out your destination on a map but with less on you than most people have for a trip to the shops.

It astonishes non-footballers how little actual footballers carry with them. When playing away in Europe in my days at Liverpool and Spurs, I would leave the house in my club-issue tracksuit. In my hand would be a wash-bag or small man-bag, containing toothbrush, phone and possibly iPad. There'd be no plug adaptor, because you can't expect a footballer to know the standard socket arrangement for a place as exotic as Paris or Milan: in the kitman's bag would be one packed for each of us. There was no passport, because you've already had to hand that in to a lady at the club earlier in the week, on the basis that waiting until the actual day to find your passport would be to leave at least three players in the departure lounge. Maybe one man out of twenty might be carrying a book, which will mark him out as a dangerous maverick who should sit with the staff rather than his fellow players.

No one has any luggage. And by luggage I mean any of the normal items you might take with you for three days away: socks, shirts, trousers, shoes, sun cream, travel guide. You don't even have a spare pair of pants, because all your pants will be provided for you: the ones you wear in training, the ones you wear round the hotel, the ones you wear in matches. We literally cannot be arsed with the things that cover our arses. All of us will be given the same brand and colour, usually a slimline black Y-front, which means that when you see a team run out for a Champions League match, every one of them will be wearing identical underwear. If you were to both read books and wear your own pants you should expect to be treated like the lunatic you clearly are and be asked to make your own travel arrangements in future.

There is a routine to away days that all footballers find comforting. You train at the normal time on Friday, polishing off by midday. You shower and put on the club-issue tracksuit. If the game is a decent distance away, requiring a train trip or flight, you will then be taken to the station or airport in the worst bus you will ever board.

The usual team coach is a beauty: sleek, black, tinted windows. Leather seats inside, arranged in groups of four around wide tables, a coffee station halfway down and a kitchen with chef at the back. That won't be with us, because it's been sent on ahead to meet us at the other end, with kit stashed underneath, regular driver at the wheel. That's the coach you arrive at the ground in. The one that picks us up from the training ground is the sort you took on school trips – seats in pairs, all facing forward, no leg room, seat covering a strange pattern of orange and brown triangles, a slight aroma of long-forgotten sweaty passengers in the air. It goes down with footballers as well as walking there with backpacks.

You don't use the same airport terminal as everyone else, of course. If your club is in the north-west, you fly in and out of the private terminal at Manchester. Not for us the signs to T1 or T3, the dual carriageway off the M56, the epic distance from park-and-ride to check-in desk. We wriggle past the Marriott in Hale, under a bridge, past the Holiday Inn and into a secret world of ease and luxury. You're straight into a hangar by the plane, possibly seeing someone like Sir Alan Sugar stepping out of his private jet, and keeping your head down in case he remembers that he only got sixty grand when he sold you from Spurs to QPR. You sit down with a cup of tea and give your washbag to a girl who puts it in a bigger bag with everyone else's washbags, which causes panic because everyone has the same brand of washbag. In an hour's time you will witness the unsavoury sight of ten grown men fighting over identical Louis Vuitton washbags and the rest scrapping over Gucci ones. 'That's mine!' 'Nope, definitely mine.' 'What colour's your toothbrush?' 'Erm, no idea …'

The planes for domestic flights are small. Too small. When you fly to Europe it's a decent-sized thing with proper jet engines, and you relax as a result. When you're popping up to Newcastle it's so cramped I enter the cabin at a crouch and progress down the aisle like a soldier under fire. You squeeze into your seat, glance out of the window, see a propeller and make a small cry of distress.

It's only Newcastle. It's only England, even if it is November, but there's something about those flights – how easily the plane gets knocked about by even the lightest of winds, the coming back in darkness, the fog, the wailing of the engines as they fight to get us airborne – that brings big strong footballers to their knees. You will see fearsome central defenders with sweat pouring down their faces. You will see strikers holding hands with wingers. The plane yawing from side to side, prayers being shouted, the desperate clutching of armrests even from those who have stayed solid through everything else.

There have been times when I've thought it was all over. Flying with Burnley from Manchester down to Gatwick en route to Brighton, I remember vast black clouds all around us. Realising we were circling at the same height with too many other planes, the captain came over the intercom to tell us that we were going to try to land, but to expect a sudden roar of engine and steep climb if it wasn't looking too pretty.

You're stuck in that situation. What are you going to do, barge your way into the cabin and fly back to Manchester, or pull a parachute out of the overhead bin and launch yourself out of the fire exit? And so you sit there, eyes clenched shut, thinking, why are we talking about making attempts? Can't we just land successfully or go somewhere else?

I saw Gatwick from all angles that day. Sideways, nose down, sliding past the end of the wing. At one point the runway appeared to be at forty-five degrees to the wheels. The relief on landing was almost indescribable – and then, being footballers, we immediately forgot all the trauma and started trying to flick each other's ears instead. Only when the assistant manager mentioned the next away game did it all come rushing back to us. We're at Newcastle on a Wednesday night? Oh God …

At least the Nice Coach is waiting for you on the tarmac. You are taken straight to the hotel, where all the keys are laid out on the counter next to your name. No checking-in required, no swipe of a credit card for any extras. The shout will go out – 'Dinner at seven o'clock!' – and the next three hours open up for you to spend as you choose … as long as you don't wish to leave the hotel, do any exercise or make a beeline for the bar.

At Stoke it was almost our favourite time of the week. Every time it was the same: break out the Trivial Pursuit board, split into teams, roll the dice. At the risk of sounding boastful, Joe Allen and I ran the show. What that man doesn't know about animals simply isn't worth storing. I'm a pure sport and geography man, an orange and blue slice-of-pie specialist. Joe's interests ranged far wider. You could throw him a literature question – the death-knell for most players – and he would have a decent stab at nailing it, particularly if it was related to science-fiction.

The teams tended to be the same. The Kids: Jack Butland and Tom Ince. The Scots: Darren Fletcher and Charlie Adam. The Bournemouth Connection: Benik Afobe and Adam Federici. I have been around football for a long time, but few things have astonished me like hearing the words, 'It's either Pope John Paul I or II,' coming out of Darren Fletcher's mouth. Yet all of us would surprise ourselves. Jack Butland would pull some absolute blinders out of the bag. I would get things I didn't even realise I knew, at least until someone picked up the Masters edition and the standard suddenly went through the roof. There were times then when I couldn't understand the question, let alone fathom the answer. I'd be sat there with Benik and Charlie staring at me, thinking, do I answer with a colour or a city?

Trivial Pursuit could last all day for us. If we had wrapped it up by dinner, it would be a football quiz in the evening – a proper multi-faceted one, conducted in the sanctuary of the massage room. Name the only player to have scored in the Premier League, Championship, League One, League Two, FA Cup, League Cup, Football League Trophy, FA Trophy, Champions League, Europa League, Scottish Cup, Scottish League Cup and the Scottish Premier League, Conference National and the Conference South. (It's Gary Hooper, by the way.) Name the twenty French players to have made more than 100 appearances in the Premier League. I'm a tough quiz-master. I don't allow any clues until you're maybe one player short and have admitted defeat.

At some stage the physios will go for a beer, or to bed. The massage room then becomes our playroom. You might start a game of two-touch – all of you in a circle, firing the ball at each other, first mistake bringing a collective punishment. This is where the ear-flicking of earlier becomes critical, because an ear-flick – aggressive, vindictive – is the usual penalty of choice. I've seen blood drawn, I've seen men on the ground. Phil Bardsley had a particularly effective strike, his forefinger winding back and smashing down like the sting on a scorpion. The really nasty players strike with power, dig in with the nail and then follow through to leave their finger in there, like a destructive midfielder leaving their studs up in the challenge. The dream is what you might call the Canal Shot: flicking across the lobe, finishing deep in the hole beyond.

The Queensberry Rules of two-touch are one flick for one mistake, flicked by everyone in a row for two. It was quite acceptable to try to stitch up your fellow players by giving them a horror-pass, particularly if they were Marko Arnautović, but his touch was so good he would usually rescue it, and then seek cruel revenge. You would rather hit the floor and curl into a ball than take the full aural assault from a group of angry players. At least that way you could protect yourself from the rogue Bugle Shot, where some sniper would take you out on the nose instead. One good Bugle Shot is worth three Canals. It can be hours until your eyes stop watering.

If the following day's game is a night one, you will be up early, assuming the adrenaline from the ear-flicking has worn off and you actually slept. There will be breakfast, a team meeting to discuss formation and tactics, a light lunch at twelve. You will then, like a crotchety toddler, be sent back to bed for four hours.

Not everyone can drop off. Some will watch box sets, play *FIFA*, or text the kitman to ask him to charge their smartphone. No one interacts in the corridors, for you are now a prisoner of your own room. I always enjoyed a sleep, the longer the better. Two hours was ideal, possibly brought to a conclusion by a gentle knock on the door and a parental murmur through the crack: 'Peter ... Peter ... It's time to get up for West Ham United ...'

The pre-match meal is always at four. I would shower before, waking myself up from the long snooze. Others will gamble on having time to shower post-food. Then it's onto the nice coach to arrive at the stadium an hour and a half before kick-off.

It's rare that we go our separate ways afterwards. The club like to supervise your post-match recovery, make sure you're eating the right foods and getting your protein-shake down you at the right time. The coach takes you back to the private terminal. The propeller plane awaits for your next rollercoaster ride through the bumpy skies.

When you travel by train, as you often will into London, it blows people's minds. Hang on, there's the Manchester City squad at Euston station! Look, it's Harry Kane walking past the West Cornwall Pasty Co. outlet by platform five! But train travel makes sense. Most footballers in north-west England live close to Macclesfield and Wilmslow stations. That's about an hour forty to the middle of London, whereas a coach can take four or five; with a plane, even a private one, you're still looking at three hours once you've got from terminal to ground. Clubs will book out two first-class carriages right at the front of the train, which can really annoy passengers who would ordinarily sit there. Even if we don't need all the seats, no punters are allowed in our carriages, the vestibule guarded politely but also with great firmness by the woman who looks after all the travel arrangements. She will witness some remarkable sights in those carriages, but never do they leak, for which all clubs are forever grateful.

You can't take advantage of the usual first-class buffet options. That menu does not apply on the football special, where the best you can hope for is a tea, water or occasional juice. No small can of Coke, no complimentary pretzels. The best bit is when you pull into Euston, normally close to platform one if you've come from Manchester Piccadilly, and the posh coach is already waiting for you by the buffers. Harry Potter has Platform 9¾ at King's Cross. The Premier League has a secret gate on the east side of Euston that opens only to let posh coaches in. You bowl off the front two carriages and walk straight up the stairs to your next seat. It drives the already angry usual first-class passengers into a frenzy, although not as furious a frenzy as when you ship a bad defeat in London, and then get off the train in the north at the same time as 500 fans who have made the same trip and had to pay for the pleasure. In the year that Stoke were relegated it could get quite nasty at Stoke station at ten on a Saturday night, and rightly so. We were letting the fans down. We were first class in ticket only.

You end the day on a high. The rubbish bus is there in the station car-park to take you back to the training ground, but you suck it up because the journey is only ten minutes, and your own vehicle awaits. When you do disembark, it's like a Premier League version of *Wacky Races*: twenty sports cars being started simultaneously, the quiet night air suddenly split with *VRRROOOM* and *NIIAAOOOW*, everyone thrashing it along the access road and then piling out onto the A-roads and motorways. Most of the local area is now wide awake, thinking that somehow they've moved to Silverstone overnight. Classic footballers: all of us doing exactly the same thing, at exactly the same time.

THE END

You make very few key decisions as a footballer. Most of the big thinking is done for you. If you're lucky, someone decides to offer you a pro contract. If that goes well, you might get lucky again and have two or three clubs try to sign you. They'll decide when you're picked and where you'll play if you are. You never get the chance to choose to play for your country. If one man likes you, he'll select you. If the next man doesn't, he won't. It's all out of your hands. You just play football as well as you can.

Until you can't.

Most players I know didn't want to retire. It was forced on them, like so much else. Jermaine Jenas couldn't get up in the morning without pain. Ledley King's knees meant he could barely walk. Bobby Zamora was gone in the back and the hip. These were young men, but they were living on anti-inflammatories just to get round the house. They couldn't put themselves through the pain any more.

I was the lucky one. My body still works. I thought I could have got through another season in the Premier League, and I reckoned I could have done okay. I could have scored goals. I understood that if I chose to step away then it would haunt me, and every Saturday afternoon at three o'clock, on midweek evenings in the depth of winter, I would think, why am I here rather than out there?

I retired because I just knew. I knew that there was a natural end in sight, that there were new adventures opening up in front of me. You can love where you are and still know that it's time to leave.

I realised I would miss the big games, but I was missing those anyway. I love watching the top Premier League matches, the special nights of Champions League action. I know how good those evenings are. But I was still playing and I was already feeling jealous, because I was no longer at that level. I didn't want to go down any further.

There were moments in my final season at Stoke – a club I loved playing for, a place that I felt so at home for so long – when we were struggling to snatch draws from Championship teams we should have been comfortably putting away. I would look at players I didn't think were better who were getting selected ahead of me, and I couldn't really argue. I feared I had lost a yard – not of pace, because that was never there, but of timing. That critical slight reaction was no longer there. I became an angrier player, and I was never an angry player. I was flying into tackles in a way I would never have done at my peak, and I couldn't work out why. Maybe it was the frustration of realising I was no longer the main man. Of knowing it was coming to an end.

Football was all I had ever done from the age of sixteen. It was all I ever wanted to do. When I was twenty-four I assumed I would be retired at thirty-two, because everyone was in those days. I came up with Ledley and he retired seven years before me. Instead I made it into my thirty-ninth year, just like Jermain Defoe, as Teddy Sheringham and Mark Hughes had in generations gone before. We were all the type of players who could make an impact with our attributes at any age: Defoe would always bag you a goal, Teddy was all first touches and vision. In your later thirties it's about football intelligence rather than speed of foot.

I knew that some managers would still consider me as an asset coming off the bench, someone who could shake things up. That in itself was a reason for me to stop. I didn't want to be the fifteen-minute man. I didn't want to be a head on a stick. If you come on that late you're usually chasing a game, so the ball gets lumped up to you, and you flick them on or knock them down. You can earn a good living doing that in the Premier League. But I felt I was better than that version, that I'd forgotten that I always wanted to be Gazza or Luca Vialli, not Ian Ormondroyd or Kevin Francis. I'd forgotten how to play, and so had those who wanted to use me. It was as if we had gone full circle, back to the clichés and misconceptions that dogged me at the beginning of my career: bang it long to the big man, don't bother playing it to his feet. I didn't want to be remembered like that.

Twenty-three years as a professional footballer. That felt like a remarkably good innings. There are times as a footballer when you wish no one knew you, so you could walk down the street and go out messing around without being filmed on a phone or stopped in every aisle of the supermarket. They were rare regrets for me. I understood every single day how good football had made my life: playing for some of the great teams of the world, winning the FA Cup, perhaps the most famous trophy of all, playing at World Cups. Going to places I would never have seen, meeting people who would otherwise never have looked at me. Experiencing highs and setting off celebrations that make my heart fizz just thinking about them again.

I had done my coaching badges while I was at Stoke, aware that a sudden end to it all would be much harder to cope with than a gradual transition. And then my book happened, and the BBC podcast with Tom and Chris kicked off and kicked on, and I enjoyed it all so much. I stood on a stage at the O2 in London at a festival named after me and had Liam Gallagher and Katherine Jenkins stroll on as guests. All for a skinny kid from Ealing who used to cry himself to sleep because he was teased so much about the shape of his body, who used to lie in bed wishing he could be a normal height like everyone else.

On the opening day of my first season outside football, I felt the sadness heavy on me. I was fine not going through pre-season. I went on holiday in July for the first time. I was looking forward to having a proper Christmas for the first time in my adult life, no longer training on Christmas Day, playing Boxing Day, training the day after, spending New Year's Eve in a distant hotel, far from family and boozy celebrations. Saturday mornings were now with my two daughters and two young sons, Bank Holidays going away with them rather than without.

I still went to a game, because I sensed I had to. If I had stayed at home I knew my thoughts would have run away with me. Someone compared it to attending the wedding of a girl you had once been in love with, but I saw it more as a little personal wake. No one wants to go to a funeral, but you have to, and when you do, and sob your eyes out, you feel better afterwards. You've got through it. You have closed that chapter.

Abbey expected more emotion from me in the summer, when I made the announcement. More tears on the day it became official. I thought about seeing a counsellor, because I've witnessed what happens to some players when they step away. They are rudderless ships, no idea where to go now the greatest adventure of their lives has come to an end. I knew that, much as Saturday mornings with the kids all climbing into our bed would be wonderful, I would be twitchy come the afternoon, waiting for an adrenaline kick that was gone for good. Every day in football I had laughed, usually proper belly-laughs, crying with the joy of it all. What else can replace that?

You begin to adjust when you come to peace with the fact that nothing will. Retirement is not better or worse than playing. It is just different. You can't compare your new life to your old because it serves no purpose. I love to look back but you need to look forward too.

Little things catch you by surprise. You've never had to think about staying fit. It's just happened as part of your day-job. Each morning you run hard, stretch, eat the most nutritious food without having to give a moment to its preparation or sourcing. Hang on, I thought. I'm going to have to get myself a Gold's Gym pass. I'm going to be down the local Bannatyne's, picking up my free towel in reception and asking if the Zumba class is already full. Member of the month, P. Crouch. Comes every day, crying.

You can leave the game with good intentions, forget that you can no longer eat what you like because you're no longer burning it off and end up doing what we might call the Full Ruddock: re-emerging into the public sphere a few years later, looking like someone's inflated you with a pressure hose. You start off thinking you'll just pop the TV on in the morning, and before you know it you've smashed through the whole of *Lorraine* and are gutted that it's over so soon. A couple of times I found myself so engrossed that I was calling Abbey through to discuss items I'd seen. 'Abs! ABS! Check out the makeover they've given this woman. She looks a-mazing!'

I began playing tennis again, a sport I played so much as a kid. I embraced the big cliché of all retiring players and started trying to get my golf handicap down. But I've kept the football skills ticking over as well. I lined up a few legends matches. I looked at the front lawn of my house and thought, we could squeeze a little five-a-side pitch in there – it'll obviously be for the kids, but I may as well make it man-sized, so I can invite a few of the lads over, and it's probably going to be quite intense, so should we look at the planning regulations for the installation of floodlights? I still let the rhythm of the football season dictate to me: summer off, getting stuck into work in August, working hard through autumn. I'm just more like the Bundesliga: mid-winter break to go somewhere warmer and eat ice-cream, mini pre-season on return and then piling back into business.

There aren't many careers that define you as totally as professional sport and then have to come to a complete halt. Musicians can keep going until their fingers or vocal cords finally fail. Even if their initial fame is a fleeting one they can come back for reunion tours when the nostalgia kicks in. You can't do that with football. You can't get the Liverpool Champions League final team of 2007 back together and take the match on tour. I'm not sure Harry Kewell would be fit for it anyway.

I was lucky that my obsession was football and that football can reward you as it has me. I could have been obsessed by dinosaurs and ended up as a palaeontologist. It might have been Dungeons and Dragons, which may have made it harder for me to meet the woman who is now my wife. But the thing I loved most became my life, and it was the best life. It happened to pay me well, yet I would have done it for free.

There was a point playing for England when I was first given the number nine shirt. My dad and I, even with all that had gone before, realised what this meant. We thought about how many kids of all ages dream of playing for England, and what a miniscule percentage ever get to do so. You think how many of those wanted to play up front, and how many dreamed of wearing the number nine shirt. And I thought: on this particular day, I've got the shirt that millions of boys and girls want. That made me understand how significant it was. I scored for England with '9' on my back. I'd made it.

I thought about the sacrifices I made early on. I didn't go to a single house party in my teens. I didn't mess about in the park after dark. As we grew older and mates started going to festivals, I stayed at home. I didn't even risk the illicit thrills of the Ealing Jazz Festival. Once I made it into the Premier League, I made up for it a little. I found my relaxation level. I found a balance that worked.

There were sliding doors moments. The constant abuse from the terraces in my early days left me asking myself if I could really put myself through it. I remember crying in front of my dad: why do I look like this? Why can't I be normal? So many doubts, so many fears. And then coming on for QPR at Gillingham and miskicking a volley, hearing a groan from the crowd, before steadying myself and lashing it in. Climbing high to set up the equaliser a few minutes later. Hitting the ground running at Portsmouth, stepping up to Aston Villa and dying inside again.

In my home debut in the Premier League I looked down the other end at Alan Shearer and it hit me: I'm a million miles away from that standard. I remember looking at my strike partner Dion Dublin and knowing I wasn't fit to play off him. Getting my confidence back up on loan at Norwich, moving to Southampton and crashing straight back down again: James Beattie leaving for Everton and me still not getting a game, Dexter Blackstock and Leon Best starting ahead of me. It took Harry Redknapp coming in to get me and Kevin Phillips together and the goals to start flowing. Eight months later I was at Liverpool as an England player. What if Saints chairman Rupert Lowe had decided to give Steve Wigley more time before sacking him? What if Harry had fancied someone else instead?

My whole world changed at Liverpool. I had been playing well at Southampton, scoring goals, getting in the newspapers. When you play for Liverpool everyone in the country knows you. It was all a high – scoring at Anfield and en route to the Champions League final, riding high with the best Portsmouth side of all time, the Champions League again under Harry and Spurs. At Stoke we finished in the top ten of the Premier League three seasons on the trot. Right at the end, Burnley gave me a new lease of life. I loved it there. My regret is that I couldn't show them what I could do.

I wouldn't change much. It was all new and I was naïve. Success can seem a million miles away, and then you roll the dice, land on a square with a ladder rather than snake and you're away. If you're smart you appreciate how fortunate you are. Football, I realised early on, is a ruthless business. Clubs will spit you out in seconds. You can be unlucky with one injury and they'll still bin you off.

It got worse as I grew older, and so many could see the rewards that were there for the chosen few. I saw average players earning millions. I saw players who didn't care about the clubs that were responsible for making them rich. I haven't missed that side of the game – the selfishness, the nastiness. I've met some of my best friends through football and I've met some where it's almost impossible to accurately describe how big a fool they are. In no other walk of life can you get away with it. In football, you do a job on the pitch and people will turn a blind eye to your behaviour off it. They'll praise you and encourage you. Then there are the ones who don't even possess the ability to get away with it who still behave appallingly. I've sat on team buses listening to players who have done nothing in the game, loudly talking about the things Sergio Agüero apparently doesn't do well. They would say, without apparent irony, that he doesn't work hard enough. I'd sometimes turn round incredulously and say, excuse me? *You* are talking about Agüero, when you've played ten Premier League games and he's scored more goals for Manchester City than any other player in history? Perhaps cut him some slack, yeah?

I made a conscious decision never to be bitter old pro. There were plenty around as I came through into the pro ranks, stuck in their ways, resentful of everything that was new. I tried to embrace the future as much as possible. I still struggled with the direction some parts of the game were going. I basically had fewer and fewer friends every year. I ended up being mates with more of the backroom staff – the physios, the doctors, the assistant coaches. I'd sit and chat to them, it gradually dawning on me that they were far closer to my age and background than the lads coming through. We'd arrive at a stadium to play a game, and I'd mention playing there before. The young player next to me would point out that he'd been minus two years old at that point. That hurt.

Even as I look forward, there are a few lingering regrets. Leaving Liverpool when I did, not realising that Fernando Torres would soon be sold and that I could have been a regular once again. There is no bigger club than Liverpool. The whole city is electric, drenched in football the same way as I am. I would have loved to play for them for ten years rather than three and a half. What happened at Stoke: going from a team with some ability and great lads to the opposite, bad characters and not much more ability. That was the saddest thing for me. Going to Burnley reminded me of Stoke at the start, in the good years – good players who were better than they were being given credit for, a hard-working manager getting the best out of his team.

There were players at Stoke who took the club down from the Premier League. I was there, and so I must share some of the blame, but the lack of care from some for the owners, the supporters and the staff was a disgrace. Joe Allen cared, Jack Butland and Charlie Adam cared. Mame Diouf was a great character. Joe even signed new four-year contract after we went down. He was the only one in the entire squad who played every single Championship game that first season, a Premier League player fighting with all he had just to get a club to sixteenth in the second tier.

I had moments that I will never forget, little personal prizes that I will always hold close. Scoring 100 Premier League goals. Making my England debut, and not becoming a one-cap wonder. Getting the record for most headed goals in the Premier League, being pretty confident it won't be broken, not with the way football is now played. Scoring for England at a rate that many more celebrated players did not match. Proving people wrong – proving that I could play, that I could volley, that I could spin and turn, that I could score with overhead kicks. Fitting in, after all those adolescent fears. Fitting in at World Cups and in the Champions League.

I met my heroes: Luca Vialli, Chris Waddle, the original Ronaldo, fat and glorious on an Ibizan beach. I lifted the FA Cup with Robbie Fowler, I played golf with Marco van Basten. My dad got to meet Peter Osgood, after years of making me watch the 1971 Cup final again and again. I never met Diego Maradona and I've yet to shake Paul Gascoigne's hand. Maybe the time has gone. But I did the Robot in front of the future king of England. Maybe that was better.

When I was at Villa I looked up to the older established stars. David Ginola, Paul Merson, Dion Dublin. As a youngster I looked up to tall players who could still had ability – Tore André Flo at Chelsea, Niall Quinn. Even van Basten was six foot two. Now I've had young players come up to me and say they used to watch me. A couple of tall, slim lads have even said I've helped them, because they've been compared to me. That feels good.

I didn't set out to be liked. I've never faked anything. I just tried to be who I am. I felt lucky to be where I was, tried as hard as I could and attempted to enjoy myself doing it. Maybe you can relate to that. If you were given the chance, you'd do the same: relish every day, give absolutely everything you had. I don't think I've done anything out of the ordinary.

I do wonder which team my kids will support. They've been bought QPR shirts, Spurs kits, Liverpool and England. They'll be so confused. I love the idea of taking them back to all of my old clubs and saying, Daddy played here, you know? Maybe they can take their dad away to European games. We'll do Loftus Road as our lovely bread and butter.

When I walk down the street, I try to have time for people. You will always piss some people off. There's always someone who hates you. But I'm glad the majority don't seem to. When I saw players treating others with a complete lack of respect I hated the game. To see it happening around the training ground was staggering. We are all working for the same club and the same aims. We are in this together – secretary, cleaner, groundsman, player.

We had a player at Stoke who was wonderfully talented but just couldn't care. We would see him hammering through the 50mph speed restrictions on the M6 in his chauffeur-driven car and try to tell him – mate, you're 30mph over the limit, you're going to get speeding fines every day. He would shrug. I've got a driver. We would say, yeah, but your driver will get done. He'll be skint. He might lose his licence. The player would shrug again. Ah, but I do not care for him. That became our go-to phrase for the footballer who has lost his senses. 'I do not care for him.'

I was always a fan first. I remember what it did for me meeting Justin Channing. I remember the Panini stickers and obsessing over the cool shirts and staring out at the outline of Wembley across the North Circular from Ealing and wishing I could just watch a game there, let alone play in one, let alone score for my country. I never even thought about robotic dancing for Mickey Rourke or being teased by Prince Harry about my ability to attract Abbey Clancy or standing in front of 3,000 people at my own festival as they sang, to the tune of 'Let It Be', *'Peter Crouch, Peter Crouch, Peter Crouch, Peter Crouch … There will be a podcast, Peter Crouch …'*

This chapter has come to an end. I'm ready for the next one. I've still got a smile on my face as I get out of bed every day. Something wonderful is over but something great is about to begin.

ACKNOWLEDGEMENTS

Thanks to Tom Fordyce, without whose help I would not have a book, let alone two. Or a podcast, come to think of it. Perish the thought.

Thanks to Andrew Goodfellow, Clare Bullock, Lydia Ramah, Becky Hibbert, Emma Finnigan and all the brilliant team at Ebury, who have done such a great job.

As I'm now retired from football, I'd also like to thank a few people who believed in me even when I didn't believe in myself: my mum and dad, Des Bulpin, Andy Campbell, Mr Wareing and everyone at Stellar.

PICTURE CREDITS

Football is a serious business. (Photo by Harriet Lander/Copa/Getty Images) • I once had a night out in Brighton dressed as a chicken. (© Peter Crouch) • A magnificent welcome in Burnley. (Photo by Alex Livesey/Getty Images) • A fan in Speedos and a snorkel (Photo by Warren Little/Getty Images) • Former QPR defender Justin Channing. (© Peter Crouch) • Showing Fabio Capello my right-arm off-spin. (Photo by Michael Regan/Getty Images) • You didn't argue with Fabio. (Photos by Michael Regan/Getty Images and ADRIAN DENNIS/AFP/Getty Images) • Rudi Voller reaches into his magnificent perm. (Photo by Bob Thomas Sports Photography via Getty Images) • 'I'm not sure why I'm on this pitch.' (Photo by Shaun Botterill/Getty Images) • When I found out about Gareth Bale's magic beans, it blew my mind and changed my world. (GLYN KIRK/AFP/Getty Images) • I could out-jump him even if I couldn't quite out-pace him. (Photo by Jamie McDonald/Getty Images) • Jermain Defoe and I had a prolific record playing together. (GLYN KIRK/AFP/Getty Images) • He could have passed a few more times. (KIRK/AFP/Getty Images) • I originally asked for the England shellsuit top at Christmas 1990. (© Peter Crouch) • Mike Dean. (Photo by James Williamson - AMA/Getty Images) • Jeff Winter. (Photo by Stu Forster/Getty Images) • Play to the whistle, they always say. (Photo by Stuart MacFarlane/Arsenal FC via Getty Images) • After I scored against Arsenal from a corner, Arsene Wenger described me as a 'basketball player'. (Photo by Ben Radford/Getty Images) • Harry Kane. (Photo by Charlotte Wilson/Offside/Getty Images) • Steven Gerrard. (Photo by Clive Brunskill/Getty Images) • Legendary Coventry goalkeeper Steve Ogrizovic. (© Getty) • Here I am sporting the latest designer luggage from the Parisian fashion house G'Arbage. (ANDREW YATES/AFP/Getty Images) • Tackling is part of the game (Photos by Athena Pictures/Getty Images and IAN KINGTON/AFP/Getty Images) • You put the luminous subs' bib over your choice of wet-top or big coat. (PAUL ELLIS/AFP/Getty Images) • You look like you can't even dress yourself. (Photo by Robbie Jay Barratt - AMA/Getty Images) • Loved this day. (Photo by Michael Steele/Getty Images) • Another trophy. (Photo by Popperfoto via Getty Images/Getty Images) • The fab four, or at least the quite good quartet: me, Steve Sidwell, Glenn Johnson and Sean Davis. (© Peter Crouch) • I interviewed Andy Cole and Les Ferdinand for my new Amazon show. (© Peter Crouch) • My last game in football! (Photo by Alex Livesey/Getty Images) • Possibly my favourite non-footballing moment. (© Peter Crouch) • Iniesta and me ... twice (© Peter Crouch) • I arrived at Crouchfest fearing no one was going to turn up. (© Peter Crouch)